Post-Industrial Precarity

New Ethnographies of Urban Lives in Uncertain Times

Edited by
Gillian Evans
University of Manchester

Series in Anthropology

VERNON PRESS

www.vernonpress.com

In the Americas:
Vernon Press
1000 N West Street,
Suite 1200, Wilmington,
Delaware 19801
United States

In the rest of the world:
Vernon Press
C/Sancti Espiritu 17,
Malaga, 29006
Spain

Series in Anthropology

Library of Congress Control Number: 2019951405

ISBN: 978-1-62273-768-0

Also available:
Hardback Premium Color: 978-1-62273-871-7

Cover design by Vernon Press. Cover image reproduced with the kind permission of Les Johnson: A detail of the sculpture 'Landed' which commemorates the dock workers of London. Created by Les Johnson FRBS 2009.

Table of contents

List of figures

Contributors

Dr Gillian Evans is an urban anthropologist. She is especially interested in the transformation of post-industrial cities in Britain, and particularly London. Gillian explores and explains what it means for the society we live in that once thriving industries, and manufacturing sites in Britain, like the docks, the coal mines, the steelworks, the potteries and so on, have declined and closed down whilst a new service sector, and knowledge and financial services economy has grown. Her research addresses the pressing question of what it means to inhabit a post-industrial society at the beginning of the twenty-first century. Gillian's most recent research is about the planning and development of London's Olympic legacy in East London. This was a five-year research project exploring the urban regeneration associated with the London 2012 Olympic Games. The book arising from this research, entitled *London's Olympic Legacy: The Inside Track*, argues London will become the test-case city for other host cities bidding for the Olympic Games. Her previous research, set in the former Docklands of Bermondsey, was a turn-of-the-century project to investigate what it means to be working class in Britain at the beginning of the new millennium. A book entitled *Educational Failure and Working Class White Children in Britain* was the outcome of this project. The book focuses on the discrepancy between children and young people's experiences at home and on the street, and their experience of learning at school. The research asks whether schools are failing working-class children or whether working-class life presents alternative means for gaining social status that conflict with what it means to do well at school. Focusing on Southeast London, this book provides insight into class values as they are embodied, lived and experienced in a post-industrial neighbourhood. When extracts of the book were published in the national media, controversy and debate were provoked. This was because the book touched a nerve in the nation by exposing the complex cultural politics of white working-class pride at the beginning of the twenty-first century.

Lucilla Barchetta is an urban ethnographer who recently completed her PhD Candidate in Urban Studies at the Gran Sasso Science Institute (L'Aquila, Italy). Her research develops an interdisciplinary perspective on urban natures, by exploring the complex interface between biophysical processes, culture and everyday urban space.

Donna Carmichael is a PhD Researcher at the London School of Economics. Her research examines economic and spatial inequality in deindustrialised British cities, with a particular focus on the impact of escalating inequality on marginalised communities.

Dr Emma Fraser recently completed her PhD in Sociology at the University of Manchester. Emma's work is focused on urban memory and ruins, and 3D and digital space and the image. In particular, Emma considers the depiction and navigation of ruined cities in games in relation to urban experience and the writings of Walter Benjamin. Emma's research has been published in games studies, urban studies, geography, sociology, and art media. Emma has undertaken fieldwork in Detroit, Chernobyl, Berlin, Paris, New York, Sydney, Christchurch (NZ), and elsewhere. She has also worked collaboratively with *Practising Place* and *The Arca Project* and is a member of the Playful Mapping Collective.

Dr Luciana Lang is an anthropologist working in the broad area of socio-ecological anthropology in urban contexts. She is interested in community use of resources and management of the commons, from mangroves to public parks. By favouring a political-ecological framing, she explores homespun strategies to cope with socio-economic effects of precarious scenarios and human-disturbed environments.

Julian May is a professional photographer, currently based in Spain. He has worked for public-sector organisations such as the NHS as well as shooting his own commissions, focusing recently on humans' impact on fragile environments. See julesmayphotography.blogspot.com.

Dr Abigail Schoneboom is an ethnographer whose research focuses on work, with a particular emphasis on resistance, technology, sustainability and work-life boundaries. She is particularly interested in the relationship between urban space, wage labour and critical consciousness, with a growing focus on the connection between humans and nature. She is currently Research Associate on a major Economic and Social Research Council-funded project at Newcastle University. Her research on work-life boundaries, creativity and the urban environment has been published in *Ethnography, Organization,* and *Work, Employment and Society*.

Dr Alice Stefanelli has recently obtained her PhD in Social Anthropology from the University of Manchester. Her research interests lie at the intersection of political and economic anthropology, human geography and urbanism. She is Editorial Assistant at *Contemporary Levant,* journal of the Centre for British Research in the Levant.

Dr Jessica Symons is an anthropologist and Honorary Research Fellow at the University of Manchester. She is involved in several projects exploring how to support people in low-income and rural areas to engage with the creative digital economy. Jessica is also Director of Visioning Lab Ltd (www.visioninglab.com) providing consultancy and services to the cultural industries and creative digital sectors.

Dr Angela Torresan has taught Visual Anthropology at the Granada Centre for Visual Anthropology in the University of Manchester since 2007. She received a Master's in Social Anthropology at the National Museum, UFRJ, Brazil, and her PhD in Social Anthropology with Visual Media from the University of Manchester. Her publications and films explore issues of middle-class migration, favela gentrification, and urban studies. She is currently doing research on state violence and resistance in Brazil.

Glossary

BNP	British National Party
CCT	conditional cash transfers
CDR	Council for the Development and Reconstruction
CPO	compulsory purchase order
CWG	Commonwealth Games
DIWO	Do It With Others
DIY	Do It Yourself
ECoC	European Capital of Culture
EU	European Union
GCC	Glasgow City Council
IMF	International Monetary Fund
ITERJ	Land and Cartography of Rio de Janeiro State
NGO	non-governmental organisation
PPPs	public-private partnerships
UKIP	United Kingdom Independence Party
UPPs	Pacification Police Units
USA	United States of America
VDU	visual display unit

Introduction

The failed promise of post-industrial society

Gillian Evans, University of Manchester

> Like many advances in human history, post-industrial developments promise men and women greater control over their social destinies. But this is only possible under conditions of freedom and open political institutions, the freedom to pursue truth against those who wish to restrict it. This is the alpha and omega of the alphabet of knowledge.
>
> (Bell 1999: xxxiv)

> What the new society will be remains to be seen, for the controlling agency is *not* the technology but the character of the political managers who will have to organize this new strategic resource and use it to buttress their political system.
>
> (Bell 1999: 112)

> We are witnessing the gradual disappearance of the postwar British welfare state behind a webpage and an algorithm.
>
> (Alston 2018: 7)

In June 2016, UK voters decided in a referendum to leave the European Union. Early in 2017, in an attempt to explain this outcome, known as Brexit, to an American audience, I argued (Evans 2017) that the result of the referendum is to be understood, in part, in terms of the failed promise of post-industrial society. The failure relates to the abandonment, by 'political managers', of the predominantly working-class populations inhabiting the regions of the UK that were once the industrial and manufacturing powerhouse of the nation. Relative to optimism about the remarkable social potential of post-industrial change, which was expressed by Daniel Bell in the 1999 foreword to a new edition of his seminal book—*The Coming of Post-Industrial Society* (originally published in 1973)—this political abandonment represents a policy attitude in the UK that has been variously described as 'benign neglect' (Comfort 2013), or 'managed decline' (Travis 2011). As Berlant (2011) suggests, optimism can be cruel; the freedoms envisaged by Daniel Bell in his imagining of post-1980s social change remain mostly unrealised. For swathes of the population, despite shared dreams of a better life, the prevailing political conditions of the contemporary moment thwart the desire for increased control over social destiny.

For example, in Liverpool on the Northwest coast of England, which was once, among other things, the site of the docks and shipbuilding yards that serviced trade with Ireland and America, national recession and the decline of the docks as a result of containerisation led, by the beginning of the 1980s, to high levels of unemployment (30–50 per cent in some neighbourhoods), rising crime, deteriorating social outcomes and finally, explosive riots in the inner city. Similar race riots, which were the worst urban disturbances of the twentieth century, spread through England's cities, in Birmingham, Leeds and London, and led to publication of the Scarman Report (1981). Scarman recommended urgent action and concluded that the consequences of national recession and uneven economic deprivation in British cities had most affected Black and Minority Ethnic populations from the Commonwealth who were targeted by racist policing and thus felt excluded from any sense of belonging to Britain. Scarman advised that racism in Britain was a 'disease' that if left unchallenged threatened to pull the nation apart.

Against the advice of the Environment Minister of that time, Michael Heseltine, who had argued for immediate and sustained investment to address the chronic problems of economic and social decline in northern cities, the Conservative Prime Minister, Margaret Thatcher, adopted instead a strategy of 'tactical retreat'. This proposed what Heseltine described in his White Paper (*It Took a Riot)* as a combination of 'economic erosion and encouraged-evacuation' leading to tens of thousands of people leaving the city of Liverpool in search of opportunities elsewhere. This course of action led to the retrospective accusation, when Thatcher's political papers were released for public scrutiny in 2011, of a scandalous level of political neglect, because the former Prime Minister had clearly attempted to leave industrial cities like Liverpool to die a slow death (Travis 2011).

The political system that Thatcher ushered in to support the transition to post-industrial society in 1980s Britain came to be understood as a USA-inspired form of neoliberalism (Evans 2017). This entailed a newly liberal attitude to capital interests, freeing business from government regulation, promoting the free market, which spelt the end of the preceding era of Keynesian economics, and that led to the increasing privatisation of national and public assets. The proposition was that a new economy in the form of post-industrial knowledge and service sectors, and financial capitalism bolstered by the revolution of new digital information, could, if freed from restriction, provide the kind of prosperity that would free the nation from its former responsibilities towards, reliance on and, indeed, identification with industries and manufacturing threatened by the dislocating forces of globalisation.

At the same time, in a sustained program of municipal withdrawal, the state and its participation in the provision of social welfare were massively reduced with devastating cuts to local government budgets. The usual terms of political solidarity in England and the spirit of resistance from below were broken when the trade union movement was defeated by the government's military-style responses to the 1984 Miners' Strikes and the 1989 protests against the imposition of the Poll Tax. In 1987, Thatcher had also casually announced in an interview for a women's magazine that there was no such thing as society, explaining that people had to learn how to stand on their own two feet—as individuals—without the safety net of the state. Consequently, it became clear that the post-industrial regions of Britain were to be blamed for their own disadvantage in a system that rewarded individual competition and entrepreneurial initiative and punished the poor for having been left behind by the forward march of progressive society.

The work of Stuart Hall and colleagues (1978) described how popular consent for this radical transformation of British society and politics was generated by the manufacture of a moral crisis such that young black males in the urban areas of Britain were scapegoated and made 'other' to the idea of national belonging. In their seminal text, *Policing the Crisis: Mugging, the State and Law and Order*, Hall and colleagues explained the legitimation of rule created by dramatic government responses to a series of manufactured moral crises that had to be policed. The ideological battle involved the re-signification of the problems of social and economic inequality. These were to be understood not in terms of the immoral consequences of changing forms of capitalism, but rather as the evidence of the immorality of those persons or groups posing a threat to the nation's peace and prosperity. By implication, the new national collectivity constituted by a style of politics that Hall *et al.* described as 'authoritarian populism' emerged from the success of a strategy to symbolically generate the categories of persons and behaviours labelled as 'other' to the patriotic mission.

For example, the sudden disproportionate sentencing that Hall *et al.* (ibid.) describe, of three young black men from Birmingham, for an unexceptional street robbery, and the proliferation of the new discourse of 'mugging' that was imported from the USA, distracted public attention from the problems of urban racial inequality in Britain. Instead, the concept of mugging made young black working-class masculinity into a primary symbol of the kind of rebellious 'otherness' that posed a threat to the British public. This explained the popularity of the exceptional law-and-order response, which made it appear that only a more punitive, authoritative leadership could quell the kind of unrest that was continuously framed as the evidence of immoral forces at work within the nation. Hence, as capitalism was unpicked and freed from the responsibilities of welfare, and the economy was dis-embedded from society, a fetish was created out of political authority, which concealed the fact that the immorality of burgeoning inequality was becoming taboo as a point of ethical discussion in neoliberal times.

One consequence of this authoritarianism, and the racialisation of policing in British cities, was the riots that exploded only a few years after Hall's work was first published. Regardless, despite changes to policing arising from the recommendations of the Scarman Report (1981), and despite the recommendation of the Conservative Environment Minister for massive and sustained investment in inner-city neighbourhoods, the neglect of post-industrial urban areas continued throughout the era of Thatcher's government and growing urban social inequality was the result. Thus, the exclusion of the former industrial and manufacturing working classes from the promise of a post-industrial society came with a heavy social price.

The new political order created freedoms for those who had the means of social mobility and could join a liberated technocratic class, in service to the new knowledge economy, but it also seriously limited the 'social destiny' and 'political freedom' of those who were excluded from this progressive vision of the future. Most interesting about this divide in the nation between those who felt themselves to be part of the excitement of the post-industrial future of Britain and those who perceived themselves to be 'left behind' was the fracturing of the most disadvantaged cities and populations along racial lines such that by the end of the first decade of the twenty-first century it was becoming clear that in the period of time during which successive governments have been determined to ignore the working class, it had become white. How was this possible?

Multiculturalism and the political vacuum created by New Labour

Strong support for Thatcher's Conservative ideology of helping those who could help themselves proved popular enough to change long-lasting traditions of voting behaviour. The economic and political chaos of late-1970s Britain, with high unemployment and high inflation, had bought the ruling Labour Party to its knees; it was no surprise, then, with the rapid decline of industry in the north of England in the 1980s, that many working-class people, especially in the south of England, started to switch political allegiance. In the general election of 1987, for the first time, 42 per cent of working-class former Labour voters started voting for the Conservatives. This new cross-social class coalition of voters led to a sustained 18-year period of rule for the Conservative Party—from 1979 to 1997.

For working-class voters in the safe Labour seats of the Midlands and north of England, this was a double betrayal. They felt abandoned by the government's policy of 'managed decline' and faced a loss of solidarity from working-class voters who moved towards the new consensus of self-determination through personal gain. Then, in a final insult, the New Labour government (1991–2010) completely failed to address and represent the interests of its traditional supporters in the post-industrial heartlands of Britain. Instead, New Labour was preoccupied with maintaining what the Conservatives had created, which was a centre ground composed of middle-class professionals and other voters aspiring to middle-class status.

My own research in the post-industrial docklands of Southeast Central London (Evans 2006) defied the political trend: it broke the taboo about speaking of the ongoing alienation of the post-industrial working classes, and caused a furore by bringing uncomfortable truths to the surface of political and public discourse. Just as in other post-industrial cities of England, like Stoke-on-Trent in the Midlands, a predominantly white, working-class population in the docklands of South London was coming to terms with the collapse of industry, in this case docks and food-processing factories, and struggling to adapt to a post-industrial service economy that was transforming the meaning of life and work.

In the docklands, social hierarchies had always mapped onto economic and political distinctions (Evans 2012a). For example, in the food-processing factories, Bermondsey grandmothers had always occupied the most prestigious positions of employment on the production lines, while Irish women from immigrant families were relegated to lower positions, and newly arrived Jamaican immigrant women were kept out of sight, labouring unseen and unable to socialise with the general workforce. Similarly, the functioning of the Labour Party, before the 1980s, was traditionally inseparable from an extremely localised way of doing politics. To be popular, politicians had to live locally, conform to ideas about whose needs came first in the hierarchical scheme of community inclusion, and attend actively to grassroots concerns (Evans 2012b). This meant that people felt taken care of by old-style Labour politicians in a system of paternalism that suited the social prejudices of the area and preserved the status quo.

The fate of Irish and Jamaican women in Bermondsey demonstrates a more general point, which is that the logic of a system of place-based, born-and-bred belonging in working-class industrial neighbourhoods necessarily implied, in a country that was far from united, a fraught tension between the categories and lived experiences of class, race, and nationalism. The unhappy marriage of class and race, even in the trade unions, explains why black and Asian migrants, arriving from the former colonies of the British Empire to the relatively impoverished neighbourhoods of the United Kingdom, found themselves caught between two forms of historical struggle for social justice and greater equality. Economically, the Labour movement ought to have provided the rational means for political integration in Britain, but the experience of xenophobia and exclusion from place-based systems of local belonging also made necessary a fight for racial equality. This took the form of the struggle for religious, ethnic, and cultural recognition, a struggle that was supported by the Labour Party with policies of multiculturalism from the 1960s onward. As long as the struggle for economic equality and the struggle for racial equality intersected as the measures of what defined a progressive society, there existed a fragile foundation of community cohesion. Without this overlap, it was clear that neighbourhoods, and potentially Britain itself, could begin to break apart.

In the docklands, I heard people lament time and again that their community had died. The fear was not about economic precariousness, but about increasing numbers of black and Asian immigrants and the policies of multiculturalism that encouraged the celebration of black and Asian people's diverse ways of life. Discontent was also expressed about a modern system of social welfare that meant that those classified as being most in need had priority access to prized public services, such as social housing. By definition, this system of needs-based welfare allocation eclipsed the historical precedence of local birth and long-standing intergenerational family residence. As a result, resentment was growing and emotions running high, because new residents who were considered outsiders were perceived as receiving preferential treatment. This led to the constant refrain of my fieldwork interlocutors, who asked, either in resignation or desperation, "What about our culture? Who cares about us?"

In places like Stoke-on-Trent, these questions had led, by 2008, to the growing success of the far-right British National Party. New Labour had become associated with a continuation of the Conservatives' economic strategy, as well as a progressive social collaboration between white middle-class aspiration and black and Asian multiculturalism. This left the white working class in post-industrial neighbourhoods in a political vacuum working out how to fight for equality when solidarity within the labour movement no longer appeared to be an option. The only solution seemed to be the multicultural bandwagon, learning how to compete with black, Asian, and white immigrants for resources and cultural equality. This meant that the choice facing white working-class voters was either to aspire to middle-class status or to learn, in the multicultural climate, how to be ethnic too.

The latter was the British National Party's strategy. Nick Griffin, the party leader, was a Cambridge law graduate. Cleverly, he was manoeuvring within the law to reconfigure the politics of working-class solidarity into a new form of ethnic association (Evans 2012a). He knew that it was now illegal to be racist in everyday life and in British politics. This meant that to be considered a legitimate political option among a population with a complete distaste for fascism, the BNP had to disguise its racist inclinations. Griffin fashioned a discourse of ethnic and cultural belonging that turned the postcolonial trope of indigeneity on its head. He described England as a land that belonged to those people whose ancient ancestors were born and bred there and who were therefore entitled to have their needs met before all others. The relative success of this strategy suggested that Labour's traditional voters were collaborating in the reconfiguration of politics away from class altogether and toward a new form of solidarity built on cultural nationalism, in which their version of cultural belonging took precedence.

In Stoke-on-Trent, the considerable success of the BNP by 2008 had been a wake-up call to the Labour Party, and, indeed, the whole political establishment. By the time of the general election in 2010, the BNP was defeated by the antifascist organisation Hope Not Hate, which acted swiftly and worked with the Labour Party in key constituencies to restore Labour's local grassroots activism. This was not enough to save Labour from defeat at the general election, but neither has it been enough to save the Conservative Party from the onward march of protectionist forms of cultural nationalism in various transforming guises. The decline of the BNP immediately led to the reconfiguration of the right wing in British politics (Ford and Goodwin 2014). Already, those older, male, white working-class voters in the south and east of the country who had voted Conservative were becoming disillusioned by what they perceived to be a growing disconnection between ordinary people and a self-serving elite in Westminster. They had begun to switch allegiance to the populist, right-wing UK Independence Party (UKIP), which campaigned as an anti-elitist, radically anti-European Union, anti-immigration, libertarian (i.e. anti-state) nationalist party.

As support for the BNP collapsed, UKIP was keen to extend its influence and began campaigning in post-industrial areas, formerly Labour heartlands, where the BNP had enjoyed a measure of success. Not surprisingly, the party's unprecedented rise in popularity caused another stir in the political establishment. Most significant about this was that UKIP began to bring together, across the political divide, older, white, better-off working-class men of formerly opposing Conservative and Labour persuasions. This was no longer simply about post-industrial urban alienation, but more generally about an anti-establishment populism. It was becoming clear, by 2014 that a broader political coalition was on the rise. All UKIP had to do to capture the centre ground and move it to the right, was to add a middle-class support base to this new coalition of working-class voters. This it had in microcosm in the form of the Conservative Party's Eurosceptic rebels, who opposed Britain's membership in the European Union, but how to connect this to a broader base of discontent in the population?

Nigel Farage, leader of UKIP, needed to distance himself from the racism of the far-right BNP, and, like the party leaders who politically sanitised the Front National in France, he knew that the legitimacy of his party depended on cleaning up the reputation of his members and politicians, who were renowned for their shockingly illiberal outbursts. Farage emphasised that his version of nationalism was not like the "blood and soil" nationalism of the BNP. Given that the party manifesto was blatantly anti-multicultural and anti-immigration, UKIP cleverly disguised its emphasis on cultural hierarchy and racial difference. This concealment meant UKIP could also appeal to long-standing black and Asian migrants who wanted to enjoy a privileged position relative to increasing numbers of new immigrants making claims on resources and jobs. Despite the Labour Party's attempts to revitalise its appeal and principles (especially with the election to party leader of left-wing socialist Jeremy Corbyn in 2016), UKIP's growing success suggested that the political landscape of Britain was shifting inexorably to the right.

Conservative leader David Cameron was under increasing pressure throughout 2015–16 to maintain a sense of unity in his party. Conservative members of Parliament had defected to UKIP, and the influence of the long-established Eurosceptic opposition was growing again. Determined to keep Britain in Europe and to call his opponents' bluff, Cameron gambled on his success in negotiating reforms to the terms of Britain's membership of the European Union and called the June 23 referendum. The tragedy of this political miscalculation was that the referendum created an opportunity for UKIP, with only one Member of Parliament in the House of Commons, to bypass the system of parliamentary democracy and join forces with elite rebels in the Conservative camp. Hoping to further his ambitions to challenge David Cameron for the leadership of the Conservative Party, Boris Johnson, a former mayor of London, ruthlessly betrayed the metropolitan multicultural values of the London majority to ride the populist wave of the UKIP leader and join forces with Farage.

Taking advantage of the perfect storm of a migrant crisis in Europe and concomitant growing anti-Muslim sentiment in reaction to terrorist incidents in France, Johnson and Farage campaigned on a platform of anti-Europe, anti-migrant cultural nationalism, and the vote to leave the European Union won by a narrow majority. This expression of discontent in post-industrial urban areas was matched by a whole range of other protest votes about life in Britain. As a result, an unintended alliance formed that combined an emerging cultural nationalism with a hotchpotch of previously unconnected complaints against austerity, the establishment, the EU bureaucracy, and capitalism more broadly.

The Brexit result sent a shockwave through the nation. This was an important victory for UKIP and Farage. The Westminster establishment and the liberal, multicultural, metropolitan elite never expected this outcome. They had underestimated the extent of alienation in the population, which revealed what the right-wing political opposition had known all along. It had learned to capitalise on the segregation of the political elite and the middle class from the everyday lives of those who have been left behind by a form of politics that gambled on financial capitalism and European integration, and hoped to consign the industrial working classes to the scrap heap of history. Now it appeared that all kinds of people who had been ignored or forgotten were suddenly given a voice, and they were going to have their day as the establishment, and its progressive idea of the future, was turned upside down. The real result is that everything, including our theory of society, is now open to negotiation. In this sense, the consequence of the Brexit vote is that all of us in Britain are disoriented and post-industrial now.

Brexit in Britain and Trump in the USA

I made this argument about Brexit in Britain, in order to provide the context for a comparison with a similar turning point in American politics. In November 2016, Donald Trump won the presidential election in the USA, and I wanted to make the claim that important similarities underlie the electoral results in Britain and America. My argument was that the results mark a turning point in the contemporary unfolding of post-industrial society. This is because both campaigns—the campaign in Britain to Leave the European Union—and, in the USA, Trump's campaign for the presidency—cleverly mobilised a significant and growing crisis of post-industrial alienation to craft a new political-cultural formation based on emergent forms of cultural nationalism.

These populist ethno-cultural reconfigurations of the nationalist project both depended for their success/political authority on making a moral crisis out of immigration. This crisis purposefully reconfigures the tri-partite relationship between government, population and territory (by moving in defence of sovereignty), and turns the forces of law and order, and popular opinion, and media attention, towards the borders, and against unwanted 'outsiders'. Significant about the manufacture of this new consensus—about the need for an increasingly authoritarian approach to the problem of 'outsiders'—is that it tries to resolve in cultural terms underlying problems of profound social, economic and political transformation. These underlying problems are to do with the twin crises of the failed promise of post-industrial society, and the post-2008-financial crash entrenchment of neoliberal governance of the knowledge and service economies. Rather than presenting these problems in terms of the threat they pose either to the American Dream, or the European project of economic prosperity and political stability, the political threat posed by extreme and growing economic inequality is again displaced as it was before under Margaret Thatcher. The problem posed by the spatial geographies of ruin and decline, for example in the Rust Belt of America, and the post-industrial northern cities of Britain, is not understood in terms of the moral crisis of advanced capitalism, whose inequalities would then have to be addressed. No, rather the problem is framed in terms of the danger that 'outsiders' pose to the patriotic mission of the nation whose prosperity now depends on defence of its borders.

In this way, the reconfiguration of nationalism entails the preservation of the project of neoliberalism, but at the expense now of its marriage with the forms of civic liberalism that formerly defined the terms of what counted as progressive society. These include, for example, the commitment to anti-racist, multicultural ethnic and religious plurality as the means for a taken-for-granted sense of how national integration ought, ideally to work. As this idea of what counts as progressive society is renegotiated a sense of moral outrage is general in the liberal establishment as the new forms of authoritarian populism take hold and begin to test the limits of what social democracy will tolerate.

Hence, in the present moment, both Britain and the USA are engaged in policy experiments that test liberal sensibilities through the internalisation of the policing of the national border by suddenly making illegal, and thus attempting to expel, migrant residents whose status in the previous political regime was never under question. In Britain this took the form, in 2018, of the Windrush Scandal that disrupted the lives of thousands of long-standing migrants from the Caribbean whose status as British citizens was never questioned before, and in the USA, Trump first announced the expulsion of 57,000 Honduran migrants who had been in the country as long as two decades. In the face of the moral outrage that these kinds of expulsions generate, it is important to understand how this kind of right-of-centre politics has gained popular appeal. My argument is that it is impossible to make sense of the contemporary turn of events without an explanation of the unfolding crisis of post-industrial society. This book adds flesh to the bones of the argument I propose here, by bringing together a collection of nine new ethnographies that chart the spatial geographies of bold ambitions for future change and alongside this, a sense of the resilience of precarious lives lived in cities that are adapting to the conditions of advanced capitalism in the USA, the UK, the Lebanon, Brazil, and Italy. My intention is to reassert what Bell (1999) proposed, which is that if the political managers of post-industrial society fail to articulate the new resources of transforming capitalism to a political system that guarantees freedom, greater control over their social identities and the pursuit of truth to all, the very building blocks of knowledge itself will have been ignored with serious ethical consequences for what counts as progressive society in the supposedly democratic nations of the world.

The chapters

As cities compete against each other for global capital, urban inequalities are increasing and the precarity and segregation of disadvantaged populations is growing. Meanwhile, the impunity of financial capitalism proceeds apace, and the business-as-usual dynamic is preserved of an intensification of wealth in the hands of a relatively small global elite. In the UK, for example, in 2018, the report of Professor Philip Alston, the UN Special Rapporteur on Poverty, revealed a shocking disconnect between the Conservative government's discourse about the prosperity of economy and nation and what he discovered on the ground through his tour of the country. Alston found and reported with shockingly consistent alarm, that in the world's fifth largest economy, in a country with a system of government that has been the envy of the world, the consequence, in the poorest neighbourhoods, of unrelenting policies of post-financial-crisis austerity has been deepening and widespread experiences of economic precarity, hardship, isolation and despair. Alston reported that the costs of austerity were falling hardest on the most vulnerable members of the population and that the safety net that was once a point of pride in British society was now seriously undermined by a political culture of indifference to the plight of the poor. He also highlighted a series of technical innovations in the digital delivery of welfare that alienated and excluded those who are least able to develop the competence to secure their present, or future stability in the new world order:

> The UK … contains many areas of immense wealth, its capital is a leading centre of global finance, its entrepreneurs are innovative and agile, and despite the current political turmoil, it has a system of government that rightly remains the envy of much of the world. It thus seems patently unjust and contrary to British values that so many people are living in poverty. This is obvious to anyone who opens their eyes to see the immense growth in foodbanks and the queues waiting outside them, the people sleeping rough in the streets, the growth of homelessness, the sense of deep despair that leads even the Government to appoint a Minister for suicide prevention and civil society to report in depth on unheard of levels of loneliness and isolation.
>
> (Alston 2018: 1)

> British compassion for those who are suffering has been replaced by a punitive, mean-spirited and often callous approach apparently designed to instil discipline where it is least useful, to impose a rigid order on the lives of those least capable of coping with today's world, and elevating the goal of enforcing blind compliance over a genuine concern to improve the well-being of those at the lowest levels of British society.
>
> (ibid.: 3)

Similarly, in the USA, the professors, Sir Angus Deaton and Anne Case, at Princeton University have highlighted the increasing number of middle-aged white people in America dying of drug overdoses, suicide and alcohol-related conditions. These are labelled 'deaths of despair'. In the UK, the Institute for Fiscal Studies think tank reported something similar arising in Britain (Joyce and Xu 2019). Sir Angus Deaton is overseeing a five-year economic review in the UK and initial findings report that in Britain extreme levels of income inequality are enriching the few at the expense of the many with serious consequences for democracy (ibid.)

Clearly, a future is no longer possible in which whole swathes of any nation's population are left behind without the means to realise what counts as a good life, and political discourse is now beginning to address the problem (post-financial-crisis) of imbalanced economies, but the question remains of how to adapt politics to what we have come to know about the complexity of the post-industrial condition. Savitch (2014) argues that post-industrial cities require the very opposite of what neoliberal policies suggest; laissez-faire cannot be the way that post-industrial cities change and develop, because the risk for capital is too high, and so unbridled competition gives way to policy direction and government collaborations. Potentially, this is the opposite of 'managed decline' and requires that private sector investment is attracted and guaranteed by state support. Usually, this means that government takes control of the land and makes it attractive to investors, but how to do this whilst also taking care of, and integrating into the city, the populations that have been fractured along the lines of social class and race, and dispossessed by post-industrial and neoliberal economic and political change?

In an increasingly urban world, a focus on urban planning, understood as the practice of envisioning and materialising new futures—as particular kinds of city spaces—is central to the work of conceptualising how the problem of post-industrial and neoliberal temporality is managed. Making a particular claim for ethnography as the method equal to the demands of the complexity posed by the experience of post-industrial urban life and the processes of urban planning and architectural process (Evans 2016), this book gathers together some of the most recent urban ethnographic research by early-career researchers in the social sciences. The chapters draw our attention to the lived experience of neoliberal and post-industrial urban subjectivities. In the first chapter, Dr Emma Fraser, a sociologist, focuses on her fieldwork in Detroit, Michigan, USA, undertaken between 2009 and 2015. The chapter considers the prospect of urban precarity in shrinking post-industrial cities through the figure of the modern ruin—the derelict though persistent relics of the recent past (houses, factories, infrastructure). As both a symbolic and material manifestation of economic and social marginalisation, urban ruins in Detroit (and other post-industrial cities) are frequently understood as liminal or abject zones, romanticised and aestheticized as dead objects (Apel 2015), rather than sites of productive—and human—encounters. As an index of precarity, these sites are model environments through which to interrogate the politics of urban decay and urban planning (especially renewal), particularly in the sensed and affective registers through which precarity can be perceived as the lived presence of insecurity and transience.

Urban precarity is framed in Fraser's chapter through an investigation of the "possibility of life in capitalist ruins" (Tsing 2015). She reveals a landscape of material and abstract ruin in terms of the everyday politics of life lived in a state of uncertainty. Fraser shows how, in this context, established notions of uneven development and gentrification come into play in ruinous urban neighbourhoods (Deutsche 1996), especially in post-industrial urban spaces. In Detroit in particular, decades of underinvestment, and anti-social economic activity and government policy, have accumulated vast fields of urban ruin, which are now up for redevelopment, resulting in evictions and expulsions of local residents, whose precarious lives often go undocumented and unvalued.

Fraser's discussion takes the interplay of fragmentation and neglect further to consider how actually existing ruins can be made use of as critical sites of manifest precarity, particularly in terms of the valuation of ruins and rubble as vital sites of critical contestation and open possibility (Deutsche 1996; Berlant 2011), even as they also speak of a Rust-Belt nostalgia that in "abandon to the performance of a world got down includes a utopia of latent and remembered possibilities" (Stewart 1996: 48). With reference to a series of interviews and informal tours undertaken in Detroit, and reflecting on encounters with ruinous landscapes across the city, Fraser's ethnographic and auto-ethnographic approach intersects with the politics of precarity, but also the radical possibilities offered by urban decay, as well as the current politics of renewal and erasure that have recently emerged in Detroit. These threaten to generate further ruination and precarity through planned gentrification and aggressive redevelopment as a new order of accumulation through dispossession (Harvey 2004).

Fraser's method of ruin ethnography focuses on what is an omnipresent and palpable manifestation of post-industrial subjectivity, a rhythm of accumulation and abandonment played out in degeneration and reconstruction, and sensed particularly through the embodied experience of material decay. She pays equal attention to both the everyday, lived encounters of local residents—their endurance and resilience—and the observed and intuited encounters of the ruin researcher.

Dr Alice Stefanelli, a social anthropologist, focuses in her chapter on urban planning as resistance to processes of displacement in Beirut, Lebanon. Whilst not a post-Fordist, post-industrial country, Lebanon is a traditionally service-oriented economy that has eagerly embraced a series of neoliberalising measures since the 1990s post-civil war period. The chapter is instructive in a book about post-industrial cities, because the case study reveals the consequences for precarious populations of entrenched neoliberal privatisation of the public good. As the preceding chapter by Fraser demonstrates, there is a danger that the 'managed decline' of previous decades will give way in the next to political collusion with privatisation of large swathes of the world's cities at the expense of, for example, green spaces, and other public resources including sites of important urban historical legacy. In other words, 'managed decline' is entering a new phase of what Stefanelli reveals in Beirut, which is government collusion with an ongoing process of urban restructuring through 'creative destruction' (Harvey 2007). The consequence in Beirut, and Fraser warns the same will be true in Detroit, is the restructuring of a city's class composition towards 'exclusification' and potentially facilitating the heightening of sectarian tensions (in Beirut) and racial tensions in Detroit. In Beirut, a significant portion of this restructuring has concerned the alteration of building and zoning laws in a gift to private developers, whose interests largely overlap with those of the political elites, which in the context of Lebanese political economy, mixes class and sectarian belonging.

Stefanelli emphasises the role of inhabitants' everyday social practices in the city such as walking, talking and dwelling, exploring how these allow for the subversion of official intended uses of city space. This approach, epitomised by De Certeau's writings (1984), identifies such forms of daily appropriation of the urban fabric as a primary locus of resistance to the top-down order imposed by the 'rationalizing urbanistic project'. Rather than considering professionals of the urban environment (urbanists, urban planners, architects, landscape designers…) as necessarily complicit in the production of dominant space (what Lefebvre calls 'representations of space', 1991: 38), Stefenelli shows how makers of the urban environment were not removed from the possibility of assuming a posture of resistance towards forms of discriminatory and damaging urban politics.

Stefanelli shows how, in Beirut, civic campaigning for the protection of urban public spaces (the 'urban commons') is spearheaded by professionals and students of precisely such disciplines of urban professional practice. Stefanelli explains that it is in fact their expertise, joined by an interest for the management of the *res publica*, that led most of her professional informants to challenge and bring to light the issue of ongoing privatisation of public space in the capital city.

As such, in Beirut, it is mostly professionals-turned-campaigners who are currently opposing authorities' policies, trying to engender a public debate on issues of urban development as well as proposing alternative solutions that might lead to the democratisation of the decision-making process around urban governance. In this context, technical expertise is used as a weapon against central planning operations based on political strategies and benefitting narrow interest groups at the expenses of the urban majority. In the light of these observations, Stefanelli proposes like others working in this field (Abram 2011; Abram and Weszkalyns 2013; Evans 2016) that anthropology pays renewed attention to professionals of the urban environment. She argues that ethnography of professional bodies and expertise might be key to shaping new understandings of the possibility for urban politics and urban resistance in our contemporary neoliberalising world.

Focusing on a gentrifying favela in Rio de Janeiro, Brazil, the chapter by Dr Angela Torresan, a social anthropologist, explains how the marginalisation and precarity experienced by favela residents is an expression of state processes of 'precarisation'. Like, Lebanon, Brazil cannot be characterised as a post-industrial country compared with post-Fordist areas in the northern hemisphere, but the ways in which urban precarity is experienced and managed has a lot to teach the Global North about the politics of precarity in relation to contemporary urban planning. The Brazilian economy is highly diversified: it has one of the largest manufacturing sectors in the Americas, coupled with a strong agribusiness and new financial, technological and consumption services industries. The economic policies that championed such growth since the mid-1990s were a mixture of conservative protectionism and neoliberalism, which coexisted with an established and large informal labour market. In 15 years of centre-left government, with the rise to power of the Workers' Party (2003–2016), there were successful conditional cash transfers (CCT) and affirmative action programmes aimed at reducing poverty and shrinking inequality gaps across class, race and gender lines. Despite this, Brazil is still one of the most unequal countries in the world. Torresan argues that economic growth alone does not tackle the problem of inequality. It requires reforms that go beyond CCT to address uneven access to resources and political power (Saad-Filho 2016).

Torresan's chapter situates urban precarity in Rio de Janeiro, not as a result of a post-industrial political-economic moment, but as a "politically induced condition"' and historical product (Di Nunzio 2017) embedded in public and private interventions to marginally integrate the urban poor into the capitalist market. Looking at a long-term case of adverse possession won by residents of a favela located in Rio de Janeiro and their recent experience with gentrification, Torresan explores how a public policy designed to integrate *favelados* into the fabric of the formal city, works as a strategic mechanism of limited entitlement (Di Nunzio 2017). Rather than addressing uneven access to resources, such policies circumscribe its limits. The policies assume that precarity is a natural modality of being poor that determines the kind of life certain people defined as marginal deserve to live.

Torresan's ethnography shows why it is important to understand that such versions of precarity do not coincide with the claims favela residents make on their right to the city (Harvey 2008). At a time when Rio de Janeiro was reinventing itself as a global city in the wake of the mega-events-led urban regeneration projects, the discrepancy between the restrictive adverse possession policy and residents' claim to their neighbourhood was even more acute. While precarity is a rubric that brings residents of the favela together, it is also perceived as an economic and political artifice that stops them from qualifying for acting as entrepreneurs in the real capitalist game they believe they have the right to play.

Focusing on initiatives of culture-led regeneration in post-industrial cities, the chapter by sociologist, Donna Carmichael, explains how culture-led regeneration strategies have been adopted by civic leaders and urban planners. Driven in part by Florida's (2002) influential work on the emergence of the 'creative cities' model to attract companies, new residents, investors and tourists, culture-focused renewal strategies have been embraced enthusiastically as an opportunity to re-imagine cities ravaged by deindustrialisation. The expected benefits are tantalisingly seductive—to attract the 'creative class' to the city; re-brand a city with a poor image; address deeply entrenched and seemingly intractable unemployment issues; tackle problems of social exclusion; attract investment and tourists; revitalise the physical environment with new cultural buildings and infrastructure; and much more. However, Carmichael draws attention to an increasing body of evidence, which suggests that the socio-economic benefits of a culture-led regeneration initiative do not necessarily trickle down to disadvantaged groups in the community, and in fact can result in increased marginalisation and income disparity. Glasgow is often referenced as the poster-child for culture-led regeneration; however, many have challenged the rosy narrative of culture-led change by pointing to the perceived silencing of working-class voices. The top-down approach of city planners and tight elitist coteries of government and business coalitions has led to biting criticism of greatly increased social and economic polarisation as evidenced by poverty, unemployment, life expectancy, etc. In these times of uncertainty, austerity and growing income disparity, along with the massive investments required to plan and deliver culture-led regeneration strategies, Carmichael argues that the assumption of trickle-down benefits and inclusive growth must be questioned as increasingly strident voices challenge the promises embedded in the new culture-infused urban imaginary.

Throwing light on the part that the concept of culture plays in post-industrial precarity in the north of England, in Salford, the chapter by social anthropologist, Dr Jessica Symons, explores the relationship between ethnographies of class identity, arts strategy and heritage-led regeneration. Symons explains the potential for cultural strategies to stimulate social change in urban contexts and provides a critique of top-down approaches of local government to post-industrial cultural change. Drawing on ethnographic insight from 18 months fieldwork in Salford, Symons describes the reaction of local people in a low-income area to yet another academic project seeking to study 'the poor'. In response to this flawed characterisation of the relationship between 'culture' and poverty, Symons explains how she redesigned the project to enable a much broader, Geertzian approach to culture, as the study of all the ways in which people make life meaningful, rather than a narrow focus on access to and participation in the 'high-culture' of art, theatre and music. This revised approach led Symons to support the development of local ideas for community projects. She shows how the insight from the project travelled into the local authority and into the development of grounded, rather than top-down cultural strategies of renewal based on a new politics of post-industrial recognition.

Focusing on projects of urban re-making in post-industrial Newcastle-Upon-Tyne, the chapter by sociologist, Dr Abby Schoneboom, with photography by Julian May, explores the spaces that exist in-between everyday urban wage labour routines (many of the makers fit their making activity around jobs in fields such as computer programming) and the creation of alternative sites of creativity in run-down city centre areas. In an era where urban centres are increasingly highly commodified and homogeneous (Augé 2008; Dale and Burrell 2002), and where organisational theory might benefit from exploring the parkour-like practices in urban placemaking that disrupt anesthetised settings (Daskalaki *et al.* 2008), Schoneboom's study is particularly concerned with the way in which the makers populate the makerspace with a spontaneous, unfettered creativity and physicality that some members feel is missing from their paid work in the information/knowledge economy.

Capturing this moment by exploring through visual ethnography the meanings that attach to objects created in the space, as well as the organisational practices that emerge alongside making, Schoneboom's study traces the ways in which these messy yet regulated, social yet individually absorbed processes disrupt non-place and militate towards a revitalised urban centre. At the same time, the study anticipates the fragility and limitations of working in the interstices, wrought by property development, which, as of 2017, was poised to evict Maker Space from its current location.

Schoneboom explains that existing literature on maker/hack spaces (e.g., Lindtner 2015; Rosner and Fox 2016) has not examined the relationship between these kinds of spaces for creativity and paid employment. Theoretically, the study reflects in particular on recent work on the making of the material world and notions of authentic/sustainable place (Carr and Gibson 2016; Paton 2013). It then makes some experimental links between this and the makers' enjoyment of their ability to make enduring physical things in the space, which contrasts with their largely immaterial wage labour in an information age. This physicality, it is argued, transforms the cityscape in an otherwise bland and consumer-oriented street. As such, the study aims to reflect in an explorative fashion on concepts of materiality, alienation and place-making, and also playfully suggests possibilities for a post-work urbanism.

Like other chapters that explore strategies of creativity and resilience in the interstices of post-industrial urban space, the chapter by social anthropologist, Dr Luciana Lang, describes an area called Cheetham Hill in North Manchester. The historical connections between Cheetham Hill and the textile trade still attract people with related skills to the area, and tailoring was one of the main sources of local labour as late as the 1970s. However, the textile trade in the area has shifted considerably with most shop units offering wholesale merchandise, and products no longer demanding a significant labour force. Consequently, unemployment in the area is high and in 2015, Cheetham Hill Road was ranked amongst the 20 per cent most deprived areas in England. The precarity of working conditions mirrors that found in people's housing experiences, and given that migrants who have not yet secured permanent residency need to regularly update documents and work permits, complex encounters with state bureaucratic processes have become part of the migrant identity.

Lang's chapter describes a shifting population stuck in an uncertain scenario of unemployment, zero-hour contracts, precarious housing, and occasionally homelessness. Lang reveals the resilience of people who resort to strategies of creativity and sharing to nourish hopes of a better life to offset this permanent state of uncertainty. Lang treats people's activities around growing and transforming food, and constructing makeshift outbuildings, as instances of "affective labour", which are described by Andrea Muehlebach as unwaged labour that produces 'good feeling' rather than goods (2011: 61). Lang explains how informality emerges as a means to create social bonds of mutual care out of precarious conditions.

The chapter by Dr Lucilla Barchetta, an urban anthropologist, also focuses on the in-between spaces of post-industrial decline and transformation. The ethnography explores the riverbank spaces of Turin and traces how, since the 1980s, the practice of urban design has been undergoing a transformation that reflects a range of opportunities generated by processes of industrial abandonment, urban redevelopment, new understanding of public space, and shifts in the urban culture of nature. Barchetta explains how, despite this change in the practice of urban design, the relationship between professional practice, public culture and local contexts remains problematic. In fact, she shows how utilitarian design productions often remain poorly informed by in-depth understandings of the actual experience of places, which can in turn translate open spaces into sites of social exclusion.

Taking tracts of riverbank spaces in Turin as primary scenes of investigation, Barchetta's study develops a materialist approach to landscape, exploring the mixing of planned and unplanned uses and relations. She shows how, despite the significance of projects of urban renewal—especially those following the 2006 Olympic Games—that have marked the progressive emancipation of Turin from its industrial identity, riverbank spaces have not been the object of a systematic plan for riverfront redevelopment, which situates them in a peculiar standby condition. Drawing on ethnographic observations, Barchetta builds a relational perspective to urban change, by taking into account not only the physical knowledge of space, but also its sensory components. She explores the liminality of riverbank spaces through experimental methods that engage with the multisensory activity of everyday life, led by individuals in interaction with the environment. In so doing Barchetta reveals what all the chapters have in common, which is a commitment to explore, and to expose the urban political ecology (Heynen 2013) of the contemporary moment as it unfolds in the precarious post-industrial, neoliberal and urban condition of our transforming worlds.

Acknowledgements

This volume is the outcome of a panel convened at the 12th Annual International Ethnography Symposium—Politics and Ethnography in an Age of Uncertainty—hosted in the summer of 2017 at the Business School at the

University of Manchester. I would like to thank all the contributors for their contribution to this volume, and for their hard work in turning short conference papers into full chapters for publication. I would also like to thank the editors at Vernon Press for their support and encouragement through the long and patient process of bringing this work to fruition. A special thanks to Amy Thomas for her time and attention as final copy editor at the last hurdle, and to the sculptor, Leslie Johnson, for his permission to reproduce an image on this book's cover of his brilliant sculpture of a docklands labourer—the Barrowman at the Victoria Dock in London.

References

Abram, S. (2011) *Culture and Planning*. Farnham: Ashgate.

Abram, S. and Weszkalnys, G. (eds) (2013) *Elusive Promises: Planning in the Contemporary World*. Oxford; New York: Berghahn Books.

Alston, P. (2018) *Visit to the United Kingdom of Great Britain & Northern Ireland: Report of the Special Rapporteur on Extreme Poverty & Human Rights*. United Nations General Assembly. Human Rights Council. 41st Session.

Apel, D. (2015) *Beautiful Terrible Ruins: Detroit and the Anxiety of Decline*. New Brunswick, NJ: Rutgers University Press.

Augé, M. (2008) *Non-Places: Introduction to an Anthropology of Super Modernity*. New York: Verso Books.

Bell, D. (1999) *The Coming of Post-Industrial Society*. New York: Basic Books.

Berlant, L. (2011) *Cruel Optimism*. Durham, NC: Duke University Press.

Carr, C. and Gibson, C. (2016) 'Geographies of making: Rethinking materials and skills for volatile futures', *Progress in Human Geography*, 40(3): 297–315.

Comfort, N. (2013) *Meeting Our Makers: Britain's Long Industrial Decline – a 60-Year Suicide, 1952–2012*. London: Biteback Publishing.

Dale, K. and Burrell, G. (2002) 'An-aesthetics and architecture', *TAMARA: Journal of Critical Postmodern Organization Science*, 2(1): 77–90.

Daskalaki, M., Stara, A. and Imas, M. (2008) 'The "parkour organisation": Inhabitation of corporate spaces', *Culture & Organization*, 14(1): 49–64.

De Certeau, M. (1984) *The Practice of Everyday Life*. Berkeley: University of California Press.

Deutsche, R. (1996) *Evictions: Art and Spatial Politics*. Cambridge, MA: MIT Press.

Di Nunzio, M. (2017) 'Marginality as a politics of limited entitlements: Street life and the dilemma of inclusion in urban Ethiopia', *American Ethnologist*, 44(1): 91–103.

Evans, G. (2006) *Educational Failure and Working Class White Children in Britain*. Basingstoke: Palgrave Macmillan.

Evans, G. (2012a) '"The Aboriginal People of Britain": The culture of class politics in contemporary Britain'. *Focaal, Journal of Global and Historical Anthropology*, 2012(62): 17–29.

Evans G., Edwards J. and Smith K. (2012b) 'Editorial introduction: "The middle classification of Britain"'. *Focaal, Journal of Global and Historical Anthropology*, Special Issue 2012(62): 3–16.

Evans, G. (2016) *London's Olympic Legacy: The Inside Track*. Basingstoke: Palgrave Macmillan.

Evans, G. (2017) 'Brexit Britain: Why we are all post-industrial now.' In Special Issue of *American Ethnologist*, 44(2): 215–219.

Florida, R. (2002) *The Rise of the Creative Class*. New York: Basic Books

Ford, R. and Goodwin, M. (2014) *Revolt on the Right: Explaining support for the radical right in Britain*. London: Routledge.

Hall, S., Critcher, C., Jefferson, T., Clarke, J. and Roberts, B. (1978) *Policing the Crisis: Mugging, the State and Law and Order*. Basingstoke: Palgrave Macmillan.

Harvey, D. (2004) 'The "new" imperialism: Accumulation'. *Socialist Register*. 40: 63–87.

Harvey, D. (2007) 'Neoliberalism as creative destruction'. *The Annals of the American Academy of Political and Social Science*, Vol. 610, NAFTA and Beyond: Alternative Perspectives in the Study of Global Trade and Development (March 2007): 22–44.

Harvey, D. (2008) 'The right to the city'. *New Left Review* 53: 23–40.

Heynen, N., 2013. 'Urban political ecology I: The urban century'. *Progress in Human Geography*, 38(4): 493–512.

Joyce, R. and Xu, X. (2019) *Inequalities in the Twenty-First Century: Introducing the IFS Deaton Review*. The Institute for Fiscal Studies. Available at: https://www.ifs.org.uk/inequality/chapter/briefing-note/.

Lefebvre, H. (1991) *The Production of Space*. Malden, MA: Wiley-Blackwell.

Lindtner, S. (2015) 'Hacking with Chinese characteristics: The promises of the maker movement against China's manufacturing culture', *Science, Technology & Human Values*, 40(5): 854–879.

Muehlebach, A. (2012) *The Moral Neoliberal: Welfare and Citizenship in Italy*. Chicago: University of Chicago Press.

Paton, D. A. (2013) 'The quarry as sculpture: The place of making', *Environment and Planning A: Economy of Space*, 45(5): 1070–1086.

Rosner, D. K. and Fox, S. E. (2016) 'Legacies of craft and the centrality of failure in a mother-operated hackerspace', *New Media & Society* 18(4): 535–538.

Saad-Filho, A. (2016) 'Social policy beyond neoliberalism: From conditional cash transfers to pro-poor growth', *Journal of Poverty Alleviation and International Development*, 7(1): 67–94.

Savitch, H. V. (2014) *Post-Industrial Cities: Politics and Planning in New York, Paris and London*. Princeton, NJ: Princeton University Press.

Scarman, L. G. (1981) *The Scarman Report: The Brixton Disorders 10–12 April 1981: Report of an Inquiry*. London: Penguin Books

Stewart, K. (1996) *A Space on the Side of the Road: Cultural Poetics in an "Other" America*. Princeton, NJ: Princeton University Press

Travis, A. (2011) 'National Archives reveals historic parallels between 2011 and 1981 riots'. The Guardian. 30th December. Available at:

https://www.theguardian.com/uk/2011/dec/30/national-archives-1981-riots-parallels.

Tsing, A. (2015) *The Mushroom at the End of the World: On the Possibility of Life in Capitalist Ruins.* Princeton, NJ: Princeton University Press.

Chapter 1

Urban decay as an index of precarity

Ruin ethnography in practice in Detroit

Emma Fraser, University of Leeds

Abstract

Developed from fieldwork in Detroit in 2009 and 2015, this chapter considers urban precarity in shrinking post-industrial cities through the figure of the modern ruin—the derelict though persistent relics of the recent past (houses, factories, infrastructure) in the city of Detroit. As both a symbolic and material manifestation of economic and social marginalisation, urban ruins in Detroit (and other post-industrial cities) are frequently understood as liminal or abject zones, romanticised and aestheticised as dead objects, rather than sites of productive—and human—encounters, or foundations for imagining futures and possibilities. As an index of precarity, these sites are model environments through which to interrogate the politics of urban decay and urban planning (especially renewal), particularly in sensed and affective registers through which precarity can be perceived as the lived presence of insecurity and transience. This discussion takes the interplay of fragmentation and neglect further than the abstract to consider how actually existing ruins can be made use of as critical sites of manifest precarity, particularly in terms of the valuation of ruins and rubble as vital sites of critical contestation and open possibility.

***

Reflecting on material encounters with urban decay during fieldwork in Detroit in 2009 and 2015, this chapter considers urban precarity in shrinking post-industrial cities. The subject of precarity is approached through a focus on urban decay and modern ruins—that is, the disused and derelict architectural relics of a recent past—that persist in the city of Detroit.

Detroit, once famous for car manufacturing, is now known as an iconic Rust-Belt city (Herron 2007; Strangleman and Rhodes 2014), and as a result, the city's decline has been widely studied, from its heyday as a bustling industrial city producing millions of cars per year, to contemporary regeneration initiatives (see for example: Clement and Kanai 2015; Draus and Roddy 2016; McDonald 2014; Reese *et al.* 2016; Schindler 2014). What this chapter offers is not a reinvestigation of the boom–bust narrative, or a detailed discussion of the city's extreme changes of fortune, but rather, through the lens of precarity, a consideration of the role of urban decay and material ruins in the lives of people who live, or have lived, in some of the most badly deteriorated areas of the city.

The notion of precarity is framed in this discussion through the work of Lauren Berlant (2011), Kathleen Stewart (1996; 2012), Doreen Massey (2002, 2004, 1994) Rosalyn Deutsche (1996), and Anna Lowenhaupt Tsing (2015), whose theoretical and ethnographic engagements with the "possibility of life in capitalist ruins" (Tsing 2015), reveal a landscape of material and abstract ruin as the everyday politics of life lived in a state of uncertainty within "newly proliferating pressures to scramble for modes of living on." (Berlant 2011: 8). In this chapter, modern urban ruins can be read as the symbolic and material manifestation of precarity, in terms of the economic decline and social marginalisation that accompany the long process of urban decay, but also regeneration (Lees and Melhuish 2015: 251). Urban ruins in Detroit (as in other post-industrial cities) are frequently romanticised and aestheticized as dead objects (Apel 2015), rather than sites of productive—and human—encounters. To focus on ruins in relation to precarity, this chapter presents the idea of a 'ruin ethnography', specific to the ruins of a recent past, which emphasises the often hidden and overlooked presence of people in sites that are otherwise abandoned or unoccupied.

This chapter argues that a particular index of precarity can be detected in the omnipresent and materially threatened ruins of Detroit. In this context, precarity is the instability characterised by urban decay and shrinkage, but also the insecurity wrought by aggressive regeneration in neighbourhoods affected by urban decay. It is also the persistence of people who work with the possibilities of life in otherwise precarious circumstances, and whose everyday lives and remembrances are linked to ruins as something more than useless relics—discussed in relation to the experiences of two Detroit locals. As an index of precarity, ruinous sites are environments through which it is possible to interrogate both the precarity of post-industrial obsolescence, and the politics of urban decay and urban planning (especially renewal), through which precarity can be perceived as the lived presence of insecurity and transience.

The discussion presented here relies on existing scholarship that frames the situation in Detroit as an example of development logics triumphing over the interests of citizens, many of them poor, and the majority black (Clement and

Kanai 2015; Kirkpatrick 2015: 262), resulting in unstable conditions for those already occupying precarious zones of marginalisation and exclusion (Fraser 2017; Galster 2012; Safransky 2014). In Detroit in particular, decades of extreme decay have been followed by aggressive renewal, accounting to some extent for contemporary conditions of precarity, or "life without the promise of stability" (Tsing 2015: 2). This is because in inner-city neighbourhoods, people scramble to persist amongst ruins, but they also do so amidst the rubble of demolition and redevelopment that emphasises growth for newcomers over ameliorating the negative effects on those directly impacted by post-industrial precarity. This is as true in Detroit as in any post-industrial city—if not more so, due to the protracted and entrenched nature of extreme inequality in the city, as a result of which Detroit has repeatedly been declared "dead", despite the city remaining home to hundreds of thousands of people (Draus and Roddy 2016: 68; Galster 2012).

In this context, established notions of uneven development and gentrification come into play in ruinous urban neighbourhoods, in which marginalised residents are further excluded through the unequal distribution of resources and services, especially in post-industrial urban spaces (Deutsche 1996; Lees *et al.* 2008; Massey 2004; Smith 1984). In Detroit in particular, decades of underinvestment, and anti-social economic activity and government policy (Sugrue 1996), have accumulated vast fields of urban ruin that are now up for redevelopment (Kinder 2014; Reese *et al.* 2016; Schindler 2014). The development-led regeneration of Detroit is very much of the type that tends to produce what Rosalyn Deutsche calls evictions (1996), and Saskia Sassen terms expulsions (2014) of local residents, whose precarious lives often go undocumented and unvalued in the push for reconstructing post-industrial urban space. This kind of marginal and insecure life is poorly reflected in financial reports, policy documents, or news articles that quantify the number of derelict structures, the absence of former residents, and the disadvantages experienced by the many long-term residents (Fraser 2017; Safransky 2014). Instead, this chapter argues that a more materially sensitive engagement is needed in order to at least partially describe the human detail of precarity, as a lived and shifting experience, something to be written out, reflected in photographs or anecdotes, and ultimately encountered in a particular site and moment.

Ruin ethnography

The use of the term *ruins* in this chapter closely reflects Marshall Berman's use of "modern ruins" to describe mass decay in New York during the 1980s; it is a material and symbolic indicator of the violence of urban inequalities, where fortunes are made or homes turned to rubble on the whim of planners and developers, usually for the benefit of commercial and economic interests (but also, sometimes, as a form of social cleansing) (Berman 1982: 290; Berman 1987). These interests, especially in contemporary Detroit, obscure forms of precarity (material, social, cultural) that are entangled with the fortunes of particular neighbourhoods, even streets and specific buildings, that are now in a state of ruin.

As this chapter discusses, modern urban ruins—whether abandoned houses, burnt-out factories, or empty schools and train stations—are extremely useful in mapping urban change, including the presence of precarious living among the large-scale detritus of obsolete industry, as in Detroit. In this chapter, sites of this kind—and the communities the persist around them—can be analysed as representations of a kind of precarity: firstly, urban ruins chart the slow decline of populations in economic terms, as well as sheer numbers, through the confronting presence of abandoned architecture. Further, a ruin tells the researcher that a profound and destabilising change has occurred—from active and prosperous neighbourhood, to sparsely habited area typified by visible decay. At the same time, while ruins can reveal the stories of those who left, never to return, they also chart the stories of those who stayed as the decline progressed, only to be made precarious in a different way—by demolition and regeneration—which is the current situation in Detroit.

The interplay of fragmentation and neglect with destructive renewal enables the ruin researcher to consider how actually existing derelict places can be made use of as critical sites of manifest precarity. For this chapter, this material/abstract approach is focused particularly on the valuation of ruins and rubble as vital sites of contestation and open possibility (Berlant 2011; Deutsche 1996). As anthropologist Kathleen Stewart describes, precarity is felt and lived through as material instability, but also persistence. To write, or undertake an ethnography of precarity demands an engagement with disintegration, but also persistence and potential amongst those whose lives carry on in areas of decline:

> Precarity's forms are compositional and decompositional. They magnetize attachments, tempos, materialities, and states of being. Their slowed, more capacious, description is a writing culture lodged in emergence, generativity, and potentiality. The writing itself attunes us to how things are hanging together or falling apart or wearing out in time that compresses or stretches out into an endurance.
>
> (Stewart 2012: 524)

Through possibility, materiality, and endurance, the practice of ruin ethnography, rather than presuming sites of decay to be absent of human occupation, seeks signs of 'falling apart' alongside 'hanging together', emergence and 'living on' amongst uneven development and the gentrification inevitably brought about by renewal. This method of 'ruin ethnography' focuses on what is an omnipresent and palpable manifestation of post-industrial subjectivity, a rhythm of accumulation and abandonment played out in degeneration and reconstruction, and sensed particularly through the embodied experience of material decay—from everyday, lived encounters of local residents, to the memories that are linked to ruins, and the observed and intuited encounters of the ruin researcher.

Through "ruin ethnography", this chapter describes two moments in the recent history of Detroit's ruins, and by association the precarity of Detroit's long-term residents who have lived amongst fields of ruinous decay for decades, only to be priced out, evicted, and otherwise expelled, threatening the possibilities for locals to reimagine the city as it regenerates.

Encountering Detroit

The two periods of research in Detroit discussed here follow a model of urban ethnography typified by relatively short field encounters as a means to intercept politics, power relations, and social and cultural formations in cities (Deutsche 1996; Jacobs 1984; Lees *et al.* 2008; Mah 2012). What is particular to this study is the focus on ruins, rather than the more active sites of the city. Similar approaches might include the extended ethnographies of more traditional anthropology, focused on ruins and relics (Stoler 2008 and 2013); geographers' industrial ruin encounters (like Tim Edensor's walking through ruins—Edensor 2008), or non-urban engagements with ruin and rubble, like Caitlin DeSilvey's call for palliative curation or curated decay (Desilvey 2014 and 2017), all of which work with ruins both as residues of prior occupation, and as live sites in transition.

In light of urban studies approaches, and the methods and practices of ruin researchers (Desilvey and Edensor 2012), the fieldwork and visual material presented here is intended to challenge the presumption that people do not engage with their local ruins (avoiding voyeuristic encounters, or what might be called Detroitism, ruin porn, or disaster tourism (Fraser 2012; Leary 2011). While populations do shrink in these areas, and active spaces become *apparently* empty in post-industrial cities, human activity continues, and can be understood through encounters with the remnants of once prosperous urban environments. Further, it is through ruin-focused images and stories of encounter that both the ruin ethnography, and the tracking of the process of change and precarity in Detroit, are facilitated.

Figure 1.1. Art installation.

2015, Packard Plant.

I first visited Detroit in 2009, before the publication of Marchand and Meffre's (widely criticised) photo book *The Ruins of Detroit* (Marchand and Meffre 2009). Just after this, their photo essay ("Detroit's Beautiful, Horrible Decline") was published in *Time* magazine (Marchand and Meffre 2010). It would be two years before the term 'ruin porn' emerged to describe the photography of modern ruins, at a time when 'urban exploration', or 'urbex' still seemed to have the potential to subvert the normative ordering of the city, rather than being a hyper-masculine, colonising practice (Leary 2011; Mott and Roberts 2013; Strangleman 2013). Yet I was already uncomfortable with the idea that people could 'explore' the ruins of someone else's biography and experience, however valuable I thought urban decay might be for empirical research (particularly as a manifestation of felt and situated precarity).

In 2009, Detroit was in a particularly bad state—before bankruptcy, before millions were pumped into regeneration and demolition projects (Reese *et al.* 2016: 369). In the midst of the financial crisis, with foreclosures threatening many residents, the situation was dire. People I met and spoke with could not understand why I was there; shop-keepers suggested to me that I would be better off visiting "anywhere else". A woman taking my order in a diner listed all the places outside of the inner city that I might prefer to visit instead. When I asked people what they thought would happen to Detroit in future, they were pessimistic—there did not seem any way out for Detroit, any possibility for change.

Local residents were welcoming, if downbeat about the future of the city. They were interested in why I was there, and what my research was about. With limited affordable accommodation downtown (the first contemporary hostel opened in Corktown in 2010) I couch-surfed with people I connected with online and slept on floors and in living rooms. During my stay, those I spoke to all echoed the same thing—this was the worst things had been in a long time. Entwined with low employment, high crime, and anger that the city had been left to fall apart, was a sense that Detroit's ruins were an important part of this story, threatened places with personal and historical worth—and described as part of the normal and everyday experience of living in a post-industrial, declining city.

Figure 1.2. Brewster-Douglass Projects.

2009, viewed from the I-75, as many residents would have seen daily.

One place I stayed in 2009 was in view of the derelict remnants of the Brewster-Douglass housing projects, described by a plaque on site as the "nation's first federally funded public housing development for African Americans". The projects were abandoned after decades of mismanagement, and partially demolished. By 2009 the remaining high-rise towers had become hollowed out shells with a reputation for being unsafe (structurally, and due to criminal activity). Still, they were highlighted by locals as a key historic landmark—partly as ruins that couldn't be ignored (people drove past them daily), but also because of the attached history (including key figures of Motown who had been raised there), and the shocking scale of the neglect and decay, which longer-term residents had witnessed over decades. The projects stood for the failures of government, the traumas of fractured communities, and the mass-decay of the city over time.

I left Detroit in 2009 with a sense of unease; although people showed that they clearly wanted to tell the story of their city, and spoke of urban decay unprompted by me, it did not seem right to talk about someone else's ruins, to speak as any kind of authority when I had not lived a precarious life in that precarious landscape myself. As debates about ruin porn started to emerge, I shelved plans for my Detroit material—it seemed an impossible space, too hard for anyone to fix, too spectacularised as a site of ruin to confront unproblematically.

On reflection, what matters is that this discourse of ruination has a social history that has come to be seen as the norm for Detroit, and similar post-industrial cities like Gary, Indiana, or Youngstown, Ohio. For example, Jerry Herron cites the extreme nature of Detroit's social inequality as a disaster that has, over time, been accepted as the natural state for Detroit (2007). Similarly, James Rhodes (2015) identifies the disaster discourse of Detroit as a means to simultaneously justify "a dramatic program of neoliberal urban development that is deepening marginalization experienced by Detroit's most vulnerable citizenry", and depict these happenings as inevitable and natural (Rhodes 2015: 118–119). As this logic extends to redevelopment, and the razing of whole neighbourhoods to make way for new uses, the contemporary renewal plans "translate into a territorially selective, planned shrinkage that will disproportionately affect the city's poorest and most isolated residents" (Clement and Kanai 2015: 377–378).

Rather than glorifying or exploiting ruins, focusing on the specifics of urban decay in a matter-of-fact fashion enables the researcher to direct their attention towards the intimate details of post-industrial cities that are often overlooked. An excellent example of the value of such an approach is Doreen Massey's discussion of Wythenshawe, in Manchester, England, in the context of the house where she was raised, which was abandoned and became derelict after her parents' death. What Massey draws out is the "immaterial architecture" of memory and lived experience, the fusion of the physical and the social, lived elements of ordinary lives, lived in ordinary places. "Place are spaces of social relations. Take this corner of a council estate: on the southern outskirts of Manchester, across the Mersey from the city. It is like many others, an ordinary place" (Massey 2002: 459). Massey goes on to evocatively describe both the social relations (her parents' lives, the life of the family and community around them), and the materiality of the house, the street, Wythenshawe and Manchester, all interlinked in her memory. The story includes schools now gone, trees and landscapes that predate the estate and remind Massey_of the farmland on which it was built, interconnecting "micro-spatiality" and "broader social history", and she uses images of everyday habitation and decay to trace development, decline, life and renewal all through one site, without devaluing any one moment.

Unlike "blank slate" (Lees *et al.* 2008: 185) renewal that perceives ruins as useless relics with no value or meaning to anyone, attending to urban decay in terms of ruin ethnography demands an engagement with the people who live amongst such places—directly and indirectly. Whether the remnants of human occupation; artwork or graffiti; vandalism; tents and other personal effects; or the actual presence of people on the ground and their memories of each location, sites of ruin that initially appear empty can be revealed through a ruin ethnography as active and habited, incorporated into people's personal stories, or understood as symbols of the wider mechanisms at play in the process of post-industrial decay and decline.

Detroit rebirth

Figure 1.3. Packard Plant.

2009, taken during a tour.

During fieldwork in Detroit in 2009, there was little sign of renewal on the horizon. People were disheartened, abandonment and decline were increasing, and the city government was corrupt and broke. However, things had changed significantly by 2015. Detroit was in the midst of a self-declared "renaissance" following the move of Quicken Loans downtown in 2010 and the city's bankruptcy (and subsequent flow of funds) in 2013 (Draus and Roddy 2016; Kirkpatrick 2015; McDonald 2014; Reese *et al.* 2016; Schindler 2014).

As a result, spaces of urban decay that had been untouched for decades had been redeveloped or earmarked for major renewal projects in the hope of attracting young white-collar workers to Detroit's derelict and under-populated inner-city neighbourhoods. As one critical article put it, "it's safe to come, we've got lattes" (Reese *et al.* 2016). This apparent renewal has been achieved by redeveloping large areas of Downtown and Midtown, using federal funds given to prevent foreclosures (Del Valle 2017), and land acquisitions from absent or destitute property owners (Safransky 2014). The latter expanded considerably as a result of the sub-prime crisis, global financial crisis, and the resulting foreclosures, the evidence of which was all too palpably present in 2009.

In considering the changes between 2009 and 2015, a good example is the 7.2 Square Mile report, which describes the plans for Detroit not in terms of the needs of current residents, but for expected new-comers, framing development-focused renewal as the means to start again, rather than working with people and sites that are already in Detroit (Hudson-Webber Foundation *et al.* 2013). As parts of the city transform under-populated zones of decay into luxury apartments and walkable neighbourhoods open to new occupation, vulnerable residents are subject to what Sara Safransky (2014) calls settler colonialism and green dispossession—ruins are redeveloped, the sites occupied by locals are colonised for renewal, and existing residents are pushed out. Simultaneously, urban decay persists outside the regeneration zones: brownfields, industrial ruins and abandonment are common and, as George Galster noted between my two visits, high concentrations of vacancy are moving outward as the inner city revives (2012).

Often—as in Detroit—it is value-based "demolition for development" (Mah 2012) that remediates dereliction and abandonment with large-scale regeneration projects. As Lauren Berlant explains, this is a feature of market vacillations, because, "capitalist activity always induces destabilizing scenes of productive destruction—of resources and of lives being made and unmade according to the dictates and whims of the market" (Berlant 2011: 192). This mutuality between renewal and destruction is not new—it is part of a pattern of urban development that has dominated cities (especially in the United States) since the mid-twentieth century.

Figure 1.4. The Imagination Station.

2009 (derelict).

For example, one run-down warehouse where I had stayed in 2009 had become a commercially sponsored "creative hub" by 2015. The nearby relics of the Brewster-Douglass housing projects had finally been demolished, after more than 50 years looking out over the city of Detroit. Their historical worth is preserved in the blue plaque, but it was the projects, and the people who occupied them (before and after abandonment) that were perceived to be troublesome—rather than socio-cultural configurations and inequalities, differential mobility, uneven development, devaluation and disinvestment. To cleanse the site of the ruins was to clear away the history of decline and precarious living, as well.

The projects themselves were not built without the politics of precarity either—they were developed in tandem with the Chrysler Freeway and other renewal projects that, much like the Cross Bronx Expressway, also obliterated existing neighbourhoods and communities. For example, the earliest stages of the housing projects were intended to take in displaced residents following the renewal of the predominantly black neighbourhoods of Black Bottom and Paradise Valley. This obliteration had also been framed as a kind of urban cleansing, offering 'opportunity' to poor, mostly black, residents and simultaneously wiping out a vibrant hub of black culture (Draus and Roddy 2016: 2531).

Figure 1.5. The Imagination Station.

2015 (following demolition and reuse).

What this particular location shows is that the ruins of Detroit reflect a complex and interwoven history of demolition, erasure, decline and precarity, manifested in visible decay, but also absences such as those exemplified by the disappeared ruins of the projects. During 2015, I went on two tours of Detroit that similarly reflected this link between ruins and precarity. The first tour guide, Avery, told me how she had spent years documenting the transformation of the city—both decline and redevelopment—and how she offers ruins tours, but also sells her images of Detroit (from pictures of the Skyline and the landmark Belle Isle, to images of ruins, including graffiti and other artwork) to local residents at art fairs, as a way to make money in a challenging economy. Over the years, many of the abandoned buildings she photographed were demolished, so her photography captures the decay before sites are renewed, but also revitalisation in process.

For Avery, many of her images reminded people of their own entanglements with ruins, and the longer trajectory of change in the city. She explained to me how the pictures of decay in particular have different affects, based on people's relationship to the sites she photographs:

> There's a lot of people who have left Detroit because they lost their job or for whatever reason and they moved out of the city ... people might buy an abandoned building photo because it might have been somewhere that they worked—there was a gentleman at an art fair a few weeks ago, he told me he used to be a pastor at St Agnes Catholic Church back in 1967 ... he came into my booth and he saw my pictures of St Agnes and he ended up buying a couple of them because you know he worked there, and he had not seen it in its current state.

Avery explained that the ruins of St Agnes are located in the area where the Detroit Uprising took place in 1967 (also known as the 12th Street riot), which began after a police raid on nearby 12th street, and ended with 43 people dead (the majority of them black residents killed by police or the National Guard). The church was notably undamaged during the uprising and featured in a number of well-known photographs from the period—but, as happened elsewhere in Detroit, the congregation declined until the building was taken out of use. Unmaintained, the church quickly became derelict, along with the rest of the neighbourhood.

The significance of the site (and Avery's photograph of it as a ruin) is to mark a complex space of history and remembrance, including segregation and police brutality—before, and after the rebellion. As Safransky notes, the events of 1967, especially in Detroit, must be understood in the context of "contemporary land crisis and the structure of feeling that shapes ongoing black struggles for land, property, citizenship rights, and liberation" (Safranksy 2018: 504). The area in 1967 had been a thriving, though segregated, black neighbourhood. Some of the businesses that were destroyed had relocated from Hastings Street earlier in the decade (Stone 2017: 76–81) just as residents were also being relocated to the now-demolished projects of St Agnes. When I visited the ruined church with Avery, there were other palpable presences to be detected as well—from tags and spray-paint cans left behind by graffiti artists, to the crumbling columns that Avery suggested were likely damaged by film crews using the building, showing that the church is not a dead relic at all, despite being a ruin.

Another Detroit resident I spoke with, Lucy, is an artist, curator, and activist who I first came into contact with as a tour guide running art-centred tours of Detroit. During our tour, as we drove through the city, she showed me places like the Dequindra Cut, Olayami Dabls' African Bead Museum, and the Grand River creative corridor, where local artists were creating works out of the disused spaces and left-behind relics of Detroit. She wanted to make it clear that of course there are still people in Detroit—living and working in the scattered blocks of activity, creating art and music in underused or derelict space and repurposing relics of Detroit's past.

At the same time, she told me how she had grown up amongst the well-established black middle class, a history that is often overlooked in discussions about Detroit, which tend to emphasise a working-class, pop-culture image of the city through Ford's factories, or sometimes Motown records. Yet, "Detroit has strong cultural history, museums, and formerly had the largest Black middle-class in the US" (Green 2015: 728), and there is still a black middle class in the city. Lucy showed me a neighbourhood partially abandoned and decaying (although showing signs of renewal) where she had lived as a child. As she tried to pick out the apartment block on the street, she told me of a lively community of artists and intellectuals who had left and moved to more populated areas of the city as the street became more run down. The middle-class history of Detroit is therefore also one characterised by precarity, with established communities moving from once vibrant neighbourhoods as they became increasingly derelict, only to move on again as the next place was impacted by economic downturn, abandonment, and decline.

For Lucy, in 2015, being in her hometown, engaging creatively with the space of Detroit, is not about useless ruins, but about the people who are based in a city that offers the opportunity to reimagine what life might be like in a more equal future. In this context, the ruins of the past—and present—city provide the foundations for the empowerment of black bodies and black identities, through the possibilities for all Detroit citizens to engage in revitalisation through resident-driven art and education programmes—a model that explicitly challenges the oppressive structures underlying Detroit's decline, and rejects the racially charged image of Detroit as a blighted city unable to control its own future possibilities.

Precarity and possibility

As these two experiences show, and contrary to development logics that see ruins as dead relics and vacant land as unexploited capital, ruins are bound to real lives, to precarious material and social conditions. As Kathleen Stewart describes in relation to the remnants of former coal-mining towns in West Virginia: "It is among these ruins, then, that the storyteller stands ... a place that in its very abandon to the performance of a world got down includes a utopia of latent and remembered possibilities" (1996: 48). In other words, in post-industrial space, where previous plans and livelihoods become impossible, people yet live and dream the possibilities of another life, in ruins.

What is obvious in Detroit, between 2009 and 2015, is that development at any cost overlooks the diverse presences within a ruinscape—buildings used for art (including graffiti), or ad-hoc music and cultural events, for squatting or even for children's play, are perceived to be just as useless as the ruins of schools, churches, and public housing that chart the story of the struggle to persist in Detroit. Nothing is spared in the conversion from worthless to wealth-generating, regardless of the latent, remembered, and even active presences in the urban landscape.

This is not just a consideration of memory or subcultural practice, but rather an acknowledgment that ruins are the site of life in post-industrial spaces, particularly cities affected by urban decay following major job losses and population shrinkage. Ruin-focused ethnographic work uncovers the confronting *material* manifestations of the abstract state of precarity that is increasingly and disproportionately defining the lives of already disadvantaged groups who are left stranded to support their own communities and interests in under-serviced shrinking cities, only to be moved along when renewal becomes viable. For every Detroit success story that ameliorates the burden of mass decay in an apparently 'empty' neighbourhood, there are people who have been moved on to make way for incomers whose presence demands the fallacy of an uninhabited, dead and empty site of ruin to be reoccupied, resuscitated.

Models of renewal that exclude precarious communities from urban transformation, primarily through the devaluation of the ruin, emphasise an "intrinsic use" value through the "lens of function", which obscures, utterly, the rights of those who cannot speak through, or about a functioning city, whose lives are instead intertwined with decline and ruin, and the precarity that is enmeshed with post-industrial urban decay (Deutsche 1996: 51-51). In the vision of the city as something that must function in terms of the moral value of economic progress, the solution is growth, cast as an apparently unbiased process that excludes no one.

Figure 1.6. Abandoned high school.

2009, graffiti on a classroom wall, viewed from the hallway.

The devaluation of areas impacted by urban decay obscures uneven development, described by Rosalyn Deutsche as the unequal distribution of prosperity, but also the aggressive territorialisation of both decaying and soon-to-be-regenerated spaces as key drivers of the kinds of economic and social exclusion that typify precarity. "Uneven economic and geographical development" is "structural" rather than "incidental", an inflection of developers' and government's perceptions that it is a lack of material prosperity, rather than social or cultural inequalities, that lie at the heart of poverty and urban decay (Deutsche 1996: 50). Uneven development was very much present amongst Detroit's ruins in 2009, and in 2015, but in different forms. Where the city of 2009 was declining and under-resourced, people I spoke to in 2015 recounted experiences of themselves or their friends and family being priced out of the run-down buildings or neighbourhoods where they had lived for years. As long-neglected areas began to revive, residents were asked to put up money for building fees or renovations that they could not afford on low incomes, and new residents brought increased market demand, higher expectations, and higher rents.

Figure 1.7. Detroit skyline.

2009, showing derelict and occupied buildings side-by-side, many of which were renewed or subject to planned renewal by 2015.

Demolition-focused renewal aggressively targets ruins as a kind of disease from which Detroit is suffering. A letter from the chairs of the Blight Removal

Task Force (one of whom is Dan Gilbert of Quicken Loans), declares that "Blight is a cancer. Blight sucks the soul out of anyone who gets near it, let alone those who are unfortunate enough to live with it all around them. Blight is radioactive. It is contagious" (Detroit Blight Removal Task Force, 2014). Saskia Sassen frames such development—in which people are displaced and moved on based on market demand and forces—in terms of expulsion, a symptom of the push towards economic growth, the triumph of a "new systemic logic" favouring corporate interest over public benefit and collective prosperity. Sassen writes "we have fallen under the sway of a dangerously narrow conception of economic growth… Anything or anybody, whether a law or a civic effort, that gets in the way of profit risks being pushed aside—expelled" (Sassen 2014: 213). The precarity I intercepted through ruins in 2009, that of market collapse, was being pushed aside in 2015 to usher in a new precarity, driven by market demand, destabilising already precarious lives.

Redevelopment of decaying sites tends to place existing residents who live in post-industrial cities in a position of further precarity, because, as Doreen Massey points out: the "mobility and control of some groups can actively weaken other people. Differential mobility can weaken the leverage of the already weak" (Massey 1994: 15). In this way, the most marginal residents are caught up in precarity, locked in by structures that have already rendered their existence economically precarious through deindustrialisation (Strangleman and Rhodes 2014), the loss of jobs and resulting urban shrinkage. These structures latterly provide them with options that are almost certain to generate a further precarious state: either gentrification and expulsion, or continued ruination of their city. The mobility of Detroit's residents is also structured around ruins: as these ruins are devalued, and their existence curtailed, so too is the mobility reduced of those who live amongst ruins. As some people exercise their relative mobility and move into a renewing neighbourhood, local people are made more precarious—priced out, foreclosed, moved on.

To return to the relation between ruin ethnography and precarity, for Stewart, "[p]recarity, written as an emergent form, can raise the question of how to approach ordinary tactile composition, everyday worldings that matter in many ways beyond their status as representations or objects of moralizing" (2012: 519). As my time in Detroit demonstrated, many local people are reliant upon the possibilities that decaying architectures might offer for what Stewart calls "worlding", an ordinary and everyday emergence of vitality and life in otherwise declining or depressed environments. A ruin-centric study of communities through urban decay demands a direct engagement with modern urban ruins as sites already populated by people whose precarity, but also whose possibilities for existence, are embedded in the uneven development of deindustrialisation, in the open and unstructured capacities of post-industrial space to support life in a vacuum of prosperity.

At one end of this spectrum, we have the seed of ruination—the American Rust Belt is a scene of made and unmade lives, where places start to lose their economic value as the economy shifts, buildings (factories, stores) become obsolete and are shut down, abandoned, leaving people out of work. If the recently unemployed cannot find more work, or sell-up and leave, their homes are, in turn, foreclosed, everything boarded up and left to rot. The cycle of abandonment leads to further ruin, as more stores, houses, restaurants are closed and unmaintained over years, then decades. As the population shrinks, amenities and services fall apart, too—train stations, hotels, petrol stations. Over time, such sites become ruins—non-functioning architectures, full of gaps and holes, missing the parts and structures to function for their designed use. Both "material and fantasmic" (Berlant 2011: 196), visible decay, as the sign of material obsolescence, can be read as an index of the precarity of accompanying everyday lives that are stranded without security. At the other end, the economy shifts again, these buildings, now in ruins, become viable commodities—subject to a new era of productive destruction that perceives not precarious residents who have waited for things to turn around, but untapped resources where a sagging building now stands—with the inevitable side effect of demolition, erasure, and lives further destabilised.

Figure 1.8. Abandoned house.

2009, opposite the high school (above), both demolished by 2015.

Berlant specifically points out that "blighted fields" are also sites of possibility, however, in which any kind of future might emerge—sites of investment by locals in "the change that's gonna come" (2011: 2)—yet when it does, the change is not meant for them, because they are seen to be part of the problem to be remediated by growth-oriented destructive renewal. As Lauren Berlant notes of post-industrial shrinking cities (as well as New Orleans after Hurricane Katrina), ruinous landscapes support active urban life, typically for people who are marginalised (in the case of Detroit and New Orleans, primarily unemployed, or underemployed, black residents), as these are the people who are least able to move away from a declining city, lacking the capital or networks to do so—impacted by differential mobility.

Conclusion

It was not until I revisited in 2015 that I began to feel equipped for the task of writing about Detroit. Unlike 2009, which in retrospect emerged as one of the bleakest periods in the recent history of the city, people were generally positive. Where, before, in the midst of the sub-prime mortgage crisis, with a corrupt and broke government, many I spoke with had been unable to speculate about the future, one word kept emerging—unprompted—in 2015: *imagine*. As my tour with Lucy indicated, everyday people, beyond the entrepreneurial vision for a gentrified and "revitalised" city, spoke hopefully of an open future yet to be mapped—though critical of aggressive change driven by imposed emergency managers and private investment. Those I spoke to felt that this official vision could not extend beyond a limited commercial zone, and that some of the energy of renewal could be harnessed for local and independent projects, for reconstruction rather than demolition. The city beyond greater downtown—more than 100 square miles—could be reimagined by anyone.

At the same time, as my tour with Avery demonstrated, by 2015 the city I had come to know in 2009 was under threat, partially disappeared by speculative investment, development logics, and the material erasure of people and places. As modern ruins disappear from Detroit, so too will the signs of a period of protracted precarity, a life lived amongst rubble and remnants, the residues left behind as a period of material growth and progress evaporated. But this evaporation is not an apolitical process—the disappearance of capital—of large factories and corporate offices, of the wealthiest citizens, of jobs and prosperity—is the structural effect of uneven development. This process—deindustrialisation, shrinking, abandonment, ruination, however it is named—is experienced by people as a process of precaritisation of existence, stripping them of their means to subsist, leaving them to make life amidst ruins. Even middle-class Detroiters who remained as the city declined were impacted by precarity, with many of their places eventually falling to ruin. This is where the politics can be located here, in an ethnographic practice that is situated within conditions of decline and decay that are easily apprehended in the material ruin, but co-exist with wider conditions that make life liveable, but also highly vulnerable, in shrinking and blighted cities.

Ruins are an index of precarity in two ways—firstly, where they stand for decades occupying the landscape, they speak of uneven development, disinvestment, and insecure conditions for those who don't have the mobility to relocate away from increasingly run-down and unstable neighbourhoods. Secondly, when redevelopment finally arrives, the sudden regeneration of a neighbourhood is a sign that those with capital are exercising their relative mobility, a manifestation of Berlant's cruel optimism (2011), where the change that residents wished for in their neighbourhood emerges as the change that devalues the sites of their everyday life and pushes them out, makes them even more precarious. Berlant's approach allows the researcher, analytically and politically, to "track the affective attachment to what we call 'the good life' which is for so many a bad life that wears out the subjects who nonetheless, and at the same time, find their conditions of possibility within it" (ibid.: 27).

Yet, ruins also support remembrance, as well as the imagining of a different future. It is not that ruins are not dangerous or unsightly, or that urban decay is necessary to provide liveable environments for the marginalised communities of Detroit, but something more nuanced than that: ruinous landscapes are open to possibility, and this is linked directly to the formation of precarious and insecure conditions of living in post-industrial cities, whether at the point of decline, or at the point of revitalisation. Unlike development-led rhetoric that derelict spaces are empty of human occupation, framing abandoned areas as the centre of a community's precarity rejects the implicit exclusion of *people* from derelict ruins. On a practical level, run-down neighbourhoods, though lacking in resources and services, are affordable for people on low incomes, with spaces available for art, music, or other creative practices. As Stewart, Tsing, Deutsche, Sassen, Massey and Berlant all emphasise in different ways, ruin and decline open up a space for everyday life, and they are not separate from the possibilities they afford.

Ruins are not ideal—even morally appropriate or guilt-free—spaces for renewal, but complex sites tangled up in precarity in ways that simultaneously disadvantage citizens and provide them with sites of possibility. In this way of thinking, the study of the transition from ostensibly inactive ruin to apparently regenerated place is not a straightforward change that replaces a lack with an abundance, but rather a transition from precarity as the emergence of alternative ways of existing amidst structural inequality, or conditions of neglect; to precarity as the exclusion from future possibilities of growth or change. These two modes of precarity are interrelated, characterised first by a vacuum of investment; secondly by the influx of capital, and are most visible in post-industrial urban decay through the transformation from architecture, to ruin, to renewal.

Thus, expulsion does not merely include physical dispossession or displacement of the already precarious, it is also the symbolic disconnection of oppressed groups in the post-industrial city through the very same mechanism—where once there was a boom, the bust generated a precarious population amidst Detroit's decaying inner city, a population that is, in turn, made more precarious by the obverse of decay—unchecked growth. The human presences in ruins—whether for creative practice, or other activities—that were obvious during my visits are implicitly threatened by aggressive redevelopment. It is not just economic collapse, the absence of employment, a lack of services, and the presence of abjection and decay that drives precarity for local populations in Detroit and other Rust-Belt cities. For those left behind amidst the ruins, only to be pushed aside just as the ruins are disappeared, Tsing's claim is particularly true: "in a global state of precarity, we don't have choices other than looking for life in this ruin" (2015: 6).

While Detroit in 2009 was typified by an absence of hope, the impossibility of even conceiving of any coming change (not even Berlant's cruel optimism), by 2015—and, indeed, in 2019—what is precarious is the possibility for life to go on for many insecure resident citizens in the inner city areas marked for renewal. The life that still persists in the real and figurative ruins of capitalism and global development, but is at risk of being extinguished by development logics that are enabled, from the beginning, by discourses about urban ruination that pre-empt evictions and expulsions. To intercept these sites at the moment of decline, through ruin-focused ethnographic work, is to understand the felt habitation of urban shrinkage and mass abandonment, revealing the contradiction of growth-driven logic that generates rubble-fields, and the alternative possibilities for life that are epitomised by those who make-do amongst ruins.

Note: The tour guide's names have been anonymized, in line with the style of this volume.

References

Apel, D. (2015) *Beautiful Terrible Ruins: Detroit and the anxiety of decline.* New Brunswick, NJ and London: Rutgers University Press.

Berlant, L. (2011) *Cruel Optimism.* Durham, NC and London: Duke University Press.

Berman, M. (1982) *All That Is Solid Melts into Air: The experience of modernity.* New York, NY: Viking Penguin.

Berman, M. (1987) 'Among the ruins'. *New Internationalist,* 178. Available at: https://newint.org/features/1987/12/05/among.

Berman, M. (2014) 'Emerging from the ruins'. *Dissent,* 61(1, Winter 2014).

Clement, D. and Kanai, M. (2015) 'The Detroit future city: How pervasive neoliberal urbanism exacerbates racialised spatial injustice'. *American Behavioural Scientist,* 59(3), 369–385.

Del Valle, G. (2017) 'Detroit is using federal funds to demolish homes'. *The Outline,* 19(July). Available at: https://theoutline.com/post/1935/detroit-is-using-federal-funding-to-demolish-homes?zd=1&zi=k7ri2ed3.

DeSilvey, C. (2014) Palliative Curation: Art and Entropy on Orford Ness. *In:* Olsen, B. and Pétursdóttir, Þ. (eds) *Ruin Memories: Materiality, Aesthetics and the Archaeology of the Recent Past.* London and New York: Routledge.

DeSilvey, C. (2017) *Curated Decay: Heritage beyond saving.* Minneapolis and London: University of Minnesota Press.

DeSilvey, C. and Edensor, T. (2012) 'Reckoning with ruins'. *Progress in Human Geography,* 1(21).

Detroit Blight Removal Task Force. (2014) *Detroit Blight Removal Task Force Plan* [Online]. Available at: http://report.timetoendblight.org/index.html.

Deutsche, R. (1996) *Evictions: Art and spatial politics.* Cambridge, MA: MIT Press.

Draus, P. and Roddy, J. (2016) 'Ghosts, devils, and the undead city: Detroit and the narrative of monstrosity'. *Space and Culture,* 19(1), 67–79.

Edensor, T. (2008) Walking through Ruins. *In:* Ingold, T. and Vergunst, J.L. (eds) *Ways of Walking: Ethnography and Practice on Foot.* Aldershot: Ashgate.

Fraser, E. (2012) Urban Exploration as Adventure Tourism: Journeying Beyond the Everyday. *In:* Andrews, H. and Roberts, L. (eds) *Liminal Landscapes: Travel, Experience, and Spaces in-Between.* Abingdon, Oxon and New York: Routledge.

Fraser, E. (2017) 'Unbecoming place: Urban imaginaries in transition in Detroit. *Cultural Geographies,* Online First. Available at: https://doi.org/10.1177/1474474017748508.

Galster, G. (2012) *Driving Detroit: The quest for respect in the Motor City.* Philadelphia: University of Pennsylvania Press.

Green, T. (2015) 'Places of inequality, places of possibility: Mapping "opportunity in geography" across urban school-communities'. *The Urban Review,* 47(2), 717–741.

Herron, J. (2007) 'Detroit: Disaster deferred, disaster in progress'. *South Atlantic Quarterly,* 106:4(Fall 2007), 663–682.

Hudson-Webber Foundation, Detroit Economic Growth Corporation, the Downtown Detroit Partnership, Midtown Detroit Inc., Invest Detroit & Data Driven Detroit. (2013) 7.2 Sq Mi Report. 2nd edn. http://detroitsevenpointtwo.com/.

Jacobs, J. (1984) *The Death and Life of Great American Cities.* Harmondsworth: Penguin in assoc. with Cape.

Kinder, K. (2014) 'Guerrilla-style defensive architecture in Detroit: A self-provisioned security strategy in a neoliberal space of disinvestment'. *International Journal of Urban and Regional Research*, 38.5(September 2014).

Kirkpatrick, L. O. (2015) 'Urban triage, city systems, and the remnants of community: Some "sticky" complications in the greening of Detroit'. *Journal of Urban History*, 41(2), 261–278.

Leary, J.P. (2011) 'Detroitism.' *Guernica*. Available at: https://http://www.guernicamag.com/features/leary_1_15_11/.

Lees, L. and Melhuish, C. (2015) 'Arts-led regeneration in the UK: The rhetoric and the evidence on urban social inclusion'. *European Urban and Regional Studies*, 22(3): 242–260.

Lees, L., Slater, T. and Wyly, E. (2008) *Gentrification*. New York and Oxon: Routledge.

Mah, A. (2012) 'Demolition for development: A critical analysis of official urban imaginaries in past and present UK cities'. *Journal of Historical Sociology*, 25(1): 151–176.

Marchand, Y. and Meffre, R. (2009) 'Detroit's beautiful, horrible decline'. *Time Magazine*. Available at: http://content.time.com/time/photogallery/0,29307,1882089,00.html.

Marchand, Y. and Meffre, R. (2010) *The Ruins of Detroit*. Go¨ttingen: Steidl.

Massey, D. (1994) *Space, Place and Gender*. Minneapolis: University of Minnesota Press.

Massey, D. (2002) Living in Wythenshaw. *In:* Borden, I., Kerr, J., Rendell, J. and Pivaro, A. (eds) *The Unknown City: Contesting Architeture and Social Space*. Cambridge, MA: MIT Press.

Massey, D. (2004) 'Geographies of responsibility'. *Geografiska Annaler*, 8(B(1)): 5–18.

McDonald, J.F. (2014) 'What happened to and in Detroit'. *Urban Studies*, (September 2013): 1–21.

Mott, C. and Roberts, S.M. (2013) 'Not everyone has (the) balls: Urban exploration and the persistence of masculinist geography'. *Antipode*, 46(1): 229–245.

Reese, L.A., Eckert, J., Sands, G. and Vojnovic, I. (2016) '"It's safe to come, we've got lattes": Development disparities in Detroit'. *Cities*, 60: 367–377.

Rhodes, J. (2015) Extending the "Urban Disaster" Paradigm: From New Orleans to Detroit (and Beyond?). *In:* Taylor, W.M., Levine, M.P., Rooksby, O. and Sobott, J.-K. (eds) *The "Katrina Effect": On the Nature of Catastrophe*. London: Bloomsbury Academic.

Safransky, S. (2014) 'Greening the urban frontier: Race, property, and resettlement in Detroit'. *Geoforum*, 56: 237–248.

Safransky, S. (2018) 'Land justice as a historical diagnostic: Thinking with Detroit'. *Annals of the American Association of Geographers*, 108(2): 499–512.

Sassen, S. (2014) *Expulsions: Brutality and Complexity in the Global Economy*. Cambridge, MA: Belknap Press.

Schindler, S. (2014) 'Detroit after bankruptcy: A case of degrowth machine politics'. *Urban Studies*, 53(4): 818–836.

Stewart, K. (1996) *A Space on the Side of the Road: Cultural Poetics in an "Other" America.* Princeton, NJ: Princeton University Press.

Stewart, K. (2012) 'Precarity's forms'. *Cultural Anthropology*, 27(3): 518–525.

Stoler, A.L. (2008) 'Imperial debris: A reflection on ruins and ruination'. *Cultural Anthropology*, 23(2): 191–219.

Stoler, A.L. (2013) *Imperial Debris: On Ruins and Ruination.* Durham, NC and London: Duke University Press.

Stone, J. (2017) *Detroit 1967.* Detroit, MI: Wayne State University Press.

Strangleman, T. (2013) '"Smokestack nostalgia," "ruin porn" or working-class obituary: The role and meaning of deindustrial representation'. *International Labor and Working-Class History*, 84(Fall 2013): 23–37.

Strangleman, T. and Rhodes, J. (2014) 'The "new" sociology of deindustrialisation? Understanding industrial change'. *Sociology Compass*, 8(4): 411–421.

Sugrue, T. (1996) *The Origins of the Urban Crisis.* Princeton, NJ: Princeton University Press.

Tsing, A.L. (2015) *The Mushroom at the End of the World: On the Possibility of Life in Capitalist Ruins.* Princeton, NJ: Princeton University Press.

Chapter 2

Urbanists and the city

Notes on an ethnographic approach to urban planning

Alice Stefanelli, University of Durham

Abstract

This chapter responds to calls for more empirically grounded research to be conducted in order to move beyond discursive analysis to understand the practical impact of neoliberal policy on urban life worldwide. The chapter provides an ethnographic investigation of the profound physical and social restructuring of life in Beirut over the past two decades and investigates the socio-historical conditions that have generated these changes. This direct ethnographic engagement does more than support the case for empirical research, specifically through participant observation, and also engages with the specific contingencies of the rise of neoliberal urban policy in Beirut. It clarifies the necessity to broaden the scope of a body of post-industrial scholarship that has largely focused on the decline of Fordist-Keynesianism in the Global North, and argues for a consideration of other neoliberal genealogies that emerge from beyond these geopolitical borders.

***

Half of the world's population now resides in cities (United Nations, 2014). As a consequence, urban life is increasingly the object of scrutiny. A fundamental part of the analysis of contemporary urban life involves making sense of the enormous spatial and social transformations that are the outcome of shifting global political landscapes and economic circumstances. Since the management of the built environment affects not only the physical, but also the social landscape of cities, urbanism is assuming growing importance.

In the past 30 years, scholarship that investigates the urban condition has particularly concentrated on the issues posed by neoliberalism to the governance of cities. At a basic level, neoliberalism may be characterised as a highly ideological form of political and economic doctrine based on the belief that unregulated markets, liberated from state interferences, free trade and a bias in favour of capital are the key elements of economic success (Moody 1997; Brenner and Theodore 2002). In this, neoliberalism is significantly different from the Fordist-Keynesian form of capitalism that had come to dominate industrialised countries in the aftermath of WW2, and which was focused on state regulation of the economy; a well-oiled welfare state system; the aspiration to full employment and institutionalised collective bargaining for wages and social security (Jessop 1996).

Upheld by a new generation of politicians such as Thatcher in the UK and Reagan in the USA, neoliberal policies have risen fast, eroding the so-called post-war 'Keynesian consensus.' In post-Fordist societies, this has entailed a comprehensive reorganisation of all aspects of life, captured by Soja's (1987) notion of 'restructuring'. In concrete terms, neoliberalisation has entailed the withering of the welfare state, the advent of post-industrialism and a new, shrunken role for the state in economic life (Jessop 2002). With regard to matters of urban governance, the growth of phenomena such as inter-city competition, the influence of the private sector on policy making and the rise of public-private partnerships_(PPPs) have been particularly stressed (Brenner and Theodore 2005).

Scholars have analysed in depth the discursive nature of neoliberal ideology, so as to not take the official narrative of neoliberalism at face-value (Brenner and Theodore, 2002). This analytical commitment has also taken the shape of calls for empirically grounded research to be done into "actually existing neoliberalism" (ibid.), with the aim of arriving at a more precise understanding of what "neoliberal governance" looks like, concretely and in specific socio-historical contexts. This chapter responds to such invitations by interrogating ethnographically the contemporary forms of urban governance in Beirut. Particular attention is paid to the profound restructuring of the built and social environment that has taken place in the past two and a half decades.

Beirut is not usually thought of as a post-industrial city, since it never embraced predominantly Western Fordist-Keynesianism. While a certain degree of industrialisation did take place and the labour movement shook the country at various times in the post-WW2 era (Traboulsi 2012), Lebanon was rather known as a "merchant republic" in the 1950s (Gates 1998) Lebanon's *laissez faire* economy_relied in fact on trade and the service sector, including high-end tourism, banking and real estate, at the expenses of both agriculture and industry (ibid.). Yet, it is interesting to look at Beirut in a conversation on contemporary post-industrialism because, albeit due to a different historical trajectory, the Lebanese capital is today faced with some of the same issues of urban governance as other post-industrial cities in Europe and North America.

In fact, in the aftermath of the 16-year long civil conflict, in 1990,[1] the country strengthened its *laissez faire* heritage by inaugurating a time of renewed enthusiasm for the private sector in general, particularly with relation to policy making in relating to the built environment (Fawaz 2016). The result is that Beirutis have been struggling with decades of incessant privatisation of public space and of the urban commons such as public parks and the seafront, as well as an unprecedented explosion of real estate development. The latter has engendered a sort of social cleansing of some areas of the city, since skyrocketing rents and property values have rendered life unaffordable for many lower-middle-class and working-class inhabitants. Beirut can thus be discussed in conjunction with post-Fordist countries where urban management is increasingly slipping away from public control (for instance, see Siemiatychi 2005).

Starting from ethnographic data on advocacy for the protection of public spaces from privatisation, this chapter will thus contextualise and detail the 'actually existing neoliberalism' of Beirut's urban governance, highlighting particularly the tensions existing between global narratives, regional dynamics and local heritage. Starting from the premise that neoliberalism manifests itself differently in different contexts, and that this plurality of neoliberalism*s* presents similar traits, but is not necessarily the consequence of the same socio-historical dynamics, the argument will be made that the post-Keynesian narrative should be understood as one of many genealogies of neoliberalism. More room should thus be made for other genealogies, not only to acknowledge their existence, but also in order to improve our understanding of neoliberal processes.

In addition, this chapter will argue for a renewed ethnographic engagement with urban governance, particularly focused on aspects of urban redevelopment that are less attended to, such as policy making, project design and implementation. Using ethnographic data on urbanism in Beirut as one of many possible examples, this chapter contends that by interrogating urban restructuring by 'studying up' we are able to appreciate that neoliberal urban policies and the expert discourses that are used to justify them are contested in their early stages in professional spheres such as conferences, meetings, workshops.

In so doing, we can identify some of the frictions already existing in the process of urban governance, which can be used by critics of the current order as pressure points to affect change. Ultimately, opening up our analytical attention to these dynamics and actors might be an opportunity to meet unexpected allies with which to form new coalitions to fight for a different kind of governance for our cities.

Post-industrial Beirut? Keynesianism, neoliberalism and urban governance in Lebanon

Much scholarship interrogating the contemporary urban condition focuses on North America and Europe, and often makes a link between the fall of the Keynesian paradigm and the rise of neoliberalism. Championed by political leaders such as Ronald Reagan in the US and Margaret Thatcher in Britain in the 1970s and 1980s, neoliberal policies marked the beginning of a new era in matters of both social and economic governance. Two distinct phases have been distinguished: one of "rolling-back" and one of "rolling out" (Peck and Tickell 2002). During the first phase, from around the 1980s, the role of the state was shrunk, a process that is commonly seen as one of 'hollowing out'; the dismantling of Keynesian style measures such as the state regulation of the labour market, or the welfare system of social security occurred at this time. More recently, neoliberalism has been experienced in Beirut as a phase of active state-building through which new kinds of social and penal policies were 'rolled out' that actively support a deregulated social and economic market system (ibid.).

Recently, it has been recognised that Keynesianism was perhaps never as dominant and undisputed as it had previously been thought to be, and that it has been at times romanticised (Hoffman, DeHart and Collier 2006; Leitner *et al.* 2007). Likewise, it has been noted that the neoliberal paradigm might not be as coherent and univocal as its proponents and, sometimes, analysts would have it (Peck, Theodore and Brenner 2009; Peck 2010). Scholars have thus rather proposed a notion of liberalis*ation* which describes neoliberalism as a continuous and tentative, trial-and-error process, rather than a monolithic *fait accompli* (ibid.). Calls have also been issued encouraging scholars to engage with a broader range of actually unravelling neoliberal processes, in order to bridge the gap between a—largely Western-oriented—theoretical paradigm of neoliberal urban governance and actually unravelling local processes in diverse locations (Brenner and Theodore 2002; Jessop 2002; Kalb 2012).

Lebanon sits uncomfortably within a theoretical paradigm that postulates the advent of neoliberalism as the consequence of an ideological victory over Keynesianism, an event contiguous with the end of Fordism and the erosion of the central role of the state. Fordism, for one, never took a strong ideological hold of the small Levantine country; rather, Independent Lebanon adopted a strong measure of economic liberalism and emerged as a 'merchant republic' in the post-WWII years. Gates (1998: 7–8) argues that: "Lebanon was clearly opposing the tide of history in the 1950s when, elsewhere, developed economies were adopting Keynesian demand management and welfare statism; and post-colonial nationalist governments embraced state activism and inward development strategies". Independent Lebanon chose in fact an economic model that was outward-looking and service-oriented, based on the country's intermediary role between the West and the Middle East. In line with powerful elite interests, banking, high-end tourism and real estate were given absolute priority. Gates (1998) emphasises that the choice of privileging these sectors over others was controversial and did not win everybody's favour. Embracing an economic ideology of *laissez faire* trumped the interests of those who benefitted from a more inward-looking economy, oriented towards production, such as industrialists, skilled and industrial workers. Ultimately, however, the interests of the mercantile-financial elites got the upper hand. In addition to these economic considerations, it should be highlighted that Lebanon's approach to social security is also very far from typical state-centred Fordist approaches. The access to services and welfare is in fact strongly interwoven with clientelistic networks, which are embedded in the logics of sectarian political economy (Salloukh *et al.* 2015). This means that each political party provides access to welfare services, education and job opportunities to its own clients, who typically share the same sectarian belonging. On the one hand, this set-up explains the continuing grip of political sectarianism over citizens. On the other, it highlights another area where Lebanon differed from the standard Keynesian-Fordist model.

Yet it is possible today to observe in Beirut many of the neoliberal phenomena in urban redevelopment and governance that have been noted elsewhere. A host of neoliberal-style policies were in fact ushered into the country in the aftermath of the long 1975–1990 civil conflict, initiated by businessman-turned-politician Rafic Hariri.

Hariri made his fortune working in the construction industry in Saudi Arabia and the Gulf, although through his engineering firm, Oger Liban, he was present in Lebanon throughout the war years (Makdisi 1997; Stewart 1996). After assuming the premiership in 1992, he immediately started a programme of reforms to rebuild the country. Hariri's reforms resembled IMF-style stabilisation measures, focused around the stabilisation of the Lebanese pound, the rise of public debt and infrastructural improvement with a view to restoring the country's role as a regional banking and finance node (Denoeux and Springborg 1998). During this period, the influence of the private sector on the public sector expanded dramatically, leading to the blurring of the boundaries between the two.

This dynamic is most evident in the case of the reconstruction of Beirut's city centre. The project was implemented by Solidere, a joint-stock company created by the Council for the Development and Reconstruction (henceforth CDR) headed by one of Hariri's own Oger employees. Solidere alone would oversee the reconstruction of the whole Downtown area, adopting a masterplan delivered by consultancy group Dar al-Handasah, which had been already commissioned to deliver a similar project by Oger in the early 1980s (Makdisi 1997).[2] At the time, a strong argument in favour of the heavy involvement of the private sector symbolised by the figure of the Prime Minister was that the public sector was too inefficient to see the project through successfully. Yet this arrangement between the state and private entities could also be seen as a de-facto abdication of the state of its role and responsibilities, since the major player in the private real estate sector—Oger Liban—now led the CDR, the principal public planning agency (Sarkis 1993).

Traboulsi (2014) argues that a direct parallel may be drawn between some of the historical characteristics of the Lebanese economy and political system, always strongly influenced by political interests, and the neoliberalisation of the post-civil war period. In fact, the strengthening of the influence of the private sector on public decision making and the focus on the service and construction industry can be seen as vigorous extensions of already existing trends in Lebanese history. Yet, even acknowledging the strong continuities with the pre-civil war past, the magnitude of the changes that the new economic climate has had on the city in the past 20-odd years should not be underestimated. Two decades of aggressive real estate development have altered the social and architectural fabric of the city and reshaped its landscape. It is to the details of this "creative destruction" (Harvey 2007) that I now turn.

The city today

A great deal of reconstruction, redevelopment and reconfiguration has been taking place in the Lebanese capital since 1990, starting, as already mentioned, from Downtown Beirut. The city centre, *al balad*, was the focus of Prime Minister Hariri's reconstruction project and it was from there that the reconstruction efforts began. The Downtown area had been one of the great theatres of war of the civil conflict, and the fighting had seriously damaged it. What was once the bubbling heart of a socially and religiously mixed polity now stood empty and abandoned. While beginning the reconstruction of Beirut from its symbolic heart made sense to most, the plan for the works and the manner in which the decision was agreed, despite widespread criticism, displeased large numbers of citizens. The heavy involvement of the private sector suggested a bias towards the economic interests of entrepreneurs and developers rather than citizens, while the high-end nature of the Horizon 2000 project betrayed the memory of the previous socially mixed and inclusive character of Downtown, changing the latter into a rather exclusive, separate enclave for the wealthy (Naccache 1998). The government's determination to implement Solidere's plan smoothly was such that all those who owned properties in Downtown were expropriated and compensated with company shares (Makdisi 1997).

The project in fact entailed the destruction, rather than the restoration of several historic buildings in the city centre, including the Ottoman souqs, which in the national imaginary were the symbol of a diverse yet peaceful Lebanon whose image had been shattered by the war (Makdisi 1997; Naccache 1998). This was so that a new *wassat Beirut al tijali* ('Beirut business district'), or Beirut Central District, could rise from the ashes of the old *balad.* In place of the old buildings, a new urban fabric imposed itself in the city centre as a mix of pastiche classical Lebanese buildings and glass-and-steel skyscrapers, luxury office blocks and mixed-use towers.

Eventually, some of these buildings became the headquarters of international bodies such as UNESCO, the Union of Arab Banks and several foreign embassies. A number of others, however, were never filled, even to this day. The new souqs, renamed 'Beirut Souks', bore no obvious resemblance with their predecessors. Rather, they were built as a large, modern-looking shopping mall, equipped mainly with high-end boutiques and fashionable brands, a world-wide neoliberal template for global retail consumption that Mitchell (1999) describes as a new "Disneyland of your desires". In time, the construction frenzy in the city centre exceeded its borders, extending to the waterfront and other nearby areas. This led to the redevelopment of the coastal area with the creation of high-end marinas such as the well-known Zaytouna Bay and, further down the coast, the Moven Pick Hotel.

The 'Horizon 2000' reconstruction project ultimately sought to fabricate a new identity for Beirut, which would put the country back on the map as a regional business hub (Shwairy 2008). In a speech to the World Affairs Council in 1996, PM Hariri expressed his aspiration that Beirut may soon become a new "Singapore of the Middle East" (Hakim and Andary 1997). Hariri thus bet on the development of a service economy that rested on the same sectors that had traditionally made the country the "Switzerland of the East", with an economic base focusing on tourism, finance, real estate and banking.

If the country at large was presumed to benefit from the rebirth of the Central District, previous Downtown property owners and residents of neighbouring areas experienced the process in rather different ways. Owners and displaced people were evicted; the former were given shares in Solidere, while after long negotiations with the government, the latter were compensated financially. This particular moment in time was captured ethnographically by Sawalha (2010), whose work *Reconstructing Beirut* depicts the restructuring of Downtown and adjacent neighbourhoods in the mid-1990s. Sawalha's project was to analyse the ways in which neighbourhoods adjacent to Downtown were being affected by the latter's reconstruction. For this reason, during her first field trip to Beirut in 1995, she was drawn to the low-income neighbourhood of Zqaq el Blat, located at a stone's throw from the city centre. Yet when the anthropologist returned six months later, most of the area stood empty, since residents had been evicted, included the many displaced individuals and families who had found refuge there during the war. The reconstruction machine had been activated and its displacing effects had quickly begun to be felt by the most vulnerable inhabitants of central Beirut.

Figure 2.1. Cranes and skyscrapers punctuate the skyline in Downtown Beirut.

Photo by the author.

The unravelling of Horizon 2000 thus produced much displacement and dispossession in Beirut; it also translated into a process of de-facto social cleansing at the expenses of lower-income inhabitants. As its 'creative destruction' expanded towards nearby neighbourhoods, costs of rent and property increased considerably in the city, quickly becoming unaffordable for many of the previous residents. Targeted by developers, neighbourhoods that had been socially mixed before the war suddenly became unaffordable to most. The dramatic increase in living costs, added to lacking public service provision, has significantly changed the social composition of entire sections of town (Achkar 2012; Geisser and Pieri 2014). The outcome, of course, has been that local inhabitants have been progressively pushed out of the city, as fewer and fewer Beirutis today can afford to live in the central neighbourhoods. In turn, the new properties are mainly owned—but not necessarily actively inhabited—by wealthy Lebanese, residing in Lebanon as well as in the diaspora, and foreign Arab nationals.

If the history of Beirut might seem specific to its national context in certain respects, for example, the long civil war, and the tradition of economic liberalism as well as the specificities of sectarian divides, its case should not be analysed in isolation. Nor should it be situated as a point of simple comparison with Western trends of neoliberal urbanism alone. This is because today, as it was in the past, Beirut is located within social, political and economic regional networks that allow for the flow of ideas, know-hows and capital across national boundaries in the Middle East and North Africa. It is important, therefore, to situate an analysis of Beirut in the context of a broader, regional understanding of a diverse Arab-Muslim sphere of influence.

Without falling in the perhaps Orientalist illusion of a homogenous Arab-Muslim urbanistic sphere, this regional space should be considered in the analysis of the way that Beirut has and still develops, changes, and is restructured. A closer look at contemporary regional flows and networks is therefore essential.

Beirut and the 'Arab city'

If the exploration of the significance of neoliberal urban governance in the West has been the domain of critical urban studies, the predicament of contemporary Arab cities has been analysed primarily by scholars working in the more technical fields of architecture, urban planning and other neighbouring disciplines. Although this line of enquiry has traditionally paid more attention to the technical aspects of planning and real estate development, in Beirut this endeavour has proved extremely productive with respect to a better understanding of the economic and political processes shaping Arab urban spaces today.

The first task that much of this scholarship set for itself was a thorough critique of existing literature on the development of Arab cities in the modern and contemporary period. This meant first and foremost questioning the taken for granted paradigm of the traditional 'Arab/Moslem city', which had largely dominated the classical twentieth-century analysis of Arab urban development. The 'Arab/Moslem' paradigm relies on an Orientalist, static approach to the history and development of cities in the region, positing that cities in the Arab world had reached their peak in medieval times, giving birth to the 'traditional' Islamic city as an a-temporal, unchanged and monolithic entity replicated everywhere across the entire region. One consequence of such a premise is the assumption that the subsequent experience of colonisation and, more recently, of globalisation, have represented a corruption of the 'authentic' Arab-Muslim model, and, therefore, a dramatic loss of identity (Elsheshtawy 2004; Raymond 1994).

Recent scholarship has responded to this claim by highlighting the long-term inclusion of Arab-Muslim cities in global networks of ideas, capital and investment. Elsheshtawy (2004) has noted that this inclusion is not only a product of recent globalisation, but rather is a consequence of the history of twentieth-century European colonial domination. This, of course, exposes Arab-Muslim cities to some of the same global trends that affect large cities everywhere. For instance, Barthel (2010) remarks that current urban planning in the Arab region is structured around "mega-projects", with large-scale real estate developments characterised, like many of urban counterparts elsewhere in the world, by an unprecedented scale of investment, as well as a sizeable involvement of the private sector, often through public-private partnerships (PPPs) (see also Verdeil 2006).

Daher (2011) argues that in practical terms, these major developments often create luxury "urban islands" of intense consumption devoted to the provision of high-quality leisure and business services to local and foreign elites. In fact, typically the rationale behind these radical developments—or redevelopments—is the creation of urban milieus that are sympathetic to business—and notably finance and banking—and that may be attractive to foreign investors, thus facilitating the influx of foreign capital into the country (Summer 2006). Arab 'mega-projects'_do resemble, then, a globalised style of neoliberal urbanism, but Barthel (2010) concludes that certain specificities of the Middle Eastern context do exist, such as the fact that these projects are conceived and implemented by authoritarian regimes, and typically in total disregard for participatory approaches to planning. Yet, Barthel's most salient observation is that the multiplication of Arab 'mega-projects' is frequently bonded to an emerging trans-Arab brand of capitalism revolving around the Gulf states and powered by oil revenues. In this context, urbanistic models and know-how originate in the Gulf and travel elsewhere as a diversion from historical trends in Arab urbanism, which previously held Cairo and Beirut as regional reference points (Daher 2011).

In practical terms, 'mega-projects' typically entail the construction of high-end residential high-rises and gated communities, as well as luxury business districts composed of mixed-use towers and skyscrapers. It is clear that the construction of such large and imposing complexes requires a significant expansion of empty land to be available in the first place, as a sort of 'clean slate' pre-requisite. Elsheshtawy has noted that these kinds of developments are well-suited to the environments of Gulf cities such as Dubai or Doha which, "unburdened by history, ... are free to create a new identity and in turn serve as a model for the rest of the Arab world" (2008: 2). The Dubai model has surely inspired several local adaptations of the same urbanistic principles, including Beirut—as we have explored—and Amman. Yet, no effective urbanistic hegemony has been produced by the intra-Arab circulation of capital and ideas (Daher 2013)—we are thus far from speaking of anything like a prototype of the—singular, homogeneous—'Arab city' of the new millennium.

The effects of restructuring

Urban restructuring does not only change the form of the city. This model of urban redevelopment inevitably disrupts established modes of local life. 'Mega-projects', whether enabled by capital from the Gulf or not, have a tremendous impact on the social fabric of areas where they are built. Especially in the case of cities that are densely built and where land is scarce, implementing 'mega-projects' has in fact required the demolition of the existing built environment and the de-facto eviction and displacement of the local populations who inhabited it—whether due to forced evictions or because rent and property prices skyrocket. Beirut's regeneration of Downtown is far from being the only example.

Mona Abaza's (2001) report on the changing landscape of Cairo's Boulaq neighbourhood reveals similar concerns. Since the 1990s, this popular area had been targeted by developers. New complexes were erected such as the World Trade Centre Mall, which houses the headquarters of the United Nations, the African Export Bank, or the Conrad and Hilton exclusive residential tower. The local ways of life were inevitably disrupted by these developments, as the cheap markets, cafés and shops used by local residents disappeared, to be replaced by more expensive, high-end counterparts suited to the new clientele brought by the malls. Discussing the recent building of yet another mall in the area, Abaza notes that "the people of the quarter ... expressed resentment and fear of the government. Everybody knows that the days of the popular quarters are numbered and eviction is soon to come" (ibid.: 113).

Daher (2013) argues that even though they are often disguised as best urbanistic practice under the title of "regeneration", 'mega-projects' in fact often have as their end result the division, or "quartering", of urban space (Elsheshtawy 2004) between newly created islands of privilege and the rest of the urban fabric. The outcome of this reorganisation of space is the production of new spatial divisions in the city based on socio-economic status.

Neoliberal urban governance, in the Arab-Muslim world and beyond, revolves around the implementation of urbanistic models that visibly devalue, penalise and dismiss the modes of life of disadvantaged urban populations, by creatively destroying them in order to make room for more exclusive lifestyles and ways of dwelling. If urban management is thus the tool used by authorities and powerful private actors to carry out such work of restructuring, it is to 'actually existing' policy-making processes, urbanistic practices, and to the power entanglements that support them that most attention should be directed.

A place for ethnography

Notwithstanding the contextual specificities, something that links together urban governance in cities around the world is the fundamental role of urbanism. This is to be understood as the study of urban life and the planning of cities' physical environment in terms of its development and redevelopment. Urbanism as a practice involves, of course, a host of different actors: policy makers and urbanists, politicians as well as technicians. And while more participatory modes of urban management might include the citizenry (Lynch 1981), the reality of planning often excludes local residents from the decision-making process, as this often takes place behind closed doors, without any formal consultation process. While officially planning might be presented as an objective matter that depends on the rational application of technical principles and on other strictly scientific considerations, this is often a discursive representation of how planning works. Political factors, ideological inclinations and powerful interests regularly interfere with the ideals of planning.

James Scott's (1998) analysis of Baron Haussmann's restructuring of Paris is illustrative of this point. This can be seen as a textbook case of top-down urbanism. Although Baron Haussmann did not have a clean slate at his disposal, his retrofitting of Paris in the mid-nineteenth century was an early example of comprehensive urban planning founded on modernising ideas hinging on military and economic functionalism. The new boulevards that cut through the city would allow troops to deploy quickly and effectively in case of rebellions, while the updating of the sewage system would improve the health of citizens, which in turn would enhance the economic performance of the city itself. From this perspective, the destruction of popular neighbourhoods and the displacement of their inhabitants caused by the new urbanistic plan of the city was a necessary, even welcomed side-effect. Firstly, the new boulevards constituted in fact a "sanitised" urban space that conformed to middle-class taste. Secondly, the clearing up of congested, crowded low-income areas facilitated military control over Paris, as the army could easily march down the broad avenues, deploying quickly anywhere in the city in case of revolt (Harvey 2003).

Yet, political interests trumped the rational principles that, in theory animated urban planning. Scott highlights that, beyond military logics, the building of rectilinear, imposing boulevards reflected the political interests and taste of Louis Napoleon, whose main concern was portraying the grandeur of the Empire, regardless of other technical or functional rationales. This meant that often the grand facades lining the boulevards simply masked some of the chaotic, unsanitary quarters that Baron Haussmann's plans ignored altogether. As Scott puts it, "the zoning regulations were almost exclusively concerned with the visible surfaces of buildings, but behind the facades, builders could build crowded, airless tenements, and many of them did" (1998: 62).

Condensing technical, political and ideological logics, urban plans are thus a blueprint of the web of relations that shape the social and physical landscape of cities. Urbanistic practice is thus a key site for the examination of the complex mechanisms that actually shape decision making in matters of urban governance. However, while scholars in urban studies, architecture and political sciences have shown considerable interest in studying the dynamics of urbanism in the contemporary remaking of cities, these dynamics have not typically been approached from an ethnographic point of view (with rare exceptions, such as Boholm 2013 and Evans 2016).

Most direct engagements with urbanistic practices have focused on policies as already-made products, and with a specific interest in the consequences of their implementation. The dynamics responsible for the decision making and implementation themselves have not been the object of direct ethnographic scrutiny, perhaps also due to the challenges that accessing the elite organisational and institutional urban structures of planning and politics (Barthel 2010).

However, even when the difficulties of securing access to the backstage of certain projects rule out the possibility for ethnography altogether, I contend that alternatives exist. By considering board meetings or the offices of the city council as the only sites from which to investigate the shaping of processes of urban change, ethnographers lose sight of other windows into the urbanistic process. By concentrating on council members and construction patrons, ethnographers overlook other important actors—such as the urban planners and other architects of change—whose work is fundamental to the realisation of projects and whose practice is itself shaped by the intricate web of interests at play.

Planners are usually imagined as technicians in the employment of public authorities, and thus it is assumed that they could most readily be found in the offices of public planning agencies, where architects, urbanists and engineers design plans for public works. After all, planning was one of the self-assigned tasks of modern states in the post-war period, as well as of colonial governments in the past (Robertson 1984). These settings might prove difficult to access in contexts where transparency in public administration might be a problem. The same could be said for large private consultancies that might not desire to have their work scrutinised by social scientists and then risk having their brand and credibility questioned. However, professionals involved in the designing of our cities do not work exclusively in these environments. In my own ethnographic fieldwork in Beirut, I followed a number of civic mobilisations for the defence of public space, one of which involved a campaign for the protection of the coastline from privatisation and another attempted to reopen a long-closed public park. There I encountered a diverse group of campaigners, many of whom professionals working in fields such as environmentalism, public health, architecture and urbanism, united by a common interest in urban governance. Different generations of campaigners worked side by side, as some of those who had lost the fight against Solidere in the 1990s had returned to the "barricades" next to a younger generation of 20- and 30-year-olds.

The pressing concern lying behind these campaigns was, of course, the intense redevelopment of Beirut's central areas that had been putting much pressure on the few remaining green spaces. Since the real estate industry seemed on a mission to "fill every gap" (Krijnen 2013) of this already very dense city, green areas had become increasingly rare. Hence, the protection of green spots which had survived was seen as vital. Despite the expectation that planners would be on the other side of the barricade—drafting plans for the CDR or the municipality—professionals' participation in these civic mobilisations was impressive. One of these campaigns, in fact, had been organised by a group of professionals, in which architects and urbanists represented a majority.

Campaigners had first heard about the imminent threat of privatisation of the coast from rumours that circulated in their sector, where an incumbent 'mega-project' would likely become quickly common knowledge. The second campaign had been kick-started by a non-governmental organisation (NGO) who worked on issues surrounding social cohesion, but it had quickly attracted a lot of attention from university students of those same disciplines. If young volunteers were first acquainted with the NGO through a friend, they often involved themselves in campaigning, because the issue was interesting to them. Volunteers often told me that naturally the campaign caught their attention since it was in line with their own interests; after all, their degree and future profession dealt precisely with the issue of managing the space of the city. Some of these campaigners had been involved in explicitly left-wing initiatives in the past, but for others, this was the first taste of activism and their political stance was not defined by a clear ideology. At the same time, all were united by their rejection of sectarian politics.

Firstly, although I did not work with planners directly, working with campaigners allowed me to learn a great deal about the way in which planning and urban management worked in Beirut, both in terms of building regulations and the networks of political economy that shaped real estate development.

Campaigners who worked as professionals of the built environment had at some point had direct experience of working within this context. Some campaigners, for instance, had worked for firms who collaborated with the municipality or the government, or knew colleagues who had, and were therefore well acquainted with the intricacies of power that governed the sector. Likewise, campaigners knew the details around plans they were contesting through their advocacy. Following their campaigning taught me a lot about how decisions on urban governance took place in the rooms of power. Undoubtedly, I learnt more from them on this subject than I did from keeping up with press reports on the matter.

However, I did not only learn about the workings of Lebanese urban planning. I also learnt about the opposition and contestation to it. This took place in professional environments, such as conferences on urbanism, talks organised by professional associations, and public debates at various local universities. These events usually attracted a mix of professionals, academics, civil servants and policy makers and, more rarely, politicians

I went along to many such events during my fieldwork, as often campaigners participated as panellists or members of the audience, and it was here that I realised just how contested neoliberalised urban governance was amongst those working in the sector. Listening to speakers' interventions was of course a source of information, but it was the Q&A that I looked forward to the most.

I would then sit in my chair listening to members of the audience, often campaigners, asking a host of pointed questions to speakers they disagreed with. The discussion that would ensue would give me invaluable insight into the state of the field—what issues urbanists and policy makers were grappling with at that time, what the bones of contention were, and what the terms of the debate might be.

On one occasion, for example, I witnessed how two architects in their forties and sympathisers with many civic campaigns surrounding green space, engaged with speakers at an event organised by one of the local universities. That day, the talk was a debate around the abolition of rent control. It took place in a medium-sized lecture theatre and consisted of three speakers, each giving a 15-minute long presentation to a 20- or 30-strong public, detailing their view on the issue. Audience members followed each intervention with full attention and, as I gathered from their technical and well-informed questions and comments at the end of the session, they were likely to be professionals in the field. A heated debate soon followed, and I quickly learnt that in Beirut rent control was one of the most hotly debated issues in urban management in the early 2010s.

In general, rent control is a policy mechanism by which rent prices are fixed and controlled by the state, and in 2014 it had been in place since the 1940s in Lebanon. In 1992, all rent contracts signed in the country before 23 July 1992 were frozen indefinitely in order to help tenants hit by 15 years of war. This meant that tenants continued to pay pre-war rents, regardless of the fact that the Lebanese pound had been devaluated strongly during the war. The consequence was that rents received by landlords under this regime amounted to very little money in today's terms, and were nothing compared to what the same property could be rented out for in today's Beirut.

Although the measure must have stirred the resentment of many landlords since its institution, rent control had become breaking news in January 2012 when an old mansion in Achrafieh, a historical neighbourhood south-east of Downtown, had collapsed, killing over 25 of its residents. The event had obviously shaken the country, but it had also fuelled a heated debate over the benefits of rent control, as some argued that impoverished landlords lacked the means—or the incentive—to keep up their buildings, leading to such tragedies. Others believed that dismantling rent control would put an end to social diversity in the city, as low-income inhabitants could not pay liberalised rents.

One panellist supported the change in legislation, arguing that this move would be fairer to landlords but would also benefit tenants' safety and improve the general state of old buildings. His opinion was that the original law had been short-sighted and that a change in the legislation might be unpopular but was also long overdue.

In this, the speaker and the two audience members represented the two opposite sides of the argument. When their turn to intervene came, the architects disagreed with the speakers' opinion. Rather, both argued that rent control laws were the only defence that some of the less wealthy Beirutis had against eviction from the city centre. In a city where real estate and land increased in price every day, it would soon be impossible for many to live in their own neighbourhoods. The architects' arguments, which I later heard multiple times from others, was that people would soon have to find affordable rent elsewhere, far from the central neighbourhoods, while wealthier tenants would move into their centrally placed homes. Later, another colleague intervened, finding a middle ground, and saying that the real issue was that affordable social housing was virtually non-existent in Lebanon, and that efforts might be better directed towards developing that area of policy instead.

Professional talks such as those were thus an ethnographic window onto the kinds of debates and challenges that were presented by the problems of managing urban space in Beirut. They offered valuable insight into the perspectives, reasonings and justifications that drove policy making and urban design in Beirut, as these were laid out plainly and debated amongst colleagues.

More, these events allowed me to appreciate that a strong internal debate existed amongst professionals of urban management, and that for each expert supporting a specific policy adopted by the government, there existed another who contested it. Although public planning itself can be a compound of power and technical rationale, an ethnography of planning alerts us to the fact that experts themselves are a heterogeneous group with different views and positions. An ethnographic outlook on experts and their practice also tells us that each architectural canon might appear uncontested from outside, but its hegemony is most likely being questioned internally by colleagues of different persuasions. Although social scientists have not picked up on it, this internal contestation happened with modernism (Rodwin 1981), and it is happening with neoliberalism, as my ethnography from Beirut demonstrates. The intense engagement of professionals-turned-campaigners in these contexts might be able to change the canon of neoliberalised professional practice that seems now cemented in our cities.

Old rents were eventually liberalised, and the construction of new social housing was not added to the government's agenda. However, some campaigns were more successful. Campaigners were, for instance, more effective in arguing against the construction of a motorway bridge which would have run through a traditional neighbourhood, wrecking its form of life and displacing its inhabitants (Stefanelli forthcoming). Campaigners successfully demonstrated that the bridge would not improve the city's congestion problems, as the Municipality claimed, and that the plan was rather an operation to allow real estate developers to gain a new playground. Experts were at the forefront of this opposition, and their arguments were presented to the public by campaigners in a long string of university debates, public gatherings and professional events such as those described in relation to the Old Rent Law. In the end, both the municipality and their technical team gave up on defending the highway project, as the latter's technical and political legitimacy crumbled under the pressure of experts' accusations.

Far from being a dead-end, doing ethnography within professional milieus opened multiple doors to my study of urban governance in Beirut. For one, it enabled me to begin to address the gap existing between the top-down study of urban policy and plans and the more classic bottom-up ethnography which usually limits itself to examining the concrete consequences of such planning on inhabitants. However, even more saliently, these ethnographic encounters led me to appreciate how opposition to neoliberal urban governance may emerge from within, for instance from the ranks of those professionals of the built environment that are usually thought to be part of the problem rather than the solution.

Conclusions

Despite the immense variety of local contexts and historical specificities, large-scale redevelopments are becoming a feature of urban life across continents, together with the social consequences that these engender, such as the disruption of established modes of life and the displacement of pre-existing inhabitants. The example of Beirut, discussed in this chapter, suggests that these models of contemporary urban governance do indeed have much in common with each other despite extremely different historical circumstances. If we are to examine different cases in a comparative perspective and establish links between them, we might have to think of ways in which to allow for neoliberalised urban governance to be associated with other urban histories and other conceptual terms than Keynesianism and post-industrialism.

Beyond issues of theorisation, a methodological matter is also of prime importance in the scholarship of urban governance: ethnography should be at the forefront of these comparative efforts. To this date, ethnographers have used their craft to document the negative effects of urban policies and urban redevelopment on the vulnerable populations whose displacement are often the collateral damage of 'creatively destructive' projects. This is invaluable work that has helped bring to the surface the often submerged experienced of those living at the socio-economic margins of society.

Yet, there is reason to believe that more space for ethnography exists in the investigation of the making of urban governance, in particular in the field of urban management. Urban planning itself is a practice at the very centre of urban restructuring, determined as it is by a complex entanglement of competing interests, techniques and practices that reflect the complexity of urban governance itself. As this chapter has argued, ethnographers should not shy away from applying their craft to the study of this practice, in all its different facets and scales. In embracing this project, researchers should thus be open to the multiple possibilities through which urban planning might be engaged: from the ethnography of institutional and organisational settings to more unexpected encounters in civic advocacy, neighbourhood associations or professional institutions.

Engaging with planning from an ethnographic perspective provides the means to finding new sites of enquiry, discovering new questions and identifying new analytical angles to better understand the ever-shifting entanglement of interests, processes and power relations at play in contemporary urban governance. These new avenues should not be thought of as replacing classical forms of participant observation, but rather as complementing them, to add detail and complexity to ethnographers' intellectual project. Lastly, a focus on actors whose professional duty it is to imagine and plan the city might reveal unexpected allies in the fight against the advance of neoliberal policies, with whom broader coalitions may be created and alternative modes to effect change and challenge contemporary processes of urban governance may be elaborated. Including rather than excluding these actors can only enrich the analytical power of sociological analyses of neoliberal urban governance today, as much as the elaboration of its alternatives.

Notes

1 The Lebanese Civil War (1975–1990) was a complex conflict which was local as well as regional, and that entwined elements of intra and inter-sectarian rivalry, socio-economic conflict and regional geopolitical oppositions. Its end cemented political sectarianism in the country, led by warring factions turned political parties.

2 Several masterplans for Beirut had been commissioned since the 1930s, but their application before the Civil War had only been piecemeal, as they threatened the interests of the real development industry (Verdeil 2003). Significantly, Solidere's masterplan rather encouraged these same interests.

References

Abaza, M. (2001) 'Shopping malls, consumer culture and the reshaping of public space in Egypt'. *Theory, Culture & Society*, 18(5): 97–122.

Achkar, H. (2012) 'The Lebanese State as initiator of gentrification in Achrafieh'. *Les Carnets de l'Ifpo.* [online] Available at: http://ifpo.hypotheses.org/3834.

Barthel, P. (2010) 'Arab mega-projects: Between the Dubai effect, global crisis, social mobilization and a sustainable shift'. *Built Environment*, 36(2): 133–145.

Boholm, A. (2013) Hypercomplexity in Collective Planning: A Case of Railway Design. In: Abram, S. and Weszkalnys, G. (eds), *Elusive Promises.* New York: Berghahn.

Brenner, N. and Theodore, N. (2002) 'Cities and the geographies of "actually existing neoliberalism"'. *Antipode*, 34(3): 349–379.

Brenner, N. and Theodore, N. (2005) 'Neoliberalism and the urban condition'. *City*, 9(1): 101–107.

Brenner, N., Peck, J. and Theodore, N. (2010) 'Variegated neoliberalization: Geographies, modalities, pathways'. *Global Networks*, 10(2): 182–222.

Daher, R. (2011) Discourses of Neoliberalism and Disparities in the City Landscape: "Cranes, Craters, and an Exclusive Urbanity." In: M. Ababsa and R. Daher (eds), *Villes, pratiques urbaines et construction nationale en Jordanie.* Beirut: Presses de l'IFPO.

Daher, R. (2013) 'Neoliberal urban transformations in the Arab city'. *Environnement Urbain,* 7: 99.

Denoeux, G. and Springborg, R. (1998) 'Hariri's Lebanon: Singapore of the Middle East or Sanaa of the Levant?'. *Middle East Policy,* 6(2): 158–173.

Elsheshtawy, Y. (2004) The Middle East City: Moving Beyond the Narrative of Loss. In: Elsheshtawy Y. (ed.), *Planning Middle Eastern Cities: An Urban Kaleidoscope in a Globalizing World.* London: Routledge.

Evans, G. (2016) *London's Olympic Legacy.* Basingstoke: Palgrave Macmillan.

Fawaz, M. (2016) 'Exceptions and the actually existing practice of planning: Beirut (Lebanon) as case study'. *Urban Studies* 54(8): 1938–1955.

Gates, C. (1998) *The Merchant Republic of Lebanon.* Oxford: Centre for Lebanese Studies in association with I.B. Tauris Publishers, London, New York.

Geisser, V. and Pieri, C. (2014) 'L'Etat libanais: Le grand absent des politiques de l'habitat?' *Les Carnets de l'Ifpo.* Available at: http://ifpo.hypotheses.org/5779.

Hakim, S. R. and Andary, S. (1997) 'The Lebanese Central Bank and the Treasury bills market'. *The Middle East Journal,* 51(2): 230–241.

Harvey, D. (2003) 'The right to the city.' *International Journal of Urban and Regional Research,* 27(4): 939–941.

Harvey, D. (2007) 'Neoliberalism as creative destruction'. *The ANNALS of the American Academy of Political and Social Science,* 610(1): 21–44.

Hoffman, L., DeHart, M. and Collier, S. J. (2006) 'Notes on the anthropology of neoliberalism'. *Anthropology News,* 47(6): 9–10.

Jessop, B. (1996) 'Post-Fordism and the state'. In: Greve, B. (ed.) *Comparative Welfare Systems.* Basingstoke: Macmillan.

Jessop, B. (2002) 'Liberalism, neoliberalism, and urban governance: A state-theoretical perspective'. *Antipode,* 34(3): 452–472.

Kalb, D. (2012) 'Thinking about neoliberalism as if the crisis was actually happening'. *Social Anthropology,* 20(3): 318–330.

Krijnen, M. (2013) 'Filling every gap: Real estate development in Beirut'. *Jadaliyya.* Available at: http://www.jadaliyya.com/pages/index/14880/filling-every-gap_real-estate- development-in-beirut.

Leitner, H., Sheppard, E., Sziarto, S. and Maringanti, K. (2007) Contesting Urban Futures: Decentering Neoliberalism. In: Leitner, H., Peck, J. and Sziarto, E. (eds) *Contesting Neoliberalism: Urban Frontiers.* New York: Guilford Press.

Lynch, K. (1981) The Form of the City. In: Rodwin, L. (ed.) *Cities and City Planning.* New York: Springer.

Makdisi, S. (1997) 'Laying claim to Beirut: urban narrative and spatial identity in the Age of Solidere'. *Critical Inquiry,* 23(3), pp.661-705.

Mitchell, T. (1999). 'Dreamland: The neoliberalism of your desires'. *Middle East Report*, 29(1): 28–33.

Moody, K. (1997) *Workers in a New World*. New York: Verso.

Naccache, A. F. H. (1998) Beirut's Memorycide. In: Meskell, L. (ed.) *Archaeology Under Fire: Nationalism, Politics and Heritage in the Eastern Mediterranean and Middle East*. London: Routledge.

Peck, J. (2010) 'Zombie neoliberalism and the ambidextrous state'. *Theoretical Criminology*, 14(1): 104–110.

Peck, J., Theodore, N. and Brenner, N. (2009) 'Neoliberal urbanism: Models, moments, mutations'. *SAIS Review of International Affairs*, 29(1): 49–66.

Peck, J. and Tickell, A. (2002) 'Neoliberalizing space'. *Antipode*, 34(3): 380–404.

Raymond, A. (1994) 'Islamic city, Arab city: Orientalist myths and recent views'. *British Journal of Middle Eastern Studies*, 21(1): 3–18.

Robertson, A. (1984) *People and the State: An Anthropology of Planned Development*. Cambridge: Cambridge University Press.

Rodwin, L. (1981) (ed.) *Cities and City Planning*. New York: Springer.

Salloukh, B., Barakat, R., Al-Habbal, J., Khattab, L. and Mikaelian, S. (2015) *The Politics of Sectarianism in Postwar Lebanon*. London: Pluto Press.

Sarkis, H. (1993) Territorial Claims: Architecture and Post-War Attitudes Towards the Built Environment. In: Khalaf, S. and Khoury, P. (eds) *Recovering Beirut*. New York: Brill.

Sawalha, A. (2010) *Reconstructing Beirut*. Austin, TX: University of Texas Press.

Scott, J. (1998) *Seeing Like a State*. New Haven, CT: Yale University Press.

Siemiatycki, M. (2005) 'The making of a mega project in the neoliberal city'. *City*, 9(1): 67–83.

Soja, E. (1987) 'Economic restructuring and the internationalization of the Los Angeles region'. In M.P., Smith and Feagin, J. (eds) *The Capitalist City*. Cambridge, MA: Blackwell.

Stefanelli, A. (*forthcoming*) 'Beyond the organic intellectual: Politics and contestation in the planning practice'. *City and Society*.

Stewart, D. J. (1996) 'Economic recovery and reconstruction in postwar Beirut'. *Geographical Review*, 86(4): 487–504.

Summer, D. (2006) 'The neoliberalization of urban space'. *Villes et territoires du Moyen-Orient*, 2: 9.

Traboulsi, F. (2012) *A History of Modern Lebanon*. London: Pluto Press.

Traboulsi, F. (2014) *Social Classes and Political Power in Lebanon*. Beirut: Heinrich Böll Stiftung.

United Nations (2014) *World Urbanisation Prospects: the 2014 Revision, Highlights*. Available at: https://esa.un.org/unpd/wup/publications/files/wup2014-highlights.pdf.

Verdeil, E. (2003) Politics, Ideology and Professional Interests: Foreign Versus Local Planners in Lebanon under President Chehab. In Nasr, J. and Volait M. (eds), *Urbanism: Imported or Exported*. Cambridge, MA: Academy Press.

Verdeil, E. (2006) 'Marches, lieux d'exercice et profils professionnels de l'urbanisme. In: Souami, T. and Verdeil, E. (eds) *Concevoir et gérer les villes: milieux d'urbanistes du sud de la Méditerranée*. Paris: Économica-Anthropos.

Chapter 3

Playing the game

Precarity and the dilemma of land rights in a gentrifying favela, Rio de Janeiro

Angela Torresan, University of Manchester

Abstract

Drawing on a Foucauldian analysis of precarisation, this chapter explores precarity as the outcome of a form of governance designed to restrict certain populations from gaining access to full citizenship rights. A long-term case of adverse possession won by residents of a favela located in Rio de Janeiro, and their recent experience with gentrification, shows how the current tangle of land titling and housing regulation for favelas works as a strategic mechanism of limited entitlement. This stirs favela residents to create a parallel juridical order of informal contractual arrangements. In so doing, they transform their precarious position into an alternative system of participation and integration into the housing market—one which gives them the freedom and the responsibility to struggle for their own livelihood.

***

Attending to a case of forced removal and land regularisation won by residents of a gentrifying favela in Rio de Janeiro, I explore the notion of precarity not so much as an outcome of a recent post-industrial moment, but as a strategic technique of governance (Foucault 1991; Lorey 2015). Precarity has become an important motif in social science's examination of the contemporary world. It is often contrasted with the ideal of stable industrial wage work that became common in post-WWII Western Europe and North America (Van der Linden 2014). Following from Bourdieu's (1998) now classic work, the main argument is that precarity is a new form of social and economic insecurity under neoliberalism. As such, it derives from the fragmentation and informalisation of labour markets and disinvestment in the welfare state in post-industrial societies in the Global North (Boltanski and Chiappello 2005; Castel 2003; Kalleberg 2009; Ross 2009; Standing 2011). Lately, however, authors in different disciplines have reassessed this definition of precarity and its relationship with recently developed forms of unstable labour and living conditions.

Scholars looking at the Global South (Lee and Kofman 2012; Millar 2018; Paret 2016), at post-colonialism (Barchiesi 2011), at different historical times in the Global North (Breman and Van der Linden 2014), or coming from a feminist perspective (Vosko 2010), argue that precarity has been the standard experience of work in capitalism (Amin 1994). What many claim (Barchiesi 2011; Lee and Kofman 2012; Millar 2018; Paret 2016) is that most people in non-Western countries never had access to the kind of secure and full-time employment we associate with Keynesian-Fordist economy and the post-WWII welfare state. These critics do not deny the importance of precarity as an analytical and political concept to the specific historical context of post-industrialisation, but contend that the security this context afforded in the past is more an exception to capitalism than the rule.

This has been the case in Brazil. The growth and diversification of industry incentivised by the government in the 1930s, coupled with new pro-labour legislation, created a national boom in urban industrial employment (Fonseca and Salomão 2017; Peláez 1972). However, the demand for work in Brazilian cities has always outstripped available jobs, especially in the industrial sector (Martins 2015). Throughout the mid-twentieth century, rural migrants joined an already large unemployed and sub-employed urban population living under precarious conditions and inflating a growing informal sector. The 1980s' wave of recession and deindustrialisation, which hit Rio de Janeiro harder than other urban centres (Queiroz Ribeiro and Telles 2000), only aggravated a scenario that was long in the making.

Notwithstanding the 1980s deceleration, Brazil cannot be characterised as a post-industrial country compared with economically developed areas in the Global North. Brazil has one of the largest manufacturing sectors in the Americas, combined with a strong agribusiness and new financial, technological and consumption services industries. The policies that championed such growth since the mid-1990s were a mixture of conservative protectionism, new welfare provisions, and economic neoliberal strategies. In 15 years of centre-left government, with the rise to power of the Workers' Party (2003–2016), there were successful conditional cash transfers (CCTs) and affirmative action programmes aimed at reducing poverty and shrinking inequality gaps across class, race and gender lines. They were not enough, however, and Brazil is still one of the most unequal countries in the world.

More generally, in Latin American studies, the debate on precarity has developed around the question of informal economies, and it substantiates the critiques that come from more recent studies on the Global South. Independently of whether authors adhered to the legalist (de Soto 1989, Stinchcombe 2001), the voluntarist (Maloney 2004), or the structuralist school (Centeno and Portes 2006; Portes and Castells 1989; Portes and Schauffler 1993), they demonstrated that precarity, as informality, had been part of people's lives from the start. This resonates with the literature on self-built settlements in Brazil, called favelas (Arias 2009; Burgos 2005; Leeds *et al.* 1972; Perlman 1976, 2006; Valladares 1978, 2005; Zaluar 2004). Both bodies of work explored a wide range of themes, including insecurity and informality of work conditions, but also irregular housing, poor access to healthcare, the militarisation of security and everyday interaction with violence, to a degree that in these studies precarity becomes analogous with poor people's very existence.

There is a general readiness in the literature on informality in Latin America to explain it mainly in relationship to the economy, with little attention to the relationship between precarious conditions and the state. When a few authors try to show how informality has been politically shaped by the creation and implementation of different laws and public policies that define the state intervention on low-income settlements, they tend to explain it as a measure of the failure of democratic states unable to enforce their own rules across all sectors of society and incapable of generating the conditions for "modern capitalist development" (Centeno and Portes 2006: 38). From this perspective, despite the apparent antithetical relationship between informal economies and the state, Latin American nations have tolerated and even perpetuated informality because it fulfils the function of maintaining economic viability and political stability. Precarity, as informality, is thus placed at the very heart of the state, reinforcing the old thesis of Latin America's incomplete democracies (Armony and Schamis 2005; Collier and Levitsky 1997; Diamond 1996). That is, Latin American countries have never reached the level of Fordist capital development and democratic practices of their Global North peers; hence, they have had to contend with the precarisation that only recently affected the latter.

To break with the teleological evolutionary undertone of the informality literature, it is important to explore the supposed failures of Latin American nations neither as the residue of weak capitalist democracies, nor as integral components of the institutional structures that support existing systems, which new studies of violence in Latin America have argued (Arias and Goldstein 2010). The merit of the latter is their going beyond the thesis of imperfect democracies, but in doing so, this stance risks painting an essentialising picture that resembles earlier culturalist definitions of national characters (i.e. 'the violent democracies of Latin America'). In its various forms precarity is, indeed, a condition preceded and determined by historically and politically imposed limited entitlements (Di Nunzio 2017), restricted access to citizenship rights (Fisher 2008; Holston 2008) and to the law (de Soto 1989). Albeit, one that is part of a complex set of strategic techniques of political governance, rather than a consequence of weak economic development, democratic incompetence, or as an essential component to Latin American institutions.

Drawing on Lorey's notion of precarisation (2009) as a technique of governance, I understand precarity as an outcome of an administrative state apparatus that restricts certain populations from obtaining full access to established citizenship rights.[1] I take a long-term case of adverse possession won by residents of Vidigal, and their more recent experience with gentrification, to explore how public policies designed to integrate favelados into the fabric of the formal city, work as strategic mechanisms of limited entitlement.[2] Furthermore, unlike what most of the authors who worked on informality and low-income settlements in Latin America have argued, the case I explore in Vidigal shows that many people in the favela want the regularisation of their land tenure and the formalisation of their neighbourhoods not simply to hang onto their houses and build their lives around them. Rather, they want to be able to decide on whether to do that or to turn their properties into assets they can utilise to participate in the capitalist market and improve their life conditions. Such conservative economic aspirations (Perlman 1976) go hand in hand with *favelados*' (those who live in favelas) desire to access to the full gamut of socio and economic rights.

Precarity as strategic governance

With and beyond Lorey, precarisation can be read as a practice of governance that produces what Das and Pool (2004) call the margins of the state. Rather than an exception to the order of the state, the margin is created from inside and strategically maintained to reinforce the centre. The value in converging these two conceptual frames, of precarisation and the margin, is that it provides a powerful theoretical instrument to explore how what seems outside the state is actually not only its "necessary condition as a theoretical and political object" (Das and Poole 2004: 6), but also of its systematic making. Precarity and marginality are provisos of the administration of the state that are meticulously engendered through public apparatus in partnership with private interests. As the working of this apparatus is hidden from view, precarisation naturalises and normalises precarity. Precarity, then, becomes a natural modality of being poor that determines the kind of life certain people defined as marginal deserve to live. What becomes visible is the separation; the boundary between forms of disorder, illegality, liminal belonging, partial citizenship and formality, legality, legitimate belonging, full citizen rights.

Foucault's (1985) concept of subjectification comes in handy. The idea of subjectification is connected to the way Foucault defined power as the ability to create conditions through which someone or something can act upon other people's lives. The crucial element here is the ability to persuade individuals to engage with the process of transforming themselves into specific kinds of subjects, through adopting specific conducts (Foucault 1982). Responsibility for dealing with consequences of self-management is placed on people, not on the state apparatus. This self-accountability creates the impression that illegality and informality are practices taking place outside and even against the order of the state. What is made visible is the idea that precarity and marginality are the result of personal inadequacy or disobedience rather than an outcome of a systematic mechanism of precarisation. However, as Lorey (2009) highlights, it is this very process of subjectification, the inflicted and accepted responsibility to manage one's own condition of precariousness, that opens a gap through which people can turn precarity—as restrictive entitlement—into a form of resistance.

The understanding that restrictive entitlement is what produces enduring conditions of precarity is not new. Scholars working with poor communities in Brazil and elsewhere devised different theoretical frameworks to explore the relationship between precarity and limited access to citizenship rights. Santos (1980) used the idea of a general *capitis deminutio* or a reduced legal capacity that brings on a condition of existential illegality, while Fischer (2008) introduced the notion of poverty of rights, and Holston (2008) that of differentiated citizenship. Keeping Lorey's precarisation in mind, I follow their lead to analyse the relationship between precarity and land regularisation policies devised to guarantee formal house tenure to favelados and consolidate self-built settlements into the formal urban fabric.

Favelas in Rio de Janeiro

Like many urban self-built areas around the world, favelas start as an informal occupation of unutilised land that provides affordable shelter in the face of unavailing or non-existing public housing policies. Favelas that were not eradicated over the course of the twentieth century became established areas of the urban environment throughout Brazil.[3] Today they vary greatly in density, expanse, level of urbanisation, and degree of internal socioeconomic diversity. The 2010 national census showed that favelas housed 6 per cent of the Brazilian population (11.4 million people). Almost half are in the metropolitan areas of the Southeast region; mostly in Rio de Janeiro (1.4 million) and São Paulo (1.3 million). With 22 per cent of its population residing in favelas, Rio has, proportionately, double the number of territories designated as favelas over São Paulo (Cavallieri and Vial 2012).

Regardless of the diversity of these areas, most favelas still share a lack of full rights to land or house tenure, unequal distribution of public resources (health, education, infrastructure), and militarised and often violent public security. The municipal urbanisation and social development programmes implemented in the last four decades have been intermittent. Any form of public intervention has had to contend with the illegal drug trade controlling favelas since the 1980s, the growing presence of militia operations, and complex clientelist political configurations. Access to housing for the urban poor in Rio de Janeiro has been entangled in a history of land speculation and unequal urban service provisions that have reflected and intensified racial, economic and geographical segregation. In this context, favela residents have endured the constant reconfiguration of deeply rooted negative stereotypes about themselves and their neighbourhoods that, over the years, have marked the physical and symbolic place of favelas and favelados in the city.[4]

Within this context, we find Vidigal, a relatively small favela nestled in the hills separating two of the most affluent neighbourhoods of Rio's coastal *Zona Sul* (South Zone), Leblon and São Conrado. Like many Zona Sul favelas expanding up the hills that mark Rio's particular topography, Vidigal has staggering views of the city and the Atlantic Ocean.[5] With the securitisation policy designed to pacify favelas in anticipation of the 2014 World Cup and 2016 Olympic Games, many South Zone favelas experienced a surge in real estate prices that coincided with the arrival of young foreigners interested in newly accessible and affordable areas.[6] While a new wave of favela removals went hand in hand with urban revitalisation projects in the Centre and West part of the cities, South Zone favelas were experiencing early signs of gentrification.

Figure 3.1. View of Vidigal favela and the Ipanema beach.

Photo by Angela Torresan.

Due to its development, size and location, a year after the implementation of a Pacification Police Unit in 2012, Vidigal had attracted a lot of local and international attention and it soon gained the nickname of "Favela Chique". News articles and social media discussions reported how a growing number of middle-class immigrants, mostly from Europe and the US, chose to live and invest in the pacified South Zone favelas, inevitably pushing property prices up.[7] While Vidigal's self-regulated real estate market experienced an unprecedented boom, the municipality introduced a new phase of a land and housing regularisation process. Vidigal residents who were potential beneficiaries of house tenure regularisation, began questioning whether this was to their advantage. While the stipulations of such tenure concessions aimed to preclude people from deriving financial gain from social housing, favelados saw them as hindering their formal access to changing local and global economies.

Vidigal: the Pope's favela

Barbara, a schoolteacher and political activist who I met through my Vidigal housemate, asked me to help develop her research project, called *Memórias do Vidigal* (Vidigal Memories). That was 2014. We did not know it then, but Vidigal was at the peak of its gentrification.[8]

Barbara planned to gather life stories form older residents who saw Vidigal grow from "a few wooden shacks connected by muddy paths to an urbanised favela with 30,000 people" before it gentrified and changed character. Barbara believed the favela needed to collect, catalogue and disseminate its history as a political gesture to substantiate its place in the city before its residents were "removed by the market" and Vidigal turned into "an exclusive neighbourhood for the international bourgeoisie."

Among those we interviewed were Paulo Muniz and Raimundo Duque. Both had been main protagonists in Vidigal's resistance movement against eviction in 1978. Duque was five when his family moved to Vidigal in 1950. Vidigal was a new favela, started in the mid-1940s with the first houses occupying private land. The legal proprietor first solicited judicial repossession of his land in 1957, to stop Vidigal residents claiming adverse possession, which could be granted by law after 10 years of uncontested and uninterrupted land occupation. Duque and a few other residents created the Vila Vidigal Residents' Association in 1967, when the landowner presented the second order of repossession. The next decade saw the Residents' Association gain in strength and legitimacy through the organisation of residents' communal taskforces (*mutirões*), and the local football team *Atlético Clube.*[9] The third time the owner claimed repossession, in 1977, Rio de Janeiro mayor, Marcos Tamoio, ordered the removal of Vidigal on the grounds of landslide risk.

The Association directors sought help. One of the residents lobbied her employer, a state congressman, who summoned the press to cover the next-day eviction. Vidigal residents organised a last-minute demonstration with children and women for great effect on the press. Press attention attracted more influential players, amongst them state congressmen Délio dos Santos and Flores da Cunha, and the lawyers from the recently formed *Pastoral de Favelas,* Bento Rubião and Eliana Athayde.

The *Pastoral de Favelas* was a section of the progressive Archdiocese of Rio de Janeiro, created to help favela residents resist the recent wave of removals and, ultimately, revive favela mobilisation. Together with the Federal Association of Favelas of Rio de Janeiro (FAFERJ), they aimed to raise political awareness and organisation among favelados, strengthening the basis of popular movements that had been crushed by the military dictatorship.[10] Between 1968 and 1975, more than 70 favelas were destroyed and residents removed to sub-urbanised remote popular housing projects far away from the city (Pandolfi and Grynszpan 2002). Vidigal's victory marked the transition from an authoritarian policy of favela removals to policies of favela urbanisation, beginning a long process of partially integrating favela territories into the city (Golçalves 2008). Residents from other favelas approached the Pastoral to forge their own associations and integrate the growing popular alliances.

In July 1980 an event placed Vidigal in the international news. Paulo and Duque recounted with enthusiasm how they watched the visit of John Paul II to their favela from the door of their shacks. The Pope walked around the muddy paths, visited wooden shack homes, and prayed at the small chapel. Vidigal became known as the Pope's favela (*a favela do Papa*). This significant symbolic event distinguishes its role in the history of Rio de Janeiro popular movements and gave residents reassurance of their place in the city.

Following Vidigal's victory and the Pope's visit, favela association movements became the springboard for a broad national mobilisation against the military regime. The political impact of this new popular mobilisation was significant, leading to the process of re-democratisation of the country (McCann 2013). With the end of the 21-year military rule in 1985, urban and rural organisations resurfaced and were invented anew. The post-dictatorship political climate and the strength of grassroots movements had a tremendous impact on the writing of the new, and highly progressive, Federal Constitution of 1988, which guaranteed universal rights to housing and access to land.

Figure 3.2. Pope John Paul II visit to Vidigal, July 1980.

Pope gives his papal ring to Father Ítalo Coelho. The ring is in the Archdiocesan Museum of Sacred Art. Photo courtesy of author Armando Almeida Lima.

The promise of a richness of rights

The political moment that followed the decline of the military dictatorship was unprecedented. It brought together disparate sectors of society that shared the longing for a new democratic constitution that expanded social, political and workers' rights and blocked military action against a government elected by popular vote. Resulting from popular participation, the Constitution required the expansion of the welfare state, extended workers' rights, and recognised the rights of ethnic, religious, sexual, racial minorities, etc. More remarkably, while establishing the right of private property of land as fundamental (article 5, paragraph 32), the Constitution removed its inalienability by salvaging an old principle of 'social function'. Basic qualities of this function were the assurance of housing and of the economic and social reproduction of life (agriculture for instance). Even more remarkable was that the city itself, not simply urban private property, was also defined as having a "social function" that should ultimately secure the well-being of its inhabitants (art 182).

All the subsequent new charters corresponding to the government of the states and municipalities, and the complementary federal law that regulates the Constitution's urban policy to guarantee the city's' social function, proscribed the old strategy of favela forced removals. In fact, favelas now became the object of a different kind of state intervention. This was a major shift from the dictatorship's systematic favela removal, which had been carried out with unprecedented violence and disregard for human rights.

The Rio de Janeiro State Constitution of 1989 and the 1990 Organic Law of Rio de Janeiro municipality established the requirement to create the means for the "urbanization, land regularisation and titling of low-income areas and favelas, without the removal of the residents, unless the physical conditions of the area represent a risk to the life of its inhabitants."[11] It was Rio de Janeiro's 1992 Master Plan, another outcome of negotiations between the municipal legal powers and various social movements and civil organisations, that provided the instruments to enforce the integration of favelas into the neighbourhoods in which they were located and therefore into the city. The language of removal became an exception to the more general rule of integration via urbanisation and housing regularisation.

However, there was a crucial caveat: the Master Plan broadened the Constitution's definition of exceptional cases justifying removal of favela residents from strict situations in which residents' lives were considered to be at risk to a whole set of conditions regarding the protection of superficial natural water sources; areas near roads; areas of special environmental interest or conservation units; or where the state cannot provide minimum conditions of urbanisation and sanitation; and under viaducts, bridges, walkways obstructing collective and individual safety. While this widening of exceptions gave legal mechanisms for considering situations in which removal remained the best option, it opened up scope for interpretation, with the risk of undermining the fundamental principles of the Constitution. Exceptions were utilised repeatedly to remove favelas, especially prior to the 2016 Olympics. The promise of legalised property that finally seemed to be within the reach of the poor was, in fact, a new and more insidious form of precarisation; a law that benefited favelados had gained administrative mechanisms to reinforce their precarious condition regarding their right to formal housing.

The first administration of Rio's mayor Cesar Maia (1993–1993) began an ambitious urbanisation programme that included a project dedicated to favelas. Designed as a participatory programme, the *Favela Bairro* installed schools, public places, health centres, improved sewage and water systems, electric energy, garbage collection, etc. The programme required the creation of a new decree establishing favelas as Areas of Social Interest (AIES), which stipulated which favelas would be included in the programme and under which specific criteria of land occupation (Complimentary Law 16/1992). The

Favela Bairro received funding from the Inter-American Development Bank and Rio's government totalling £140m of investment in 147 favelas over 14 years. The project's longevity was possible because the urbanist/architect who formulated it, Luiz Paulo Conde, succeeded Maia as mayor. Cesar Maia was, in turn, elected for a second round of two successive mandates.

Although land regularisation was a mandate in all the charters, it became a supplementary aspect of the *Favela Bairro* and the promise of legal property materialised for but a few. To convey just a small aspect of the mechanism of legal convolution that land regularisation in Brazil entails, one needs only list the various forms of land acquisition prescribed in Brazilian law: these include the simple purchase and sale, permutation, donation, expropriation and at least three modes of adverse possession. The most appropriate way to implement land regularisation in specific favelas depends on who owns the land, the availability of resources to carry out pecuniary compensation, the administrative process required for each case, preliminary research, surveys of residents, mapping of houses and public spaces, etc. None of the administrative mechanisms the new laws created are easy to implement. Not helped by the insufficient coordination between the different governmental branches and their communication with civil society organisations.

While most favela scholars agree that land and housing regularisation are a crucial instrument for the acquisition of further or even full citizenship rights and social/economic inclusion, all have been equally intrigued by the difficulties involved (Golçalves 2016; Holston 2008; Magalhães 2014; Santos 1980). They also agree on the diagnosis that, in Holston's words, "[f]ar from being incoherent, the Brazilian legal system deploys technical complications and its chaos brilliantly for strategic ends" (2008: 345). Ends that, I add, are compatible with techniques of governance designed to sustain a condition of precarity that places people in a porous boundary between legality and illegality.

Cesar Maia's administration (2001–2009) and the one that followed, that of Eduardo Pães (2009–2017), provide good examples of this process of precarisation. Maia used the exceptions to removals prescribed in the Master Plan regarding areas of special environmental interest and units of conservation to remove a number of favelas located in the West Zone of Rio, on valuable land ripe for real estate development. Meanwhile, Maia nominated the young 23-year-old Pães, as the first sub-mayor of Barra da Tijuca e Jacarepagua, a recently created office for which the official *raison d'etre* was the 'decentralisation' of the municipal administration. In fact, the instalment of Rio's sub-prefectures, especially this one, laid down the cornerstone of what came to be a very strong alliance between real estate and construction businesses and Rio's municipal government.

By the time Rio became the seat of various sports mega-events in the 2010s, this alliance had been consolidated and the language of favela removals gradually returned to the political scene and to the media. Furthermore, the administration, with the assistance of a conservative media, attributed the escalating violence throughout the city to the drug trafficking businesses that since the mid-1980s had gradually taken control of favelas. In his review of favela removals policies in Rio, Brum (2013) rightly observes that favelas came to be perceived as the cradle of urban violence that spilt from the 'hills to the asphalt'. To paraphrase Fischer (2008) the 'richness of rights' that the 1988 Constitution had promised, became entangled in the multitude of contradictory and fragmented administrative apparatus that an even more seemingly incoherent regulatory body tried to apply. Even more incomprehensible was the continuous condition of insecurity and vulnerability in the face of such a promising and progressive Constitution.

Broken promises: mega-events and favela removals

The end of Cesar Maia's office in 2009 marked the beginning of a new phase of urbanisation in Rio de Janeiro. It inaugurated the decade of sporting mega-events the city would host. The 2007 Pan American Games provided the first impetus for heavy investment in urban revitalisation and real estate investment through public-private partnerships (PPP), setting the pace for the 2014 World Cup and the 2016 Olympic Games. The preparation of the city for the events gave rise to a major international real estate operation involving corporate and financial capital, pushing for the appropriation and transformation of neglected territories in selective areas of Rio into lucrative PPPs (Faulhaber and Azevedo 2014; Rolnik 2015). The supporting ideology for this operation was the crafting of a new image of Rio as a global metropolis, and the construction of this image required effective security measures to tackle Rio's international reputation of urban violence.[12] Favelas, with their own reputation as cradles of violence within the violent city, were the main targets for such measures.

Right after the 2007 Pan American Games, Rio's state government launched a public security policy to 'pacify' favelas located in areas of the city strategic to the Cup/Games. Modelled on different experiences with community policing in other Latin American countries (Dammert and Malone 2006; Eilbaum 2004; Föhrig *et al.* 2006), the policy's objective was to break with the armed and violent display of drug-trafficking control and reclaim governance of the territories in order to reintegrate favelas into the city. After a heavy military operation occupied and pacified an area, Pacification Police Units (UPPs) were permanently installed within favelas.

The next mayor, Eduardo Pães (2009–2017), continued the UPP policy and intensified Maia's discourse of cleaning up the city for the Cup and Games. A clause in the Master Plan supposed to work as an exception became the rule with which the Pães administration partially or fully removed favelas on valuable land whenever possible. Different popular movements and even Amnesty International condemned Pães' lack of transparency in the preparation of the city for the mega-events and denounced the excessive use of force in the removal of more than 19,000 families—the largest number of removals in the city's history (Faulhaber and Azevedo 2015). In addition, his version of *Favela Bairro* gained the new designation *Morar Carioca* (Carioca House) mostly to facilitate his removal policy by focusing on building new social housing of unsatisfactory quality to accommodate removed families (the Constitution decrees that any process of removal should be redressed by new settlement or indemnity).

The Master Plan removal exceptions are a poignant example of the apparatus of precarisation, reinforcing the poverty of rights (Fischer 2008) that maintains favelados in a condition of precarity. Specifically, the systematic use of exceptions allowed the state to pick and choose which rights it will comply with, creating, according to Magalhães, "institutional practices that are at the frontier between right and the non-right" (2014: 77). In his detailed analysis of the Law of the Favelas, meaning the legislature concerning favela urbanisation, land use and regularisation in Rio, Magalhães shows how the state employs the law to determine which areas of the city will be privileged for public intervention and which will be abandoned. As Das and Poole (2004) remind us, it is precisely the idea of a condition of marginality that is considered a natural attribute of poor people, or, I would add, a 'natural condition of precarity', that allows the state "never to be held responsible to its own promises" (17). In the case of favelas in Rio de Janeiro, favelados' differentiated citizenship (Holston 2008), which makes their lives so precarious, seems to be the necessary condition for a state that has always been closely implicated with the expansion of capital at the expense of its poorest population.

Vidigal playing the game

Since the first residents of Vidigal won the removal case in the late 1970s, the favela expanded upwards into areas that were not included in the original process of land regularisation. The original lower area has been expropriated by the state and is now public land awaiting regularisation. As the government has not yet paid pecuniary compensation to the former landowner, it can only grant a concession of promise of use to the entitled residents.[13] The upper part of Vidigal, developed later, still belongs to private owners. Residents of this area must request land regularisation through the administrative instrument of adverse possession (usocaption). No one in Vidigal thought this intricate process worth the expense and trouble. In common with many of

Rio's favelas, a mixture of partial land regularisation and incomplete infrastructure upgrading was part of the everyday lives of Vidigal residents. As a beneficiary of the *Favela Bairro* project in the 1990s, Vidigal had its sewage and pluvial water drainage system improved, some of its hills reinforced to prevent mud and rock slides, and roads and alleys paved. However, despite land regularisation being a component of *Favela Bairro,* no one in Vidigal had gained formal ownership of their houses.

The real estate boom of South Zone favelas brought an extra complication to the already messy boundary between forms of disorder, illegality, partial citizenship and formality, legality, and full citizen rights, as I mentioned at the beginning of the chapter. Foreigners and outside Brazilian investors were buying properties in Vidigal observing the rules of the local real estate market. As with any other Brazilian favela, this market operates under a parallel juridical order of contractual arrangement unrecognised but tolerated by the municipality. The Residents' Association acted as a registry and signed off negotiations for a small fee. Lack of titles, in the case of Vidigal, neither hindered nor protected against gentrification (Gonçalves 2008). This was a piecemeal kind of gentrification with very little direct influence from the state. As such, it differed from the gentrification of downtown Rio, for instance, which ensued from the partnerships the city government developed with private property developers.

Figure 3.3. Signs of gentrification in Vidigal 1.

The first upmarket hotel Mirante do Arvrão opened in 2014 co-owned by a renowned Brazilian architect and a successful businessman. Accommodation ranges from deluxe suites (£120 per night) to a 12-bed dormitory (£16 per night per bed). Photo by Angela Torresan.

Figure 3.4. Signs of gentrification in Vidigal 2.

Ninho shows me an alleyway at the top of Vidigal. On the left is the DaLaje hostel also inaugurated in 2014. The main attraction of DaLaje is the upstairs bar/restaurant that caters to a middle-class clientele. On the right a small house for sale. Photo by Angela Torresan.

Figure 3.5. Signs of gentrification in Vidigal 3.

The construction of a free art school for Vidigal children by an internationally famous Brazilian artist. Favela architecture does not normally make use of steel beams. Photo by Angela Torresan.

While I was filming the then president of the Residents' Association with Ninho, another friend and collaborator from the favela, we came across two technical agents from the Institute of Land and Cartography of Rio de Janeiro State (ITERJ)—a public but autonomous institute responsible for land tenure and granting ownership titles. The agents were verifying house occupation cartography of the lower part of Vidigal, which had won the removal case and gained the land regularisation process in the late 1970s. We joined one of the Residents' Association directors, Walmar, who was guiding the agents through Vidigal's alleyways. While the agents were busy talking to a few residents, trying to ascertain which part of which building belonged to which family, Walmar asked us to say a few words on camera about the promise of concession of use the ITERJ had been granting to residents. Looking at Ninho, he said, "You are a lessee, you're not an owner. Concession is something I can give you and can take away. 'Promise of Use', this title is a bit strange. This is my point. I support the idea, but I'd like a clearer title."

In other words, what good does it do to receive a paper from the government that only promises a concession of use? Not only it does not recognise or promise to grant house ownership, but it can take the promise of concession away at any time. The paper certified in writing the restricted right they had over their properties.

After a while, we arrived at Ms Amelia and Mr Aloisio's doorstep, a couple who had been living in Vidigal since the 1960s and had witnessed the Pope's visit from their shack. The ITERJ agent asked them who owned the eight units that comprised the building in which they lived. Ms Amelia confirmed they were all theirs. They lived in one, their son lived in another, and they rented the others. When asked what was the purpose of his questioning, the agent explained that once they received the promise of concession of use, if they sold their property in the future, the new owner would have to go to ITERJ to transfer the ownership.[14]

In line with the feeling of most residents who I later talked to about the regularisation, Ms Amelia and Mr Aloisio wanted to receive their house title and be able to pay their property tax and utility bills properly. They wished to abide by the rules and become entitled to full citizenship duties and rights. However, all they knew was that the process was taking a very long time and "nothing has come of it until now". The problem, which the agent did not clarify, was that concession of ownership was conditional. Only one property can be regulated per family (housing or mixed housing and commercial use), the one in which the family resides. Women are preferential recipients of titling, which can be transferred to their heirs, but cannot be sold before 10 years from the concession date. Furthermore, no part of the property can be rented out. These conditions were part of the principle of the social function of the land granted by the state and designed to protect favela residents against removal through gentrification and, consequently, maintain a reserve of urban areas accessible to low-income families. However, this protection went against a whole parallel system of land use and house ownership that had established a thriving favela real estate market. Many Vidigal dwellers had additional property that they rented to others, which was an integral part of the people's income and businesses.

Figure 3.6. Land regularisation 2.

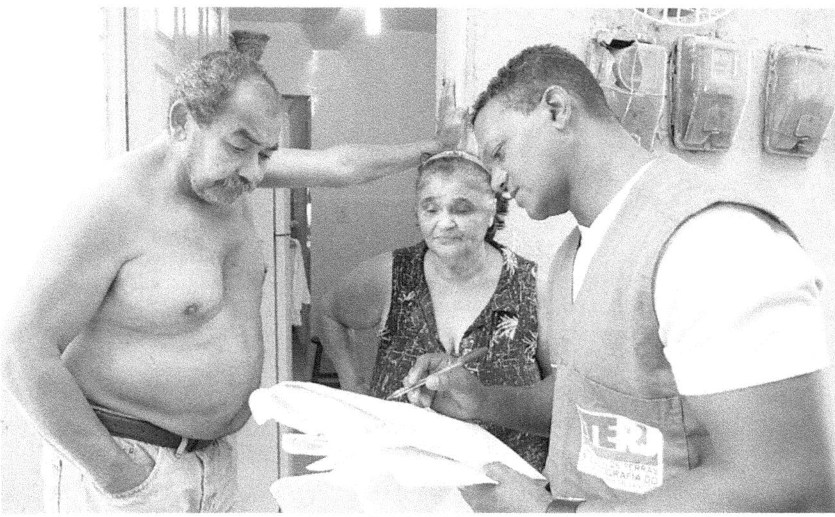

ITERJ agent asks Ms Amelia and Mr Aloisio to locate their properties on the map. Photo by Angela Torresan.

Decrees of land use and occupation that translate the legal idea of social function into protection mechanisms against the whims of the real estate market, in fact, encroach on a fundamental social and economic value for favela residents—that of the possibility of improving one's life conditions. This was an expression I heard many times in Vidigal and it referred to a value shared by family members, friends, and neighbours. There was an understanding that people should be entitled to improve their life's condition, even if that impinged a little on one's own personal wellbeing. Given people's reliance on each other in Vidigal, another's growth usually had a positive effect on one's own condition, either through there being more resources to share around, or because of the chain of obligations and reciprocity current in people's everyday relationships.

Figure 3.7. Land regularisation 3.

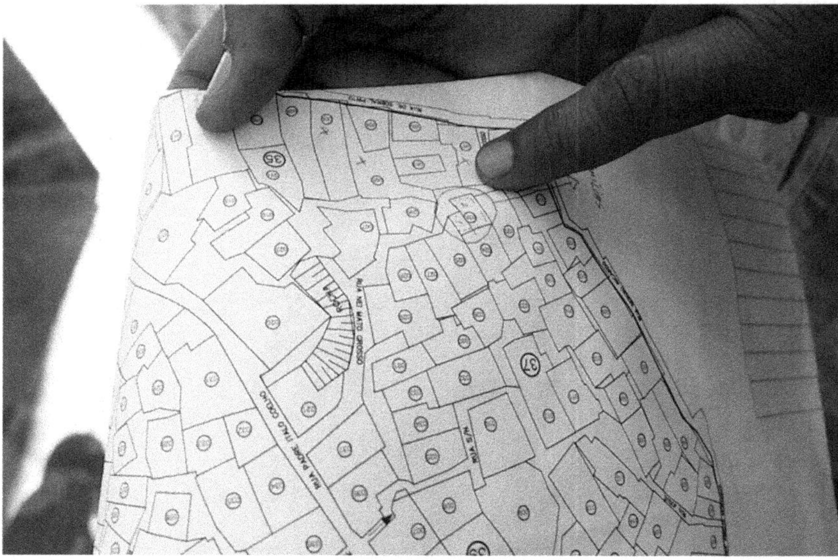

ITERJ map showing single-family units. Each building in the favela may comprise a series of units, complicating the regularisation process. Photo by Angela Torresan.

One's house is an extremely valuable resource and part of many personal improvement projects. It not only guaranteed security of shelter and an economic investment, but it can be transformed and modified to accommodate all sorts of activities and play different functions. Favela houses are self-constructed and constantly self-modified according to the current needs of their inhabitants. In 2014, with the pacification policy and gentrification, many residents who owned a number of properties for rental, were taking full economic advantage of the increase in real estate value. Others were dividing their current residences into smaller units to rent, or were renting extra rooms in their houses. A few had sold their houses to foreigners or Brazilian entrepreneurs and moved either to another area of Vidigal, to another favela in Rio, or back to their homeland in the Northeast of Brazil. No one in Vidigal could use the moral argument that they were playing into the hands of wider capital interests given that their own possibility to improve their life conditions was at stake. Therefore, being able to access a valuable asset in the capitalist property market had a local social function through which individual ambition becomes intrinsically linked to reciprocal means of improvement.

On the one hand, there is a growing discussion questioning whether land titling protects poor people's assets (Bonamichi 2016). Established favela movement leadership and scholars view land regularisation with suspicion. It appears more as a strategy to intensify processes of incorporation of favelas in lucrative real estate markets than a redistributive policy. On the other hand, Vidigal residents are profoundly sceptical of patronising terms of ownership that do not grant them the right to legally manage their assets. Vidigal favelados wanted autonomy to participate in the formal, and more lucrative, real estate market. In their view, this participation is commensurate with full citizenship. They did not see themselves solving the general problem of poverty and, if they could choose, they would remove themselves and their families from the condition of legal and economic precarity that perpetuates their poverty. The kind of protection that land regularisation bestows, limited people's resources to play the capitalist game by restricting their risks and stopping them from taking chances to improve their life conditions. Full access to citizenship rights should involve formal ownership of the properties they have amassed with great sacrifice over decades of hard work and full entitlement to manage their ownership like any other citizen in the city.

If one understands precarity as an outcome of precarisation (Lorey 2009), that is, as the result of an administrative apparatus that restricts certain people from gaining full access to formal entitlements, one can see how the current tangle of land titling and housing regulation for favelas obstructs favelados' full formal participation in the real estate market. As Perlman (1976) argued many years ago, favelados have been, inevitably, participating in the same economic, social and cultural life of the city, albeit from a marginal place (Das and Poole 2004). In order to engage in a way that they can improve their life conditions, favelados have created a parallel juridical order of informal contractual arrangements. Hence, transforming their precarious position into an alternative system of participation and integration into the fabric of the city. However, one in which their self-accountability regarding their precariousness also gives them the freedom and the responsibility to struggle for their own livelihood.

Ex post facto

In 2014, gentrification was a contentious subject in Vidigal. Although many were afraid of the long-term consequences of the new real estate boom, which could lead to dismissal of the favela as a mid-city area of affordable housing for low-income people; most realised that they could not tell residents how to manage their own assets. Given the unpredictability of pacification and the possible return of the drug trafficking business if the UPP project failed, many in Vidigal and in other favelas, saw gentrification as a unique window of opportunity.

Most people, however, could not envisage how the situation would change. Within three years since my fieldwork research, the political and economic situation of Brazil transformed drastically. In 2016, the democratically elected president was removed from office under questionable impeachment proceedings, the national economy suffered from plummeting oil prices, unemployment soared, and the inflation rate reached 10 per cent. A highly unpopular interim government had to cope with a string of bleak international news reports that devastated the image of the country. The current conservative president elected in 2018 by half the electorate who hoped for something new, is under siege with allegations of misconduct and ineptitude to rule.

Less than two months after the end of the Olympic Games, Rio de Janeiro declared a state of financial bankruptcy in a desperate move to receive federal government funding to maintain, for the time being, public security, health, education and transport management. Meanwhile, the pacification policy began to falter. Violent incidents between favela residents and the UPP police have intensified in the last few years and the administration ran out of funds to support the policy.[15] A public policy that could have been widely beneficial if community policing had been truly implemented, is instead furthering militarisation of favelas and becoming progressively punitive (Müller 2016). In December 2017 and January 2018, a new war between rival drug gangs seeking to resume control of Rocinha, a large favela adjacent to Vidigal, resulted in a series of shoot-outs. In 2019, Wilson Witzel, the conservative ex-marine and newly elected governor of Rio has declared war on the 'bandits', reinstating ostentatious violent military police incursions in favelas. The first three months of the year saw a record high of 434 police killings in the state.[16] In June 2019, the UPP police killed four men in Vidigal, none related to the drug traffic gangs. A community street cleaner had gone out looking for his children who were playing outside on a sunny Easter Sunday when he heard the police shootings near his house. He was shot at point-blank range.

Tourists are now advised to avoid South Zone favelas and the upmarket Vidigal hostels and bars no longer attract the same middle-class clientele. Most of the foreigners I met in 2014 who bought properties in Vidigal have left the favela and cannot recover their investments. Vidigal's informal property market is still dynamic but values are back to the levels they were at before 2012. Gentrification, to the Vidigal residents with whom I keep in contact, now seems like a short window that has been indefinitely closed. Ironically, it is the return of gang-related activities and police violence, not land regularisation, that is maintaining the social function of favela land as a place of affordable housing, and keeping favelados, irrespective of their wishes, in the margins of the city.

As a strategic technique of governance that hides the production and perpetuation of the margins under the cover of a contradictory, messy and corrupt state, precarity works to facilitate capitalism in various forms, restricting and selecting those within the nation who can participate in it with adequate economic and political resources. For many people I met in Vidigal, the end of precarity requires a restructuring of the system such that the centre would no longer need the margins to sustain itself. What favelados could in reality aspire to was to become less precarious through individual changes, which would, with luck, also help improve the lives of some of those around them. While it lasted, gentrification offered a chance of that.

Notes

1 Lorey follows Foucault's notion of governmentality as, in her words, "the structural entanglement of the government of a State and the techniques of self-government in Western societies" (2009: 188). Foucault developed the concept throughout his writings, but for a more comprehensive definition see Foucault (1991). Crucial to my own use of precarisation is Foucault's idea of apparatus, or dispositif, as a specific ordering, or relationships, between things and populations—discourses, regulation, laws, knowledge, etc.—within a social domain that makes a specific course of action possible (1979, 1980). In this sense precaritisation of favelas and favelados involves the historical development of a whole dispositif. However, here I am concentrating on the specific administrative and regulatory measures.

2 I lived in Vidigal, undertaking ethnographic fieldwork, for six months in 2014.

3 For an excellent account of the emergence of favelas and their transformation into a subject matter for social sciences research, see Valladares 2005.

4 For a review of public policies for favelas see Ayse and Cavallieri (1998), Burgos (1998), and Riley *et al.* (2001). For favela, violence and negative stereotypes see Arias (2009), Carvalho (2000), Freeman (2012), and Gledhill and Hita (2008).

5 According to the 2010 census, Vidigal has approximately 10,000 inhabitants. However, the directors of Vila do Vidigal Residents' Association estimate a much large number of 30,000 people. Neighbouring favela Rocinha has an approximate 100,000 residents.

6 The securitisation policy received the military epithet 'pacification.' Since its inception in 2008, 38 UPP units have been installed covering 233 favelas throughout Rio's South, West and North zones. Cunha and Mello (2011) wrote the earliest article on the impact of the UPP in the first pacified favela, Santa Marta. See also Cummings (2015), Burgos *et al.* (2011), and Frischtak and Mandel (2012).

7 O Globo, 26/10/2014, http://oglobo.globo.com/rio/vidigal-cada-vez-mais-cobicado-por-estrangeiros-ate-cariocas-14361731. The Guardian, 23/01/2013, https://www.theguardian.com/world/2013/jan/23/rio-favela-real-estate

8 I use the notion of gentrification here to identify changes in the real estate market of pacified favelas stimulated first by the arrival of foreigners who saw an opportunity to buy cheap properties in depreciated areas within the affluent South Zone. Subsequently, other private interests began to look at favelas as possible territories for capital accumulation. A few wealthy Brazilians invested in the growing tourist economy and the national press began running stories about 'gentrifying' favelas, in an attempt to change the negative image of no-go areas of crime and violence. The literature on gentrification is too vast to be perused in this chapter. For my purpose here, I adhere to Smith and Williams' (1986: 3) definition of gentrification as the "visible spatial component" of global capital expansion.

[9] The *mutirões* were composed of residents who would get together to improved common areas and help individual families build or extend their houses.
[10] Brazilian military dictatorship lasted 21 years (1964–1985). Fearing the current progressive government of João Gulart, the middle classes gave full support to the military coup. The authoritarian regime instituted press censorship and violent restriction to political rights.
[11] Lei Orgânica do Municipio do Rio de Janeiro, article 429 – VI. http://www.rio.rj.gov.br/dlstatic/10112/4946719/4126916/Lei_Organica_MRJ_comaltdo205.pdf
[12] Since the early 1990s, different city administrations have tried to insert Rio in the global scenario as a modern and competitive city altering municipal legislation to accommodate different urban projects. However, with the federal resources designated for the sporting events and the concentrated efforts to promote the city as distinct and attractive, and safe, the state government has managed to develop a large plan of urban renewal and gentrification in strategic regions.
[13] The value of the compensation was in 2014 US$14,548,719.64. According to the director of ITERJ, an autarchy linked to Rio de Janeiro Secretary of State for Housing in charge of regularising land ownership, although former proprietors cannot contest the expropriation they have the right to negotiate the value judicially, which can take years.
[14] The film, Marcelo and ITERJ, is part of Views of Vidigal, a six short-film series on gentrification in Vidigal. It can be watched here: https://vimeo.com/241846808.
[15] See Rioonwatch article on the current UPP crisis: http://www.rioonwatch.org/?p=28108
[16] Public Security Institute statistics (http://www.ispvisualizacao.rj.gov.br).

References

Arias, E. D. (2009) *Drugs and Democracy in Rio de Janeiro: Trafficking, Social Networks, and Public Security.* Chapel Hill: University of North Carolina Press.

Arias, E. D., and Goldstein, D. M. (2010) Violent Pluralism: Understanding the New Democracies of Latin America. In: Goldstein, D. and Arias, E. (eds), *Violent Democracies in Latin America.* Durham and London: Duke University Press.

Armony, A. C. and Schamis, H. E. (2005) 'Babel in democratization studies.' *Journal of Democracy* 16(4): 113–128.

Ayse, P. and Cavallieri, P.F. (1998) 'Alleviating Urban poverty in a global city new trends in upgrading Rio de Janeiro's favelas'. *Habitat International,* 22(4).

Barchiesi, F. (2011) *Precarious Liberation: Workers, the State, and Contested Social Citizenship in Postapartheid South Africa.* New York: SUNY Press.

Boltanski, L. and Chiapello, E. (2005) 'The new spirit of capitalism', *International Journal of Politics, Culture, and Society,* 18(3–4): 161–188.

Bourdieu, P. (1998) *Acts of Resistance: Against the Tyranny of the Market.* New York: New Press.

Breman, J. and Linden, M. (2014) 'Informalizing the economy: The return of the social question at a global level', *Development and Change,* 45(5): 920–940.

Brum, M. (2013) 'Favelas e remocionismo ontem e hoje: da Ditadura de 1964 aos Grandes Eventos'. *O Social em Questão,* XVI(29): 179–207.

Burgos, M. B. (1998) Dos Parques Proletários ao Favela-Bairro. In: Zaluar, A. and Alvito, M. (eds), *Um Século de Favela.* Rio de Janeiro: FGV.

Burgos, M. B. (2005) 'Cidade, territórios e cidadania', *DADOS – Revista de Ciências Sociais,* 48(1): 189–222.

Burgos, M. B., Pereira, L. F. A., Cavalcanti, M., Brum, M. and Amoroso, M. (2011) 'O efeito UPP na percepção dos moradores das favelas', *Desigualdade & Diversidade – Revista de Ciências Sociais da PUC,* 11: 49–98.

Carvalho, M. A. R. (2000) Cidade Escassa e Violência Urbana. In: Pereira, C.A., Rondelli, E., Schlhammer, E. and Herschmann, M. (eds), *Linguagens da Violência.* Rio de Janeiro: Rocco.

Castel, R. (2003) *From Manual Workers to Wage Laborers. Transformation of the Social Question.* New Brunswick, NJ: Transaction Publishers.

Cavallieri, F. and Vial, A. (2012) Favelas na cidade do Rio de Janeiro: o quadro populacional com base no Censo, Rio de Janeiro: IPP/Prefeitura da Cidade do Rio de Janeiro, nº 20120501.

Centeno, M. A. and Portes, A. (2006) The Informal Economy in the Shadow of the State. In: Fernandes-Kelly, P. and Shefner, J. (eds), *Out of the Shadows: Political Action and the Informal Economy in Latin America.* Philadelphia: Pennsylvania University Press.

Collier, D. and Levitsky, S. (1997) 'Democracy with adjectives: Conceptual innovation in comparative research'. *World Politics* 49(3): 430–451.

Cummings, J. (2015) Confronting Favela Chic: The Gentrification of Informal Settlements in Rio de Janeiro, Brazil. In: Lees, L., Shin, H.B. and Lopez-Morales, E. (eds), *Global Gentrifications: Uneven Development and Displacement.* Bristol: Policy Press.

Cunha, N. V. d. and Mello, M. A. d. S. (2011) 'Novos conflitos na cidade: A UPP e o processo de urbanização na favela', *Revista de Estudos de Conflito e Controle Social,* 4(3): 371–401.

Dammert, L. and Malone, M.F.T. (2006) 'Does it take a village? Policing strategies and fear of crime in Latin America', *Latin American Politics and Society,* 48(4): 27–51.

de Soto, H. (1989) *The Other Path.* New York: Harper and Row.

Diamond, L. (1996) Democracy in Latin America: Degrees, Illusions, and Directions for Consolidation. In: Farer, T. (ed.) *Beyond Sovereignty: Collectively Defending Democracy in the Americas.* Baltimore, MD: Johns Hopkins University Press.

Di Nunzio, M. (2017) 'Marginality as a politics of limited entitlements: Street life and the dilemma of inclusion in urban Ethiopia', *American Ethnologist,* 44(1): 91–103.

Eilbaum, L. (2004) La policía 'al servicio de la comunidad': tradición policial y vientos de cambio. In: Tiscornia, S. (ed.) *Burocracias y violencia. Estudios de antropología jurídica.* Buenos Aires: Editorial Antropofagia.

Faulhaber, L. and Azevedo, L. (2015) SMH 2016: remoções no Rio de Janeiro Olímpico. Rio de Janeiro: Mórula.

Fischer, B. M. (2008) *A Poverty of Rights: Citizenship and Inequality in Twentieth-Century Rio de Janeiro.* Stanford, CA: Stanford University Press.

Föhrig, A., Pomares, J. S. and Gortari, C. (2006) Citizen Security Policy in Argentina: The National Crime Prevention Plan. In: Tulchin, J.S. and Ruthenburg, M. (eds) *Toward a Society under Law. Citizens and Their Police in Latin America,* Washington, DC: Woodrow Wilson Center Press with Johns Hopkins University Press.

Fonseca, P. C. D. and Salomão, I. C. (2017) 'Brazilian industrialization: Notes on the historiographical debate', *Tempo,* 23(1): 86–104.

Foucault, M. (1979) *Discipline and Punish,* Sheridan, A. (trans.). New York: Vintage and Random House.

Foucault, M. (1980) The Confession of the Flesh. In Gordon, C. (ed.) *Power/Knowledge: Selected Interviews and Other Writings, 1972–1977.* New York: Pantheon.

Foucault, M. (1982) 'The subject and power', *Critical Inquiry,* 8(4): 777–795.

Foucault, M. (1985) *The History of Sexuality, Vol. 2, The Uses of Pleasure.* New York: Pantheon.

Foucault, M. (1991) Governmentality. In: Burchell, G., Gordon, C. and Miller, P. (eds) *The Foucault Effect.* Chicago: University of Chicago Press.

Freeman, J. (2012) 'Neoliberal accumulation strategies and the visible hand of police pacification in Rio de Janeiro', *Revista de Estudos Universitários,* 38(1): 95–126.

Frischtak, C. and Mandel, B. R. (2012) 'Crime, house prices, and inequality: The effect of UPPs in Rio', FRB of New York Staff Report, (542).

Gledhill, J. and Hita, M. G. (2008) 'Beyond victims and aggressors: Thinking about violence in poor families in Brazil and Mexico', *ReVista: Harvard Review of Latin America,* VII(2): 23–25.

Gonçalves, R. S. (2008) 'O debate jurídico em torno da urbanização de favelas no Rio de Janeiro', *Revista Internacional de Direito e Cidadania,* 2: 139–148.

Holston, J. (2008) *Insurgent Citizenship: Disjunctions of Democracy and Modernity in Brazil.* Princeton, NJ: Princeton University Press.

Kalleberg, A. L. (2009) 'Precarious work, insecure workers: Employment relations in transition', *American Sociological Review,* 74(1): 1–22.

Lee, C. K. and Kofman, Y. (2012) 'The politics of precarity: Views beyond the United States', *Work and Occupations,* 39(4): 388–408.

Leeds, E., Leeds, A. and Violich, F. (1972) *Brazil in the 1960's: Favelas and Polity, the Continuity of the Structure of Social Control.* Institute of Latin American Studies, University of Texas.

Lorey, I. (2009) Attempt to Think the Plebeian: Exodus and Constituting as Critique. In: Raunig, G. and Ray, G. (eds) *Art and Contemporary Critical Practice: Reinventing Institutional Critique.* London: MayFlyBooks.

Lorey, I. (2015) *State of Insecurity: Government of the Precarious.* New York: Verso.

Magalhães, A. F. (2014) *O direito das favelas.* Rio de Janeiro: Letra Capital Editora.

Maloney, W. F. (2004) 'Informality revisited.' *World Development* 32(7): 1159–1178.

Martins, L. C. (2015) 'Urbanização, industrialização e favelas: o Rio de Janeiro na imprensa carioca no segundo governo Vargas', Projeto História (PUCSP).

McCann, B. (2013) *Hard Times in the Marvelous City: From Dictatorship to Democracy in the Favelas of Rio de Janeiro*. Durham, NC: Duke University Press.

Millar, K. M. (2018) *Reclaiming the Discarded: Life and Labor on Rio's Garbage Dump*. Durham, NC: Duke University Press.

Müller, M. (2016) *The Punitive City: Privatized Policing and Protection in Neoliberal Mexico*. London: Zed Books.

Pandolfi, D. and Grynszpan, M. (2002) *'Poder público e favelas: uma relação delicada', Cidade: história e desafios*. Rio de Janeiro: FGV.

Paret, M. (2016) 'Precarious class formations in the United States and South Africa', *International Labor and Working-Class History*, 89: 84–106.

Peláez, C. M. (1972) *História da Industrialização no Brasil*. São Paulo: ANPEC.

Perlman, J. E. (1976) *The Myth of Marginality: Urban Poverty and Politics in Rio De Janeiro*. Berkeley: University of California Press.

Perlman, J. E. (2006) 'The metamorphosis of marginality: Four generations in the favelas of Rio de Janeiro'. *The ANNALS of the American Academy of Political and Social Science* 606(1): 154–177.

Portes, A., Castells, M. and Benton, L.A. (1989) *The Informal Economy: Studies in Advanced and Less Developed Countries*. Baltimore, MD: John Hopkins University Press.

Portes, A., and Schauffler, R. (1993) 'Competing perspectives on the Latin American informal sector'. *Population and Development Review* 19(1): 33–60.

Queiroz Ribeiro, L. C. d. and Telles, E. E. (2000) 'Rio de Janeiro: Emerging Dualization in a Historically Unequal City. In: Marcuse, P. and Van Kempen, R. (eds) *Globalizing Cities: A New Spatial Order?*. Hackensack, NJ: Wiley-Blackwell.

Riley, E., Fiori, J. and Ramirez, R. (2001) 'Favela Bairro and a new generation of housing programmes for the urban poor', *Geoforum*, 32(4): 521–531.

Ross, A. (2009) *Nice Work If You Can Get It: Life and Labor in Precarious Times*. New York: New York University Press.

Santos, B. d. S. (1980) Notas Sobre a História Jurídico-Social de Pasárgada. In: Souto, C. and Falcão, J. (eds) *Sociologia e Direito: textos básicos de Sociologia Jurídica*. São Paulo: Pioneira.

Smith, N. and Williams, P. (1986) *Gentrification of the City*. Boston: Allen and Unwin.

Standing, G. (2011) The Precariat: The New Dangerous Class. London: Bloomsbury Academic.

Stinchcombe, A. L. (2001) *When Formality Works: Authority and Abstraction in Law and Organizations*. Chicago and London: University of Chicago Press.

Valladares, L. P. (1978) *Passa-se uma casa*. Rio de Janeiro: Zahar.

Valladares, L. P. (2005) *A Invenção da Favela: do mito de origem a favela.com*. Rio de Janeiro: Fundação Getúlio Vargas.

Van der Linden, M. (2014) 'San precario: a new inspiration for labor historians', *Labor: Studies in Working-Class History of the Americas,* 11(1): 9–21.

Vosko, L. F. (2010) *Managing the Margins: Gender, Citizenship, and the International Regulation of Precarious Employment.* Oxford: Oxford University Press.

Zaluar, A. (2004) *Integração Perversa: Pobreza e Tráfico de Drogas.* Rio de Janeiro: Fundação Getúlio Vargas.

Chapter 4

Voices of dissent

Culture-led regeneration in post-industrial European cities

Donna Carmichael, London School of Economics and Political Science

Abstract

The decline of the manufacturing sector in Britain resulted in social and economic devastation, with the loss of over 6 million jobs between 1966 and 2011. Culture-led regeneration strategies have been embraced by deindustrialised cities to attract tourists, investment, creative class workers, and to re-brand the city. However, there are few studies that seek to understand the lived experiences of residents in cities undergoing culture-led urban revitalisation—especially low-income and working-class communities whose voices are rarely incorporated into urban planning decisions. This chapter argues for the value of acknowledging and listening to these voices of dissent and for understanding the strategic resistance of residents/activists as new projects of urban cultural regeneration unfold.

***

The formidable forces of deindustrialisation in the late twentieth century had a devastating impact on cities across North America and Western Europe. Many formerly bustling industrial cities experienced massive downturns in manufacturing output and the closure of countless factories, mills and warehouses as production shifted to lower-cost geographies such as Japan, Korea and Taiwan (Jones and Evans 2013). In the UK, the manufacturing sector declined by 34.5 per cent, and employment fell from 8.9 million workers in 1966 to 2.7 million workers in 2011 (Tallon 2013). The closure and abandonment of manufacturing facilities resulted in many industrial buildings falling into dereliction, which made them easy targets for arson, vandalism and other criminal activities (Jones and Evans 2013).

The consequences of deindustrialisation include erosion of the traditional economic base; rises in unemployment; shrinking of the tax base and cutbacks in government services, which often lead to an increase in social problems (Brabazon 2014). In Britain, manufacturing was a critical economic pillar for 100 years from the early 1860s, and this contributed to the steadily rising living standards over that period. However, since the 1960s, there has been a significant decline in the UK manufacturing sector relative to other sectors, and relative to manufacturing sectors in other European countries such as Germany and Japan, and, more recently, relative to the newly industrialising countries of Brazil, Russia, India and China (Kitson and Michie 2014). In the 1980s, the emergence of the services and knowledge-based sectors contributed to the continued decline of UK manufacturing (Jones and Evans 2013), and this led to the emergence of an increasingly significant imbalance in the economy. Apart from the forces of globalisation and the consequent relocation of the process of production, the lack of government investment in the upgrading of manufacturing has also been identified as a significant cause of industrial decline in the UK (Kitson and Michie 2014: 1):

> There has been a chronic failure to invest in manufacturing, with the UK economy and investment being instead skewed towards short-term returns and the interests of the 'City'. The benign neglect of manufacturing by policymakers has led to an unbalanced economy with manufacturing balance of payments deficits emerging and then persisting since the early 1980s.

Cultural regeneration as a response to economic decline

Evans and Shaw (2006: 1) define regeneration as:

> the renewal, revival, revitalisation or transformation of a place or community. It is a response to decline, or degeneration. Regeneration is both a process and an outcome. It can have physical, economic and social dimensions, and the three commonly coexist.

The authors explain that in a culture-led regeneration model, cultural activity is seen as the catalyst and engine of regeneration (Evans and Shaw 2004). Evans (2005) provides examples of culture-led regeneration initiatives, including construction of new flagship cultural venues; cultural events such as arts festivals and garden festivals; a program of cultural activities under the banner of European Capital of Culture and Expo titles; sporting events such as the Olympics and Commonwealth Games and art schemes in the public realm.

Glasgow's 1990 European Capital of Culture and the 1997 opening of the Guggenheim Museum in the former industrial city of Bilbao in Spain are examples of the emergence of this new type of regeneration strategy in response to the industrial decline in cities throughout Europe (Miles 2005). The iconic Frank Gehry-designed Guggenheim Museum Bilbao was the first international branch of the New York-based Guggenheim Museum, and it has helped to transform the local economy by contributing to the re-imagining of the formerly polluted, crime-ridden city. Since opening in 1997, the museum has attracted large influxes of international and domestic tourists (Plaza *et al.* 2015).

Evans (2005) argues that the construction of a major new cultural venue, or the organisation of a large cultural event, will frequently be cited as a visible indicator of urban regeneration. As a result, culture-led regeneration strategies have become a solution of choice for urban planners and economic development professionals around the world. Florida (2002) suggests that a 'creative class' of knowledge workers comprising scientists, engineers, academics, designers, musicians, managers, etc., "whose economic function is to create new ideas, new technology and/or creative content" (Florida 2002: 8) can be an important driver of economic growth in cities. Cities and regions now compete vigorously with each other to reinvent themselves as "creative cities" in order to attract "the creative class" as the ingredient that enables urban revitalisation and economic growth (Miles and Paddison 2005). The competition to attract these people is based on the assumption that "creative workers seek creative outlets in all aspects of their lives and therefore migrate to cities that actively support their preferred lifestyles" (Donegan 2008: 181). Florida (2002) suggests that the creative class prefers experiential activities spanning cultural, social and physical domains, and includes activities such as antique shopping, bike riding and running, and visiting cultural festivals and urban spaces such as museums, art galleries, concert halls, and frequenting unique cafes and bistros (Florida 2002). Vuyk (2010: 10) suggests that, "inspired by [the research of] Florida, governmental bodies, especially at a local level, are nowadays fascinated by the question of how they can bind this creative class to the community in order to give its economy a lasting impulse."

Across the UK, cultural policy has been embraced by city leaders as well as central and local governments as a panacea of sorts to address the contemporary urban problems of post-industrial cities (Connolly 2013). As stated by Zukin (1996: 226), "so much of the dominant capitalist economy has ... undergone a cultural turn". For many deindustrialised cities in the UK, the culture-led approach has dominated policy and investment activity over the last 30 years (Liu 2016). For example, several UK cities have undertaken culture-led regeneration projects, such as Liverpool (2008 European Capital of Culture); Glasgow (Commonwealth Games 2012; European Capital of Culture 1990); Newcastle/Gateshead (the BALTIC art gallery and Sage concert venue 2002–2005), and recently, in Dundee, the Victoria & Albert (V&A) Museum of Design opened in September 2018. However, despite the proliferation of cultural-regeneration strategies, there are few studies that seek to understand and analyse the impact on the residents living proximal to such developments especially in affected low-income or marginalised post-industrial areas. Bailey *et al.* (2004: 64), argued, for example, that if it is true that culture-led regeneration, "does change people's lives after all ... it is about time we understood how and why it does so." Similarly, if the contrary is true, and the residents most affected by cultural regeneration strategies are not seen to be the beneficiaries of the developments that are imposed upon them, it is important that we arrive at a more in-depth understanding of why this might be. If the many and varied projects of cultural renaissance in post-industrial urban neighbourhoods often fail to positively impact on those people who are most in need of the support that cultural change often promises to bring, then the onus is on social scientists to clarify how cultural regeneration can lead not to an amelioration of life conditions for people living in relative poverty, but to the entrenchment of social and economic marginalisation.

Many culture-led regeneration initiatives focus on the quantitative assessment of impacts (Garcia 2005; Lees and Melhuish 2015), but there are also increasing calls for greater focus on the 'lived experiences' of people in diverse social conditions and urban change processes (Brownhill and Carpenter 2007; Lees and Melhuish 2015). This relatively new 'lived experience' approach has gained traction, for example, in research examining the process of industrial ruination (Mah 2014), providing rich insights into the meanings attached to deindustrialisation, urban decline, and the reconfiguration of the urban physical and socio-economic environment. Nevertheless, it remains the case that grassroots views are notably absent from discourses about regeneration (Edmiston 2017), and some have argued that working-class people's lives are negated and destroyed by the process of change and its "language of revitalization, recycling, upgrading and renaissance" (Smith 1996: 30).

Researchers have noted that much of the promotional messaging and impact assessment studies have clearly demonstrated an advocacy-for-cultural-regeneration perspective, which resolutely refuses or conveniently ignores any possibility of negative impacts, despite the current political emphasis on evidence-based policy creation and assessment (Belfiore 2012). This observation is echoed in other studies which also veer close to an advocacy stance (Campbell *et al.* 2016), with a bias to show positive impact rather than any potentially detrimental or negative repercussions of cultural policy related to urban regeneration. The silencing of working-class voices, combined with the predilection towards 'boosterism' is amplified by the often-facile affirmation of the value of culture and the sentiment that those opposed to culture-related initiatives are an "unpatriotic bunch of philistines" (Kelman 1992), cited by Mooney (2004: 330). All of which results in few studies that incorporate the dissenting voices of marginalised communities affected by cultural-led regeneration.

Giving voice to the 'recipients' of culture-led regeneration

The objective of this chapter is to draw attention to the downside of culture-led regeneration, and to give voice to some of the marginalised communities that are adversely affected by these initiatives. The literature on culture-led regeneration reflects a variety of disciplines, including scholarly research about the production of symbolic branding and representation of cities and spaces (Jones and Wilks-Heeg 2004; Kavaratzis and Ashworth 2015; Lennon 2014; Lucarelli 2011). Essentially, the research encompasses questions regarding who participates in the development of the new urban imaginary that supports culture-led regeneration initiatives. This body of literature explores the issue of power imbalances across groups in society, described as the

> point of collision, between the mobilizations of the deprived, the discontented and the dispossessed, on the one side, and on the other, ruling class strategies to instrumentalize, control and colonize social and natural resources, including the right to the city itself, for the benefit of the few.
>
> (Brenner, Marcuse and Mayer 2009: 182)

Another key research thread examines the social and political economy perspective (Frenzel and Beverungen 2015; Gray and Mooney 2011; Lees and Melhuish 2015; Miles 2005; Mooney 2004; Paton *et al.* 2016), which includes a research focus on the question of who benefits from culture-led regeneration—with many struggling cities embracing culture as a tool for economic revitalisation, and a diverse range of stakeholders engaged in vigorous dialogue and debate.

The idealised benefits of a culture-led regeneration strategy are tantalisingly seductive with promises to attract creative people to the city; take advantage of the opportunity to re-brand a city with a poor image; address deeply entrenched and seemingly intractable unemployment issues; tackle problems of social exclusion; nurture community; attract investment and tourists; revitalise the physical environment with new cultural buildings and infrastructure; and much more (Connolly 2013). However, the difference between the ideal and the reality can often be significant and hard to document, much less act upon.

The city of Glasgow was awarded the 1990 European Capital of Culture title. This gave rise to criticism of Glasgow's culture-led approach as indicative of a turn towards the instrumentalisation of culture as a tool for city re-branding. Urban marketing and economic renewal were key objectives for a city in desperate need of reinventing its economic base and negative city brand (McGuigan 2005). Glasgow is often pointed to as the poster child for culture-led regeneration, although many have challenged this rose-tinted narrative by pointing to the perceived silencing of working-class voices, the top-down approach of city planners and tight elitist coteries of government and business coalitions (Mooney 2004). Other criticisms include the prioritisation of international cultural events over the local culture of Glasgow (Garcia 2005). The most vociferous critics argue that the approach adopted by the city has led to greatly increased social and economic polarisation as evidenced by poverty, unemployment, poor health and life expectancy, and deprivation statistics (Shaw *et al.* 2005). Such promises have been decried as attempting to address social problems through the façade of superficial efforts to 'dress up' a city, with culture acting as a "surrogate for social policy" (Matarasso 1997: 85).

In a similar vein, Rius-Ulldemolins *et al.* (2016) describe how, in Valencia, a turn-of-the-century focus on economic development resulted in the construction of several new culture-focused buildings (aquarium, museum, arts centre, etc.) within a large 35-hectare urban space labelled as the City of Arts & Sciences, and designated as the flagship project to invent the 'new Valencia'. Valencia's culture-led regeneration strategy has attracted stinging criticism, including complaints about the over-building of expensive cultural venues, including 'white elephants'—which are major infrastructure components requiring large investments and maintenance costs, but that do not provide public value. Instead, they pile-up major public debt as a result of over-spending on iconic buildings and never-realised festivals; the destruction and/or gentrification of historic lower-income neighbourhoods; the diverting of much-needed public funds away from grassroots neighbourhood renewal and social support towards programs and amenities that support the cultural and business elites of the city (Ruis-Ulldemolins *et al.* 2016).

This 'instrumentalisation' of culture has been attacked as a one-size-fits-all cookbook approach to social and economic revitalisation (Pratt 2011), which rarely produces the promised results for marginalised communities (Ferilli *et al.* 2016). However, cultural organisations have seemingly eagerly embraced this broader societal mandate as it can facilitate their access to increased public funding (Evans 2005; Gray 2008). Gray (2008) has described this phenomenon as 'policy attachment', whereby cultural sector actors associate their actions and objectives with the policy objectives of other seemingly unrelated realms, such as economic growth and social inclusion, such that culture is essentially being utilised to achieve other non-cultural objectives. Kawashima (2006) points out that the cultural sector has been mandated to help address broader issues related to the alleviation of poverty, crime, unemployment, etc., providing culture with its "long sought-after economic justification" (Connolly 2013: 163).

The willingness of the cultural sector to appropriate other non-cultural policy mandates, such as economic and social revitalisation to generate employment and provide enhanced access to cultural activities, has been criticised by scholars because the mechanisms whereby cultural investments translate into positive socio-economic impacts are poorly understood (Belfiore and Bennett 2007; Colomb 2011; Skrede 2016). For example, Colomb's (2011) study of culture-led regeneration in the former industrial town of Roubaix in northern France investigated the 'trickle-down' assumption that underpins such initiatives, with trickle-down defined as "the explicit mechanisms promoted by local actors to ensure that cultural investments benefit vulnerable social groups through job creation and cultural democracy" (ibid.: 77). Her study indicated that investments in cultural regeneration do not automatically trickle down to the vulnerable populations in Roubaix, and in fact, may result in negative impacts (Colomb 2011).

Perhaps the most contentious aspect of the debate about who benefits from a cultural revitalisation initiative relates to the physical regeneration of cities to eradicate urban decay and clean-up the urban environment. Vast swathes of land are often acquired by governments and developers for the building of new cultural facilities such as museums, sports stadiums, and concert halls. Abandoned factories and related industrial buildings, along with derelict housing stock in former industrial districts, are viewed as a blight on the physical landscape of the city, and an embarrassing reminder of the decline of a city's former industrial economic engine. A primary objective is to upgrade the physical environment by demolishing derelict structures, accompanied by cultural venue development and infrastructure improvements in order to catalyse private sector investment and attract tourism (Connolly 2013). It has been noted that, during the 1990s, culture-led regeneration efforts were focused primarily on enhancing the design of the urban physical environment through demolition and the construction of new cultural facilities or installing public works of art (Campbell *et al.* 2016), with little requirement or expectation to address social or economic problems in these areas of redevelopment. It has been suggested that many such regeneration projects are actually more rightly described as 'development' projects, given the primary role of private sector real estate developers and investors (Brownhill and Carpenter 2007; Pratt 2011). Klunzman (2004: 2) wryly notes that "each story of regeneration begins with poetry and ends with real estate". A further criticism of such initiatives that focused on physical revitalisation without social consequence for anyone other than those who were to profit from transformed land use, was that many such projects failed to consider or address the pressing issue of economic and social inequality that exists in many deprived urban areas in deindustrialised cities (Skrede 2016). Garcia (2004) points out that despite the intention to use new cultural projects in derelict areas to improve the conditions for poorer communities, it has often resulted in the displacement of these communities and the inflow of higher-income groups into the area. Clearly, not everyone benefits from culture-led regeneration, as reinforced by Miles and Paddison (2005) who question the degree to which these kinds of initiatives work for diverse social groups.

For example, as part of its bid for the 2008 European Capital of Culture, the city of Liverpool culture-led regeneration strategy included commitments to economic and social regeneration. Claims about the many anticipated benefits of creative activity included strengthening and empowering communities, encouraging integration and diversity, and engaging local people in the regeneration process. All of this is promised to lead to better neighbourhoods, higher employment and prosperity, and higher aspirations (Connolly 2013). Boland (2010) studied Liverpool during its year as European Capital of Culture, and his travels during 2008–2009 in the city centre and throughout the peripheral housing estates including Toxteth, Speke, etc., revealed the dramatic spatial disparity between the core city and the peripheral communities:

> My journeys exposed a life a world away from the stylish regeneration in the city centre. The contrast was startling with impoverished housing estates suffering unemployment, deprivation and crime against a city centre thronged with yuppie apartments, four- and five-star hotels, plush eateries and exclusive stores.
>
> (Boland 2010: 633)

Similarly, a study of culture-led regeneration in Salford by Henderson *et al.* (2007) included 45 in-depth interviews with a variety of stakeholders, including local council representatives, property developers, and community representatives, and the qualitative data revealed the tension between these groups, and intimated that there were clear winners and losers from the Salford Quays development:

> They sold it to local people on the surmise of jobs that would become available, both in the construction industry and later on in the actual firms that moved onto the Quays. The jobs didn't develop in the construction industry … the only actual jobs have been the ancillary jobs for the housewives at night, cleaning and things like that.
>
> (former member of Tenants Association: 1458)

> The real uncertainty there is that while the community put some ideas forward, at the end of the day the key drivers are going to be the people who propose developments.
>
> (Tenant Management Cooperative Manager: 1458)

> The Council has got a hidden agenda for this estate to go completely private anyway ... we are just a little enclave facing the Quays that would be ideal for privatisation.
>
> (former member of Tenants Association: 1458)

In analysing their data, the researchers noted the existence of a deep cynicism and a feeling of 'them' and 'us' among the local people, which intimated that, whilst Salford Quays is a generally perceived as a successful development, it is not intended for them. The quotes above certainly lend support to that interpretation, and the cynicism and sense of betrayal is clearly evident in their choice of words to describe their reactions to the regeneration project.

Regeneration or gentrification

Paton *et al.* (2016) suggested that mega-sporting events, such as the Olympics and the Commonwealth Games, are an arm of gentrification, and their research examined as a form of displacement, the culture-led regeneration of the East End of Glasgow as part of the Commonwealth Games (CWG) urban development plans. Glasgow's bid for the hosting of the CWG in 2014 focused on a number of key 'legacy' improvements to the city and its residents, including increased prosperity, increased physical activity of residents, greater community inclusion, improvements to the environment, and enhancements to the city's image and global brand (Glasgow City Council, 2009). From an urban improvement perspective, a key objective of the Games strategy was the urban regeneration of the deindustrialised East End of Glasgow, and this goal included a primary focus on making effective use of otherwise derelict land "... with new housing, sports and community facilities, business spaces, public realm and transport infrastructure" (Glasgow 2014 Ltd. 2014: 18). Paton *et al.* (2016) examined the reality and lived experiences via focus groups with local East End residents, as well as through 22 resident diaries over the period before, during and after the Games (June 2014 to September 2014). The East End of Glasgow was designated as the site for several new Games-related venues, including the Athletes' Village, and the issue of displacement of residents and the demolition of housing was extremely contentious, and serves to illuminate the 'winners vs. losers' debate in terms of who benefits from such culture-led regeneration.

Resident diaries included reference to the upset in their lives caused by the Games, often resulting in economic loss and social disruption for many vulnerable residents, such as bus route detours, road closures, blocked access to parks, and roads crowded with trucks and construction vehicles. It is easy to overlook the real-life day-to-day negative impacts of the Games, when the focus of the approved narrative is on economic benefits such as job creation, inward investment, physical regeneration, and tourism; however, this type of qualitative research brings these supposedly mundane issues into sharp focus, and serves to bring a much-needed personal and human perspective to culture-led regeneration.

As mentioned above, the issue of displacement and dispossession (achieved through Glasgow City Council (GCC) compulsory purchase orders of property designated for Games purposes) was a contentious issue during the planning and build-out for the Games. Again, it is easy to ignore the human impact of these actions, especially as the East End of Glasgow was populated with poor and working-class residents, with many living in the social housing that dominated the residential areas (Paton *et al.* 2016). As these residents inhabited socially-rented homes, it was relatively simple for the GCC to evict and disperse these people to other neighbourhoods; however, the issue of displacement and dispossession gained international attention when Margaret Jaconelli, a long-term home-owning resident of the East End, refused to comply with the compulsory purchase order (CPO) to vacate her home to make way for demolition and the subsequent construction of Games venues. Chris Leslie,[1] a Glasgow photographer and journalist, followed Margaret's story from March 2008 to her eventual eviction in March 2011, and documented this situation in photography, video reportage and interviews:

> Margaret Jaconelli purchased her Dalmarnock home in 1976 and has lived as the sole remaining resident of Ardenlea St since 2002. With the Commonwealth Games fast approaching, the council wished to demolish the whole street which occupies the site of the proposed Athlete's Village. All the other residents have been re-housed but Margaret, as one of the few who owned her property, refused to move until offered adequate compensation. For four years she was on a one-woman crusade to save her family from being evicted whilst the rest of Dalmarnock was flattened around them. But in March 2011 the battle was lost, and Margaret's family evicted from their home.[2]

The story of Margaret's resistance to compulsory eviction provides insight into the human side of dispossession, and the devastating impact on individual lives that rarely hits the headlines and is not counted in the overarching metrics of economic development and growth promised by mega-sporting events: "I'm just a wee person from the east end of Glasgow and all I'm doing is fighting for a home that my husband has worked hard for for 34 years. They're stealing my property after us working so hard for it" (Margaret Jaconelli).[3]

Figure 4.1. Tenemental Blight, Dalmarnock, Glasgow East.

Photo by Neil Gray (used with permission).

Most of the residents of Dalmarnock, living in typical four-storey multiple occupancy tenement housing in Glasgow's East End, were evicted and re-housed following a decision by the local Housing Association to demolish the area in 2000. Margaret Jaconelli and her family, however, remained in their home in an empty building surrounded by advancing dereliction. Her last neighbour departed in 2002, leaving the family to face damp, cold, vermin, insecurity, no social services, and winter fuel bills of £140 per week (Porter 2009). Unlike many others in the area who socially rented, the Jaconelli family owned their own property, with no mortgage. They refused a paltry offer of £30,000 compensation, although the house had been independently valued at £90,000, and removal to other tenures was deemed to be neither like-for-like, nor a legitimate exchange for full home ownership. In 2008, they were made subject to a CPO and it became apparent their home was situated on the site designated for the CWG's 2014 Athletes' Village (Gray and Porter 2015).

Figure 4.2. Site of Commonwealth Games Athletes' Village, Dalmarnock.

Photo by Neil Gray (used with permission).

The story of Margaret Jaconelli's battle with the GCC was brought to broad public attention via the multi-media documentation of her situation, and the ability to share the digital record of her struggles across geographic boundaries and on multiple platforms was made possible only in the last few years as a result of new technologies and applications. This reflects the power of digital capture of such real-life stories about the struggles of real people, and the ability to present the issue from the viewpoint of the less powerful in society. There are now many examples on various social media platforms of the 'little people' experiencing social injustice, thereby making possible a remarkable opportunity for activists, journalists, filmmakers and other mission-driven associations and groups to broadcast these situations to global audiences. This can provide a much-needed counterbalance to the established media and communication channels that typically pay minimal attention to such 'human interest' stories.

Powerful online crowd-funding platforms can also provide a means for fundraising to cover costly legal expenditures, etc., that would normally be impossible to afford by marginalised individuals and groups who are under threat of displacement and dispossession. The explosion in the availability of digital capture of text, video, image, music, etc. has revolutionised qualitative research, and the emergence of digital ethnography is a powerful and exciting new method that allows researcher access to potentially new populations in an internet-mediated social world (Airoldi 2018).

Building a brand

By the 1980s, with the loss of industrial activity, the physical environment of many formerly bustling cities had decayed dramatically, and the external image of many of these cities was highly unflattering. This was based on an image of crumbling and overcrowded slum housing, severe levels of deprivation, unemployment, drugs and gangs, crime and vandalism, labour unrest, and widespread urban decay (McCarthy and Pollock 1997). Increasing globalisation has resulted in intensified competition between places around the world—as the economic base of many cities around the world has eroded, many places are now competing with each other for survival, and it is no longer a question of *whether* to brand, but *how* to brand (Hanna and Rowley 2013). Place branding, or *re-branding* in the case of many post-industrial cities struggling to address years of economic decline due to massive deindustrialisation, has become an important element in culture-led regeneration strategies.

The corporate world has long embraced the concept of brands and branding to help differentiate and communicate unique and compelling aspects of products and services (Arvidsson, 2006). The application of branding in the public sector is evident in the branding of places—cities, regions, and nations (Braun 2008). Place branding has emerged as an important policy component to help to transform negative imagery of cities and regions (Peel and Lloyd 2008) and has figured prominently in culture-led regeneration initiatives in many European cities (Anholt 2011; Jones and Evans 2013). Increasingly, local authorities, urban planners and economic development professionals are embracing the concept of reimagining and re-branding of cities in conjunction with regeneration activities, often including flagship cultural developments, with the objective of creating a more favourable identity that will be attractive to investors, businesses, tourists, and new residents (Jones and Evans 2013). The example frequently referenced in the literature is the iconic Guggenheim Museum in Bilbao which is often described as having been instrumental in helping the city recover from longstanding economic and social decay as a result of the loss of substantial industrial activity. Pratt (2011: 125) observed that such iconic cultural buildings need to be as "unique and controversial as possible" to generate maximum media coverage and marketplace awareness to help propel the rebranding effort. Plaza and Haarich (2015: 1457) suggested that the Guggenheim Museum Bilbao has "succeeded as a tourist magnet and an image-making device" with increased tourism, and improved awareness and perceptions of the city as a result of the stunning Gehry-designed building.

However, a key issue in the literature relates to the debate about whether the new city brand actually reflects the reality, heritage and culture of the city and its citizenry (Lennon 2014). Jancovich (2015) has pointed out that, despite the establishment of participation targets by the UK government, the situation persists that a narrow range of voices remain involved in urban decision making, which continues to be dominated by the cultural and economic elites and rarely includes participation by lower socio-economic individuals and groups. Cultural regeneration remains, therefore, a process implicated in the reproduction of urban social class divides with benefits often accruing to a wealthy middle class with money to spend on the kinds of activities that are associated with dominant cultural distinction.

Aiello (2012), points out that it is paradoxical that, in the pursuit of differentiation, cities have ended up adopting very similar culture-based regeneration strategies that ignore local cultural endeavours, which may not be confined to conventional categories of art, music, and theatre. Thus, a key issue within the city branding domain is the question of authenticity of the brand, as reflected in the work of Lennon (2014) with respect to the rebranding of Glasgow; Lennon raises cogent questions regarding who owns the brand narrative, whose culture is reflected in the brand, and whose voices are sought and whose are silenced. Concerns of this nature can be described as arising from questions regarding decision-making power within the city branding firmament, and who can select and dictate a new brand story for a city undergoing culture-led regeneration and rebranding. Place branding is often simply 'tacked-on' once the regeneration strategy has been developed, or applied post-hoc simply as a method to measure audience impressions and perceptions or to attract visitors (Garcia 2017), rather than as an integral part of the regeneration process.

Significant investments in flagship cultural institutions, infrastructure (new roads and bridges and rail lines, train station improvements, etc.), demolition of housing stock for redevelopment, reclamation of brownfield land, and many other elements could fail to generate the expected new jobs and economic benefits if a city cannot overcome its historically negative image as a declining post-industrial city. The stakes are high, and there is a risk that the culture-led city branding will alienate the existing residents, which could jeopardise the brand positioning as a result of a disconnect with the reality of the brand experience. In his article on place branding, Rius-Ulldemolins (2014: 1) decries the prevalence of "local elites using culture as an instrument of urban regeneration and urban branding." He examined, as a counter-example, the process for defining an 'authentic' place brand for the Raval, a formerly run-down area within central Barcelona, by intentionally basing the brand on an idealised historical memory that resonated strongly with the local residents—linking the place brand to a 'real' historical aspect of the area that related to the collective memory of local residents resulted in tremendous local adoption and internalisation of the 'new' brand. Far from being a planned and imposed top-down process, the local residents were central to the creation of an image that celebrated The Raval's uniqueness as multicultural urban area. The process was characterised by local resistance to the erasing of the district's historical assets, and proud ownership of the unique, albeit somewhat sordid, social history of the area.

De Rosa and Di Palma (2013) discussed the challenge of finding a balance between regeneration for economic development purposes and the protection and enhancement of local identity and community experiences. Braun *et al.* (2013) commented that place marketing might be a field where the participation of residents can enrich the creation of a place brand, so that rather than being seen as passive spectators in the branding process, local inhabitants can become active participants in the planning and branding process. On the other hand, Eshuis *et al.* (2014) discussed the fact that consensus among multiple and varied stakeholders is difficult to achieve, and may in fact result in the definition of a place brand with very general and non-descript attributes. A balance definitely seems to be required between the top-down imposition of potentially elitist place brands, and the bottom-up emergence of a meaningful and authentic place brand.

For example, the city of Dundee has undertaken a major regeneration initiative, which includes a substantial cultural component including the building of the V&A Museum of Design on a transformed waterfront. Historically, Dundee's economic fortunes were closely tethered to the jute industry, and up until its demise in the late 1970s, a large proportion of the population was employed in mills scattered throughout the city. Given the timing of the loss of these textile manufacturing jobs in the city, there are many residents who likely have vivid memories of the industrial nature of Dundee's economy, and likely have had minimal exposure or experience with the newer cultural amenities and experiences offered in Dundee, including art galleries, theatres and museums. Therein lies a major risk—the creation of a top-down city brand that does not reflect the reality of the residents' experiences and memories of the city, resulting in a lack of alignment between the desired brand position and the actual brand experience of visitors, new residents and companies. This was expressed in a news article (Morkis 2017: 1) about the 'two Dundees' and the massive drug abuse problems in a city trying to project an image of a prosperous and culture-rich environment:

> There are so many good things happening but, sadly, we still have this terrible problem with drugs. The waterfront and the V&A will mean nothing if the lasting impressions visitors take away from our city is addicts passed out in car parks or shambling glassy-eyed through the city centre.

European Capital of Culture (ECoC) host cities have been increasingly criticised for failing to enable local cultural ownership (Garcia 2005; O'Callaghan 2012). According to Pratt (2011), there is an implicit bias favouring a specific cultural representation which appeals to a cosmopolitan, international audience rather than presenting a more local representation of culture, which has resulted in community tensions. For example, the city of Cork was awarded the 2005 European Capital of Culture, and researchers highlighted the tension between local culture versus international culture which intends to appeal to the global cultural tourist, with increased tourism as a major objective of the ECoC title. In response to perceived 'sanitisation' and genericisation of the local culture in favour of a focus on a more internationally appealing cultural expression, the grassroots *Where's Me Culture?* group was established as a vehicle to present an alternative and more localised vision of Cork as the 2005 European Capital of Culture. This perceived slight of local culture polarised the arts community, dividing the city's arts practitioners between those who saw it as an opportunity for Cork to stage an international arts event, and those who saw it as an opportunity to stage Cork's local culture for an international audience (O'Callaghan 2012). As a result, the struggle over cultural expression remains a contentious aspect of the various 'city of culture' titles (Comunian and Mould, 2014; Connelly 2013; O'Callaghan 2012).

A study by Frenzel and Beverungen (2015) described the value struggles about cultural branding in the Stokes Croft area of Bristol, UK, resulting from local values clashing with the imposition of value as defined by the cultural and financial elites of the city, which they describe as a classic case of the shared notion of the public good being appropriated by capital. This is illustrative of Harvey's (2012: 78) comment that "those who create an interesting and stimulating everyday neighbourhood life lose it to predatory practices of the real estate entrepreneurs, the financiers and upper-class consumers bereft of any social imagination". This is an interesting case where a community 'self-branded' as a cultural zone, based on the presence of a large number of local artists and a thriving graffiti and music culture, and faced a battle against the threat of being colonised by the capital of private sector financial interests via the building of a large Tesco store nearby. The problem was neatly expressed by Chris Chalkley, a local community representative (Frenzel and Beverungen 2015: p. 1029):

> The corporate forces of the city are marching up the road from Cabot Circus [a big shopping mall at the city centre end of Stokes Croft] at present and Tesco is moving in from the other direction ... we are fighting a rearguard action here.

Similarly, in Belfast, a government and private sector-led effort was undertaken to create a cultural zone focused on the city's many cathedrals (Cathedral Quarter), and the project reflects the tension and value struggles between involvement and representation of the local arts community and the tourism and profit-oriented motives of the private sector, and the socio-economic objectives of the local authority (Laganside). McManus and Carruthers (2014: 85) articulated the struggle as follows:

> Cathedral Quarter was clearly a formal designation with the intervention and remit of Laganside, but the evidence here does question the extent to which the approach has reflected local aspirations, encouraged partnership and brought the sense of ownership that Bianchini and Ghilardi (2004) suggest are much more likely with a more organic approach. Whilst such tensions are inherent and inevitable in these types of policy interventions, perhaps more could have been done to include, involve and engage with the local arts communities to this end.

The authors' qualitative research provided a clear articulation of the issue of community representation by several informants (ibid.: 86):

> We took a lot of flak from the arts groups because they thought that we were coming into impose our way, they would have liked more say and control over what was done. At the start they wanted our input, but then when it came down to the activity and when it came to decisions, we were being informed about it afterwards.

Conclusions

The objective of this chapter is to draw attention to the negative socio-economic impacts and oft-neglected voices of marginalised communities experiencing culture-led regeneration efforts in their cities and neighbourhoods. Specifically, there is a focus on quantitative economic measures, a predilection towards positive assessments and city boosterism, and the unassailable 'feel-good' aspect of cultural endeavours. These all have the effect of diminishing the value and credibility of the lived experiences of the affected marginalised communities regarding who benefits and whose voices are incorporated into urban planning decisions. It is my hope that this chapter helps to give credence to the value of acknowledging and listening to these voices of dissent and to fuelling the strategic resistance of residents/activists as new projects of urban cultural regeneration unfold.

Notes

[1] http://www.chrisleslie.com/

[2] https://woffglasgow.com/programme/films-a-z/jaconelli/

[3] http://www.gamesmonitor.org.uk/node/1119

References

Aiello, G. (2012) 'All together now: The recontextualization of branding and the stylization of diversity in EU public communication', *Social Semiotics*, 22(4): 459–486.

Airoldi, M. (2018) 'Ethnography and the digital fields of social media', *International Journal of Social Research Methodology*, 21(6): 661–673.

Anholt, S. (2011) Beyond the Nation Brand: The Role of Image and Identity in International Relations. In: Pike, A. (ed.) *Brands and Branding Geographies.* Cheltenham: Edward Elgar.

Arvidsson, A. (2006) 'Brand value', *Journal of Brand Management*, 13(3): 188-192.

Bailey, C., Miles, S. and Stark, P. (2004) 'Culture led urban regeneration and the revitalization of rooted identities in Newcastle, Gateshead and the North East of England', *International Journal of Cultural Policy*, 10(1): 47–66.

Belfiore, E. (2012) '"Defensive instrumentalism" and the legacy of New Labour's cultural policies', *Cultural Trends*, 21(2): 103–111.

Belfiore, E. and Bennett, O. (2007) 'Rethinking the social impact of the arts', *International Journal of Cultural Policy*, 13(2): 135–151.

Bianchini, F. and Ghilardi, L. (2004) The Culture of Neighbourhoods: A European Perspective. In: Bell, D. and Jayne, M. (eds), *City of Quarters: Urban Villages in Contemporary Cities.* Aldershot: Ashgate.

Boland, P. (2010) 'Capital of culture—you must be having a laugh! Challenging the official rhetoric of Liverpool as the 2008 European cultural capital', *Social & Cultural Geography*, 11(7): 627–645.

Brabazon, T. (2014) Introduction: Sliced Cities. In: Brabazon, T. (ed.), *City Imaging: Regeneration, Renewal, and Decay.* Dordrecht: Springer.

Braun, E. (2008). *City Marketing: Towards an Integrated Approach.* Rotterdam: Erasmus Research Institute of Management (ERIM).

Braun, E., Kavaratzis, M. and Zenker, S. (2013) 'My city – my brand: The different roles of residents in place branding', *Journal of Place Management and Development*, 6(1): 18–28.

Brenner, N., Marcuse, P. and Mayer, M. (2009) 'Cities for people, not for profit', *City*, 13(2): 176–184.

Brownhill, S. and Carpenter, J. (2007) 'Participation and planning: Dichotomies, rationalities and strategies for power', *The Town Planning Review*, 78(4): 401–406.

Campbell, P., Cox, T. and O'Brien, D. (2016) 'The social life of measurement: How methods have shaped the idea of culture in urban regeneration', *Journal of Cultural Economy*, 10(1): 49–62.

Colomb, C. (2011) 'Culture in the city, culture for the city? The political construction of the trickle-down in cultural regeneration strategies in Roubaix, France', *Town Planning Review*, 82(1): 77–98.

Comunian, R. and Mould, O. (2014) 'The weakest link: Creative industries, flagship cultural projects and regeneration', *City, Culture and Society*, 5(2): 65–74.

Connolly, M. G. (2013) 'The "Liverpool model(s)": Cultural planning, Liverpool and Capital of Culture 2008', *International Journal of Cultural Policy*, 1(2): 162-181.

De Rosa, F. and Di Palma, M. (2013) 'Historic urban landscape approach and port cities regeneration: Naples between identity and outlook', *Sustainability*, 5(10): 4268–4287.

Donegan, M. (2008) 'Which indicators explain metropolitan economic performance best? Traditional or creative class', *Journal of the American Planning Association*, 74(2): 180–195.

Edmiston, D. (2017). 'Welfare, austerity and social citizenship in the UK', *Social Policy and Society*, 16(2): 261–270.

Eshuis, J., Klijn, E. and Braun, E. (2014) 'Place marketing and citizen participation: Branding as strategy to address the emotional dimension of policy making?', *International Review of Administrative Sciences*, 80(1): 151–171.

Evans, G. (2005) 'Measure for measure: Evaluating the evidence of culture's contribution to regeneration', *Urban Studies*, 42(5–6): 959–983.

Evans, G. and Shaw, P. (2006) 'Literature review: Culture and regeneration', *Arts Research Digest*, 37(1): 1–11.

Evans, G. and Shaw, P. (2004) *The Contribution of Culture to Regeneration*. London: DCMS.

Evans, G. (2017) 'Brexit Britain: Why we are all postindustrial now', *American Ethnologist*, 44(2): 215–219.

Ferilli, G., Sacco, P. L. and Blessi, G. T. (2016) 'Beyond the rhetoric of participation: New challenges and prospects for inclusive urban regeneration', *City, Culture and Society*, 7(2): 95–100.

Florida, R. (2002) *The Rise of the Creative Class*. New York: Basic Books.

Frenzel, F. and Beverungen, A. (2015) 'Value struggles in the creative city: A People's Republic of Stokes Croft?,' *Urban Studies*, 52(6): 1020–1036.

Garcia, B. (2004) 'Cultural policy and urban regeneration in Western European cities: Lessons from experience, prospects for the future', *Local Economy*, 19(4): 312–326.

Garcia, B. (2005) 'Deconstructing the city of culture: The long-term cultural legacies of Glasgow 199', *Urban Studies*, 42(5): 841–868.

Garcia, B. (2017) '"If everyone says so ..." Press narratives and image change in major event host cities'. *Urban Studies*, 54(14): 3178–3198.

Glasgow's Legacy Framework (2014). Available at: https://www.glasgow.gov.uk/CHttpHandler.ashx?id=26935&p=0.

Gray, C. (2008) 'Instrumental policies: Causes, consequences, museums and galleries', *Cultural Trends*, 17(4): 209–222.

Gray, N. and Mooney, G. (2011) 'Glasgow's new urban frontier: "Civilising" the population of Glasgow East', *City*, 15(1): 4–24.

Gray, N. and Porter, L. (2015) 'By any means necessary: Urban regeneration and the "State of Exception" in Glasgow's Commonwealth Games 2014', *Antipode*, 4(2): 380–400.

Hanna, S. and Rowley, J. (2013) 'A practitioner-led strategic place brand-management model', *Journal of Marketing Management*, 29(15–16): 1782–1815.

Harvey, D. (2012) *Rebel Cities: From the Right to the City to the Urban Revolution*. London: Verso.

Henderson, S., Bowlby, S. and Raco, M. (2007) 'Refashioning local government and inner-city regeneration: The Salford experience', *Urban Studies*, 44(8): 1441–1463.

Jancovich, L. (2015) 'Breaking down the fourth wall in arts management: The implications of engaging users in decision-making', *International Journal of Arts Management*, 18(1): 14–28.

Jones, P. and Evans, G. (2013) *Urban Regeneration in the UK*. 2nd edn. Los Angeles: SAGE.

Jones, P. and Wilks-Heeg, S. (2004) 'Capitalising culture: Liverpool 2008'. *Local Economy*, 19(4): 341–360.

Kavaratzis, M. and Ashworth, G. (2015) 'Hijacking culture: The disconnection between place culture and place brands', *Town Planning Review*, 86(2): 155–176.

Kawashima, N. (2006) 'Audience development and social inclusion in Britain: Tensions, contradictions and paradoxes in policy and their implications for cultural management', *International Journal of Cultural Policy*, 12(1): 55–72.

Kelman, J. (1992) *Some Recent Attacks*. Stirling: AK Press.

Kitson, M. and Michie, J. (2014) 'The deindustrial revolution: The rise and fall of UK manufacturing: 1870–2010', Centre for Business Research, University of Cambridge Working Paper No. 459.

Klunzman, K. (2004) Keynote speech to Intereg III Mid-term Conference, Lille, in: Regeneration and Renewal, 19 November, p. 2.

Lees, L. and Melhuish, C. (2015) 'Arts-led regeneration in the UK: The rhetoric and the evidence on urban social inclusion', *European Urban and Regional Studies*, 22(3): 242–260.

Lennon M. (2014) Glasgow the Brand: Whose Story Is It Anyway? In: Brabazon T. (ed.) *City Imaging: Regeneration, Renewal and Decay*. Dordrecht: Springer.

Liu, Y. (2016) 'Cultural event and urban regeneration: Lessons from Liverpool as the 2008 European Capital of Culture', *European Review*, 24(1): 159–176.

Lucarelli, A. (2011) 'City branding: A state-of-the-art review of the research domain', *Journal of Place Management and Development*, 4(1): 9–27.

Mah, A. (2014) 'The dereliction tourist: Ethical issues of conducting research in areas of industrial ruination', *Sociological Research Online*, 19(4), doi: 10.5153/sro.3330.

Matarasso, F. (1997) *Use or Ornament? The Social Impact of Participation in the Arts.* Stroud: Comedia.

McCarthy, J. and Alan Pollock, S. (1997) 'Urban regeneration in Glasgow and Dundee: A comparative evaluation', *Land Use Policy,* 14(2): 137–149.

McGuigan, J. (2005) 'Neo-liberalism, culture and policy', *International Journal of Cultural Policy,* 11(3): 229–241.

McManus, C. and Carruthers, C. (2014) 'Cultural quarters and urban regeneration – the case of Cathedral Quarter Belfast', *International Journal of Cultural Policy,* 20(1): 78-98.

Miles, S. (2005) 'Our Tyne: Iconic regeneration and the revitalisation of identity in Newcastle Gateshead', *Urban Studies,* 42(5): 913–926.

Miles, S. and Paddison, R. (2005) 'Introduction: The rise and rise of culture-led urban regeneration', *Urban Studies,* 42(5): 833–839.

Mooney, G. (2004) Cultural policy as urban transformation? Critical reflections on Glasgow, European City of Culture 1990', *Local Economy,* 19(4): 327–340.

Morkis, S. (2017) '"The sad truth is there are now two Dundees" — Shameful image shows depth of drug depravity', Available at: https://www.thecourier.co.uk/fp/news/local/dundee/426624/sad-truth-now-two-dundees-shameful-image-shows-depth-drug-depravity/.

O'Callaghan, C. (2012) 'Urban anxieties and creative tensions in the European Capital of Culture 2005', *International Journal of Cultural Policy,* 18(2): 185–204.

Paton, K., McCall, V. and Mooney, G. (2016) 'Place revisited: Class, stigma and urban restructuring in the case of Glasgow's Commonwealth Game', *The Sociological Review,* 65(4): 578–594.

Peel, D. and Lloyd, G. (2008) 'New communicative challenges: Dundee, place branding and the reconstruction of a city image', *The Town Planning Review,* 79(5): 507–532.

Plaza, B., González-Casimiro, P., Moral-Zuazo, P. and Waldron, C. (2015) 'Culture-led city brands as economic engines: Theory and empirics', *The Annals of Regional Science; An International Journal of Urban, Regional and Environmental Research and Policy,* 54(1): 179–196.

Plaza, B. and Haarich, S.N. (2015) 'The Guggenheim Museum Bilbao: Between regional embeddedness and global networking', *European Planning Studies,* 23(8): 1456–1475.

Porter, L. (2009) 'Planning displacement: The real legacy of major sporting events', *Planning Theory & Practice,* 10(3): 395–418.

Pratt, A. C. (2011) 'The cultural contradictions of the creative city', *City, Culture and Society,* 2(3): 123–130.

Rius-Ulldemolins, J. (2014) 'Culture and authenticity in urban regeneration processes: Place branding in central Barcelona', *Urban Studies,* 51(14): 3026–3045.

Rius-Ulldemolins, J., Hernàndez, I. M. and Torres, F. (2016) 'Urban development and cultural policy "white elephants": Barcelona and Valencia', *European Planning Studies,* 24(1): 61–75.

Shaw, M., Smith, M. and Dorling D. (2005) 'Health inequalities and new labour: How the promises compare with real progress', *British Medical Journal*, 33. doi: 10.1136/bmj.330.7498.1016.

Skrede, J. (2016) 'What may culture contribute to urban sustainability? Critical reflections on the uses of culture in urban development in Oslo and beyond', *Journal of Urbanism: International Research on Placemaking and Urban Sustainability*, 9(4): 408–425.

Smith, N. (1996) *The New Urban Frontier: Gentrification and the Revanchist City*. New York: Psychology Press.

Tallon, A. (2013) *Regeneration in the UK*. 2nd edn. London: Routledge.

Vuyk, K. (2010) 'The arts as an instrument? Notes on the controversy surrounding the value of art', *International Journal of Cultural Policy*, 1(2): 173–183.

Zukin, S. (1996) Cultural Strategies of Economic Development and the Hegemony of Vision. In: Merrifield, A. and Swyngedouw, E. (eds) T*he Urbanization of Injustice*. London: Lawrence and Wishart.

Chapter 5

Culture as meaning-making

A new-old paradigm to reconcile working-class priorities with creative hubs and cultural industries

Jessica Symons, University of Manchester

Abstract

This chapter argues that an understanding of culture as how people make their lives meaningful allows for a wider engagement with community practice. It draws on fieldwork among people in a low-income area in Salford, North West England and explains why attempts to run a research project exploring cultural activities produced local consternation. The research shows how a reframing of the project to support community members to develop their own ideas for cultural activities, meant that the research team then found considerable enthusiasm for creative and self-expression. The chapter suggests that respecting local pride and locally generated priorities (such as caring for community members) produces significantly more citizen engagement and new formulations of cultural creativity than is the case when people and places are conceived of as 'deprived' or 'hard-to-reach'.

***

> A local authority will subsidise a community group, because it has labels of poverty and inequality. The organisation that is doing the negotiation cannot reveal that to the group... If you had the same conversation that you have with the local authority, with the community group, they would be really unhappy and upset that the provision of their stuff is basically a subsidy for a poor area. This is dishonouring people because it's insulting to them, exposing the reason why money is drawn down.
>
> Hannah, 52, Community organiser, Salford (Interview 2014)[1]

In this chapter, I share insight from my time as a Research Fellow in a £1m UK university-led research project on understanding cultural dynamics undertaken in 2014–16 around a low-income area of Salford, North West England.[2] I describe how reactions from community members in Salford to the research project design led to a reframed understanding of culture as the processes through which people make their lives meaningful. This new emphasis on culture-as-meaning-making helps reconcile an ongoing dichotomy in the UK's creative sector which situates narrow versions of culture as primarily relating to performance art, theatre, music and dance. Insight from the research suggests a much broader, more grassroots understanding of culture to include what everyone does all the time where culture is about 'just everybody'.

The project reframing of how to understand culture in this low-income community was inspired by the Geertzian (1973) proposition that culture is about the general process of human 'meaning-making'. Geertz's argument provided the groundwork for enabling self-expression among research participants from working-class backgrounds who might have otherwise felt excluded from more conventional and dominant modes of cultural expression. The approach helped tackle the frustration often felt, in marginalised working-class areas in response to clumsy government interventions that attempted to increase rates of 'cultural participation' to address the more general problem of 'social exclusion' caused by post-industrial decline.

By 2010s, certain groups of people living in particular areas of the UK had become labelled as 'hard-to-reach' because their socio-economic status remained stubbornly low. Repeated government interventions had not seemed to work in improving people's circumstances. This analysis draws on research among these so called 'hard-to-reach' people living and working in Salford, a city in the north of England. The research site was a geographical area targeted for government intervention due to its high score on the English indices of deprivation.[3] I was recruited to carry out grounded research to develop 'cultural activities' with people living and working in the area.[4] I worked alongside another academic whose research focused on governance and social change, the project administrator and four 'cultural intermediaries' from the local area who responded to an advert inviting them to participate in the project.[5]

During fieldwork, it became clear that state-led processes that categorise areas as 'deprived' are actually a significant *barrier* to engagement with local people. As Hannah, a community organiser describes above, people are insulted by the "labels of poverty and inequality" and people perceive that these terms are used to "dishonour" them. While these residents may face considerable adversity with ongoing and significant health issues, living in high crime areas, and experiencing poor work opportunities, they also have ambitions and aspirations, the same as everyone else. Hannah, explained further:

> The only way in which local people's perspective of the government will change is if their real experience changes. It's just getting worse. So they are rightly suspicious, generally insulted and oppressed by the nature of that relationship and the 'tokens' of support and funding offered by government.

The 2010s were a challenging time in the UK. The UK government's decision to resolve a banking crisis by injecting funding into the financial sector had led to significant retraction of budgets in most other areas of government spending. Local councils were particularly badly affected with cuts to budgets running across adult social care, housing, environment and culture. Since many people living in low-income areas are almost completely reliant on government support, they were disproportionally affected by the UK government's 'austerity' drive. As a long-term community worker, Hannah had witnessed first-hand the devastating impact of a sudden withdrawal of state support on community members.

For the research project, I was tasked with setting up a "panel of local people to commission cultural activities". Through encounters and conversations with people such as Hannah, I wrestled with intersecting dynamics between ethnographic principles of non-interventionist participant observation and research project obligations to 'deliver' action research. Discordance between these two objectives heightened awareness of how 'outsiders' are perceived in this particularly tight-knit (Young and Wilmot 1957) area of Salford and stimulated sensitivity to the tone and style of state-led, bureaucratic engagement.

In the following analysis, I explain how people reacted to terms such as 'hard-to-reach' and 'culture' and argue that these responses reveal assumptions that run through state-led interventions. I suggest that characterisations and depictions of certain areas of the UK as 'deprived' or 'poor' are actually middle-class conceptualisations of working-class lives and that these negative characterisations generate negative responses.

This chapter also describes how the research project team reacted to local people's frustration and anger at the project intervention and how a reframing of the research project made it more acceptable. In particular, we found that making the research process reciprocal rather than extractive, working with local organisations and supporting people to develop their own ideas rather than expecting them to deliver ours, made a substantial difference to local engagement. While the project had its limitations, the research team progressed from hearing statements like "I hope this project f***ing fails", as one resident put it, to a community celebration event attended by the project participants, their families, the local mayor and university officials. By engaging with local people on their terms, we made a difference to how they engaged with us.

Introducing Salford

Salford is a city in Northern England adjacent to the larger city of Manchester. Its development arc can be summarised as a story of boom to bust then boom again. In the nineteenth century, the two cities' infrastructure of navigable rivers, canals and railways sat at the heart of the North West's developing industrial revolution (Kidd and Wyke 2016). It was Salford's docks that enabled the distribution of cotton that built Manchester's fame as 'Cottonopolis' (Maw 2013; Webb 1990). However, this boom was followed by a slow decline as changing technologies and globalisation diminished Manchester's role in international trade. The working-class communities that constituted this "original modern" city (Leadbeater 2009) were particularly affected by a slump in trade. These changes devastated the local economy leading to widespread unemployment that persisted well into the 1990s and whose effects are still felt today (Peck and Ward 2002).

From the 1950s, in line with national policy, local governments in Salford and Manchester dealt with the wide-scale decline of housing stock and significantly impoverished populations by introducing a 'social housing' policy which involved carrying out 'slum clearances' and rebuilding new estates (Parkinson-Bailey 2000). However as Ravetz (2003) argues the social housing project was part of a utopian aspiration to change working-class lives through the provision of 'ideal' homes as the 'seat of personal and marital fulfilment'. She argues that the subsequent 'failure' of social housing to change lives can be read as failed utopian aspirations by interventionist governments; people brought their existing troubles and cultural understandings into these new residential settings (Ravetz 2003).

Paid for by local governments or 'councils', these areas of social housing became 'council housing' and state intervention, initially focused on improving *housing stock*, became state intervention focused on improving *working-class people*. How this moral tone continues to imbue government interaction in these communities can be found in ethnographic research by anthropologists such as Evans (2006). Her groundbreaking work shows in detail how resident lifestyles in a housing estate in Bermondsey, East London come to be mediated through middle-class expectations that start at school and continue into adulthood through engagement with government benefits and housing offices (Evans 2006). It was this elision from government *support for people* in difficult circumstances, to government *control over people's behaviour* as they experience difficult circumstances, that directly affected our research as we entered a social housing estate in Salford. The project's aspiration to explore cultural activities in a low-income 'hard-to-reach' area bumped up against local frustration at government-led ideological framings of social housing communities as problems to be solved.

As an anthropologist, I took an ethnographic approach to the research. I spent time hanging out, visiting different areas, talking to people in the library, café, in local organisations and at public meetings. I volunteered in community spaces and interviewed people living and working in the area. We also paid Hannah's community organisation to hire four local women who carried out similar 'community researcher' activities focusing in particular on what people considered to be 'culture'.

While people were largely polite towards me as an outsider, Hannah's team encountered an immediate and strong hostility to their questions with people making comments like "I hope this project f***ing fails" and refusals to talk. I was asked if I was undercover police and faced a persistent disinterest in the project even though we had significant amounts of money to spend in the area (Symons 2017). A few months into the project, we became concerned that our style and approach was alienating people rather than empowering them.

It was in response to this pushback that an understanding of cultural priorities for people in this area emerged. Fieldwork helped reveal the different groups in the area and why some people were resistant to outsiders. It gave us access to a vibrant community focused on close social relationships and family ties. These findings reinforce the arguments in the contemporary anthropology and sociology of working-class post-industrial neighbourhoods such as Evans (2006), Smith (2012), Edwards *et al.* (2012), Koch (2016) on how these communities need to be understood from the inside before taking interventionary action.

Introducing Ordsall

> I remember the docks when they were working, full of fellas shouting and moving stuff about. Massive great ships sitting there with ropes the size of your arm. It were a busy place back then.
>
> Bertie, 86, remembering Salford Quays as a working port. 2014

Bertie had lived in Ordsall, 'man and boy' and remembered a working community, whose lives wrapped around the river and the canals that wrapped around their area. The stories poured out of him as we stood around in the celebrated local lads club. People would laugh, gripped by his accounts of a bygone era.

Figure 5.1. New flats materialising next to familiar landmarks.

Photo by Jessica Symons.

Bertie described how a boy went swimming in the river and came back blue ... from the dye released into the water by a nearby chemical factory. He told this story in response to the recent announcement that anyone found jumping in the dock waterways would be carrying out a criminal act. The residents of the new developments on the Quays had lobbied the local government to introduce a bylaw, as they were irritated by local boys swimming in the water on hot summer days. 'But we've been swimming there for years' people would say to me, 'long before they cleaned it up and made it safe for others'. The local boys ignored the rules and signs, instead jumping off the bridges and quays into the water, 'just like they always had'. The area may be changing rapidly through regeneration and property speculation, but memories seemed to be inherited in the Ordsall community along with a sense of belonging and ownership.

Figure 5.2. Fenced in green spaces in Ordsall demarcated for property development.

Photo by Jessica Symons.

Ordsall was a sprawling district in Salford just over the river Irwell from Manchester city centre. Its large housing estate was bordered on three sides by the river, the Manchester Ship Canal and Salford Quays and bisected by large arterial roads and railways creating isolated pockets of social housing in some areas and affluent residential neighbourhoods in others. The area was constantly transforming during the 2014–16 research project with new developments appearing in former derelict empty warehouses with spruce new gated apartment blocks. The people living in social housing, some of whom had lived there all their lives, would describe feeling left out by this gentrifying wave. They could not afford to move into the new apartments themselves and the tall, metal gates with keycode access indicated incomers attitudes towards existing residents. These experiences echo those of other marginalised neighbourhoods worldwide as existing low-income communities residing in newly valuable urban areas wrestle with growing property prices and rapid change led by developer speculation and local government sanguinity (DeSena 2018; Lees *et al.* 2015; Paton 2016; Wacquant 2008).

The particular instance of property speculation and change in Ordsall produced friction that included, for example, arguments over noise when a new development of artists' studios held club nights; opportunist parking by office workers in a nearby housing estate and local residents being followed by security guards when they visited the gleaming new MediaCity UK, a creative digital hub built to attract the affluent London-based media organisations to open offices in the North of England.

These were moments when underlying frustrations manifested leading to tense community meetings, complaints to the council, arguments between different groups and car windows smashed. The swimming in the docklands water on hot days can be read as one expression of defiance about what it meant to be 'from Ordsall'. Where formerly Ordsall was a place associated with crime families, drugs and violence, which were themselves a response to the collapse of paid work when the docks and factories closed; now the area was changing ostensibly for the better, but still leaving 'local people' out.

The development of the docklands into a 'cultural quarter' was particularly galling for people as the area they associated with lost work became inaccessible in the form of a cultural economy of theatre, music, art and performance, which had high entry costs and little relevance to local working-class residents' own life experiences. One community organiser described The Lowry theatre in Salford Quays as being like a 'bright spotlight' that outshone all the smaller lights of cultural activity situated around it; she spoke of it 'sucking up' all available government resources. Our arrival in the community asking research questions about 'cultural activities' mediated through our privileged status as academic bureaucrats from the nearby university, became entangled in an ongoing and frustrated wrestle for ownership and recognition among local people as the original custodians and inhabitants of the area.

On culture

Culture is big business for the UK. The 'industries' of art, theatre, music, sport and especially the growing digital sector bring in £84bn annually into the British economy (Department for Culture, Media and Sport 2016). Culture is big business for Manchester too. The city adjacent to Salford has a big reputation for cultural output worldwide through the famous Manchester United and Manchester City football clubs, a thriving night life and musical legacy that produced internationally famous bands such as the Smiths, Oasis and New Order. During the 1990s, this cultural offer played a significant role in bringing Manchester out of post-industrial doldrums and into a new phase of urban development (Lewis and Symons, 2017; Peck and Ward 2002). In 2011, Manchester launched a 'Cultural Ambition' to "ensure a year-round world-class cultural offering and to attract, therefore, more international visitors".[6]

Inspired by Manchester's successful capitalisation of a cultural offer to regenerate their city, Salford followed suit with a consortium of private and public interests led by a large and influential property developer in the area, Peel Holdings (Harrison 2014). The first phase included new developments in the former docklands and the second was MediaCity UK, a substantial 'cultural quarter' which grew further when Salford won the competition to host an anchor regional television station in the form of BBC North. Further digital media companies followed suit leading to a thriving creative digital economy and stimulating significant property speculation in the areas surrounding the Quays. By 2017, while attending a major cultural event in a gleaming arts theatre surrounded by the UK's key cultural decision makers and overlooking a metropolis of shiny buildings, I could see how others might have considered Salford's 'regeneration' as complete.

However, I was at the Lowry arts theatre to speak at the Culture and Creative Industries event run by the central government Westminster Policy Forum. The gathered throng were senior executives of public, private and third sector organisations. It was a coup for MediaCityUK that this influential organisation's first event outside London was located at their creative digital hub in Salford. My speech argued and advocated for a different way of understanding culture. I introduced the nearby low-income community residing a stone's throw away from the Quays and explained how people there felt left out by regeneration of the docklands, which was remembered locally as a site of work and community. In this area, people were proud of their industrial past and struggled with bureaucratic characterisations of them as living in poverty as "disenfranchised", "deprived" and "hard-to-reach" people (Symons 2017).

During the talk, I shared how people in Ordsall would reject the term 'culture' when asked about cultural activities, instead claiming that "we have no culture, *they* have taken it away". I suggested that what had led to these perspectives was a woeful neglect of local priorities and interests combined with patronising attempts to 'make' people participate in 'culture' as defined by the 'creative industries'. What people really wanted was policies to support their ideas and aspirations. I then described our research project and how when supported to develop cultural activities of their own, people focused on family and close social relationships, celebrating shared history, offering to teach new skills and providing opportunities for social gatherings. This was where people derived satisfaction, a sense of purpose and meaning in their lives. I emphasised that the activities themselves were not unlike what you might find in the cultural sector—a festival, social history play, photo exhibitions—it was just that the framing of the significance of these events was different.

The talk also drew attention to the fact that ongoing private sector gated developments and rocketing property prices were causing significant consternation among people in social housing who could never afford to buy a home of their own. I clarified that due to a lack of available social housing, residents were worried that they may have to leave an area to which they felt a strong historical connection and a community in which they were deeply embedded.

As I sought to reframe understandings of culture that would engender respect for the interests and activities of people in these communities, I cited the new Culture White Paper[7] that opened with an exhortation that 'Everyone should enjoy the opportunities culture offers, no matter where they start in life' (Vaisey 2016). I drew on the longstanding anthropological approach to 'culture' as inherent to every context of human life and not just particular sectors such as art, theatre, music and performance. The implication in the White Paper was that 'everyone' should enjoy art as defined by the cultural sector rather than deriving enjoyment from participating in the creative pursuits defined by what is important to them and what gives their lives meaning.

The argument elicited a strongly positive response from the cultural industries representatives. People gathered round afterwards, agreeing enthusiastically and proffering examples from their own experiences. The argument that 'culture is everywhere', as one Ordsall resident put it, resonated because this approach makes a bridge between community activities such as dog walking and barbecues and the cultural sector with its emphasis on performance through dance, music, theatre. If culture is how people make their lives meaningful, then meaning comes from everywhere also.

For Geertz, analysis of culture is an "interpretive enquiry of meaning" (Geertz 2003 (1973): 311). He proposes looking at the details of particular settings and focusing on how people interact in different contexts. For example, Geertz describes how closing one eye as a wink can be interpreted in multiple ways (e.g. suggestive, sarcastic, sneaky, amusing) and that the context is critical to understanding meaning. One person's provocative wink is another person's twitch. Geertz builds on this insight to emphasise the importance of looking at activities in a given setting and identifying meaning from the lived context through an analytical process. Building on his interpretation, I was able to explain that culture is iteratively produced and emergent as people co-construct meaning through their daily interactions. From this perspective, culture becomes the substance through which people make meaningful actions and therefore make sense of their lives.

This approach to culture, understood as to *how people make their lives meaningful*, connects multiple interpretations of cultural practices. For example, Gilmore (2017) explains the importance of parks and culture as aspects of "everyday participation". People engage with their local community because it gives them a sense of belonging to somewhere, culture is produced through their participation in the local amenities.

This approach also works for and can help articulate the value of sectors such as music, theatre, art, performance which are traditionally associated with culture. If the focus lies on how people seek to make sense of life, building on their own daily practice, then engagement with music by making or listening to it is an equivalent cultural act to walking the dog through the local park. When a fine artist looks for meaning through paint or clay, a conceptual artist through ideas, a musician through their instrument, an actor by exploring performance on stage or their audiences by engaging with these works, then the meaning made in those moments is how culture comes to be produced. Culture as how people make their lives meaningful also works for when people do activities that have significance for them, even if there is no obvious output such as an artwork or object. If these meaningful activities include hosting barbecues, going to the park, caring for relatives or just sitting at home, then this is part of people's 'culture'.

Since cultural strategies are increasingly used to stimulate urban dynamics, this produces a compelling need to unsettle assumptions about culture and tackle its nuances in government policy making. In his analyses of creative cities, Pratt calls for, "a platform for a more nuanced and subtle approach of creativity, culture and cities, one that is situated and not universal; and one that is centrally concerned not simply with the growth possibilities, but also redistributive strategies" (Pratt 2011: 2; see also Pratt 2017) By drawing boundaries around particular activities and labelling them as 'cultural' or 'creative', cities and government cultural strategies can significantly constrain a wider group of people from participating in the cultural economy.

My presentation at the Creative Industries conference resituated an understanding of culture away from narrow domains of activity to more general processes of meaning-making. It insisted on incorporating people's sense of self and community into cultural strategy and recognising local values and aspirations for achieving a sense of wellbeing. While this approach may resonate with community-oriented agendas, it is not common in discussions about the cultural industries. People are focused on arts, theatre, music and increasingly digital forms of production. 'Community' is something to be covered by a different government department, or an 'outreach' activity that aims to bring people from low-income communities to an art gallery or theatre. It becomes part of an "unguarded instrumentalism" (Gilmore 2014), which insists on a particular kind of cultural practice rather than respecting the cultural practices that are integrally important to people.

By reframing 'culture' as strategies through which people make their lives meaningful, it becomes possible to acknowledge people as cultural producers as well as consumers and so bring them into the cultural economy. The strong and enthusiastic response at the conference to this argument indicated a growing desire for such redistributive strategies. Connected Communities, the programme, which funded the research project, is also part of this changing agenda. They wrestle in particular with what constitutes a community in these contexts (Facer and Enright 2016).

Encountering culture in Ordsall

Building on this new framing of 'culture as how people make their lives meaningful', I now turn to the ideas and activities that people on the project chose to develop as part of their cultural practices. These resonated with a focus in Salford on social history that emphasised solidarity with working-class lives. During 2014/15, the city hosted plays by Shelagh Delaney and a memorial event of her life. Delaney was a local Salford playwright renowned for *A Taste of Honey,* which depicted the poverty and challenges of post-industrial, post-war Salford life with a wry tenderness (Delaney 2014 (1958)). Other events included a sold-out run of *Love on the Dole* (Greenwood 2008 (1933))—a theatre play about Salford Victorian Gangs drawing on research by Davies (2009); ongoing exhibitions about local history at the Museum and local heritage sites, Ordsall Hall and Salford Lads Club. The latter raised over £50,000 in funding from private donors and trusts to commission an artwork that celebrated over 30,000 members in 100 years and a new 'heritage room'. As May (2016) asserts, Salford people have built on their sense of belonging to the area through associations with the past. This 'past' focuses on sociality and dependency as the foundation of working-class values in the nineteenth and early twentieth century.

In Ordsall, the predominant themes that emerged during the research project focused on exploring shared history, passing on skills and expertise, celebrating place and exploring social entrepreneurship. We had £50,000 of project money to spend on cultural activities. The project team's local 'cultural intermediaries' identified a handful of individuals each who had a passion for particular activities they thought should happen in the community. Curious about what people would choose if given complete freedom, we encouraged the intermediaries not to make suggestions or carry out the work themselves, but to support the individuals or 'ideas people'. Altogether they found 27 people with specific ideas to support. These people were networked into different social groups so the project gained access to several hundred people in the two major social housing areas of Ordsall—one which we called the Ordsall triangle (the area of social housing was shaped like a triangle) and the other called Islington.

Some of the Ideas4Ordsall cohort, as they came to be known, knew each other and others did not. Many talked about how they had walked past each other in the street, but only started chatting by taking part in the project. People who lived in the Ordsall triangle oriented around the Salford Lads Club, the community café, the allotments and the local arts organisation. The participants were more likely to know each other and have experiences in common. This was the area where people felt most closely associated with the former docklands and the working-class heritage of the area, facilitated to some extent by the presence of the Salford Lads Club and its resident artist whose practice included raising awareness of local history.

In nearby Islington, part of the Ordsall district, several 'ideas people' were connected to the high-rise buildings that were the last bastion of social housing in an area which was rapidly gentrifying. Islington is very close to Salford University, so there was a high turnover of affluent foreign students. It also has a popular artist studio whose club nights were causing irritation for some residents living in the nearby high-rise, who claimed to be kept up at night by the noise.

Here, the ideas expressed by residents focused on gaining recognition such as a photo zine and exhibition entitled "How is it for you, Islington?" A local camera club took photographs of people in the streets and published them to draw attention to the diversity of people living in the area. The exhibition hung in the nearby train station displaying photos of people from low-income communities alongside students, builders and workers who pass through. Another idea was a community festival, set up by an events organiser based at the artist studios who wanted to collaborate with the people in the high-rise building. She hoped people would celebrate the area working and enjoying themselves alongside each other, rather than trading barbed comments at community meetings about the noise issue.

Figure 5.3. Organising the community festival.

Photo by Jessica Symons.

Over six months, in 2015, I moved between the 4 intermediaries and the 27 'ideas people', chatting with them about their ideas and the reasons behind them. The research team held regular gatherings to bring people together and share what they were doing. It was only when people started discussing how nice it was to meet each other and how they could talk more now to each other than before, that I started to understand how silenced people had felt. Hannah later explained in an interview that people found it easier to not speak outside trusted circles, caught between well-intentioned, but patronising 'community' projects and a vigilant element concerned about being reported to the police.

Ideas for 'cultural activities' included dog walking, beekeeping, photo, craft, cooking and bike workshops, restoring a Victorian printing press and setting up a graphic design company. Whilst appearing to mirror existing cultural understandings—photos, craft, festivals, heritage—activities were motivated for different reasons largely independent of their intrinsic or aesthetic value. People wanted to share their skills with each other, to provide services and to spend time together. It became evident that despite the inevitable fallings out and disagreements, we were collaborating with people for whom caring for others was important. Not just for people they knew, but for the 'people of Ordsall'.

Connecting community in Ordsall

Some of the cultural activities focused on connecting community members together. Each emphasised the absence of communication between individuals and how this lack of communication was affecting people's wellbeing. From accounts of depression to providing support for people coming off drugs and alcohol, to telling stories about difficult childhood experiences to bringing warring groups of neighbours together, each idea explicitly aimed not just to facilitate communication, but to ameliorate anxiety and frustration.

For example, Keira (32) was passionate about communicating what was going on in the area to local residents. She decided to set up a Facebook group to let other residents know about what was going on in the area. She would post and share messages about activities and invite people to share opinions. Keira would also talk to people in the shops, in the street and outside the school. Her enthusiasm and willingness to speak up generated a positive buzz in the Ordsall triangle area.

Figure 5.4. Making a noticeboard to let people know what's going on in the community.

Photo by Jessica Symons.

Figure 5.5. Capturing memories and sharing them on artwork.

Photo by Jessica Symons.

Edward (52) was part of a family who had lived in the area for generations and was known as one of the 'original families' who moved there to work on the docks. Edward was a talented artist whose landscape drawings captured the spirit of independence in Salford. He decided to work with local residents to capture their memories and stories about the area. He produced t-shirts and cloth with quotes from these conversations. He presented these artworks hung on a 'washing line' to reminisce about how the area looked when people hung their washing up in the terraced streets.

Keith (58) had experienced significant ups and downs during his life, including spending time in prison and battling addiction. His priority was to introduce people from his apartment block to the 'Theatre of the Oppressed'—a practice developed by Boal (2008) and commonly used to help people experiencing trauma. A previous set of workshops had helped Keith turn his life around. It was really important to Keith that he ran these sessions and while it took him a long time to deliver the sessions, he was really proud of the fact that he led them, not staff from a community or theatre organisation.

Curating history in Ordsall

Figure 5.6. Learning how to use a Victorian printing press to share with others.

Photo by Jessica Symons.

Some cultural activities emphasised aspects of neglected local history. A social housing co-operative founded by a group of local women created a booklet to celebrate 30 years of running the organisation. Two retired people captured stories from the past, one developing a local history play and animation about Ordsall and the other researching and speaking at public events about a World War One nurse heroine who had worshipped at a local church. Another 'ideas person' used project funding to buy a Victorian letterpress and explore the technical prowess and social potential of these hand-operated machines and another bought foldaway tables for his travelling mining exhibition. The latter, Bernard, (68) came from a mining family and was proud of the industrial heritage of the area. Working with his friend, he collected together memorabilia from Salford's mining history and created a 'pop-up mining museum' as well as a mining memorial in the area. In a discussion, they would emphasise the proud social history of the mining communities pointing to posters and artefacts as they described unions, strikes and how the community came together over pit accidents and the eventual closures.

Developing social enterprise in Ordsall

The project also attracted people whose ideas had clear potential to develop into social enterprises. Several ideas built on existing aspirations that people had tried to develop and struggled to get support either financially or to find time to develop while working full-time. The research project provided funding and access to trusted support where residents could work their ideas through in more detail, consider potential income sources and how to develop their business. During the project, they advertised their services and developed activities, which allowed them to test the market and see what opportunities were available. In all cases, the economic climate proved too challenging to set up a new business, but each built on their experiences to develop further work opportunities for themselves.

For example, Cathy (24) was a local young woman born and raised in the area. She was passionate about becoming a photographer and wanted to explore how to set up a photographic studio. She ran several pop-up studios at a local arts organisation and at the annual community festival where she photographed people with their families. While other community arts project may feature photographs of local people, these were taken by someone from the area and the warmth of her relationships radiates through the pictures.

Barrie (51) came from another 'original family'. He had trained as an artist but worked for 20 years in the local supermarket to support his children as they grew up. He saw an opportunity in the project for setting up a long-desired art collective with a view to developing and selling work. With support, he brought together other aspirational artists who were in a similar position—working in retail while trying to develop their art—and negotiated several opportunities for people to sell their work.

Capturing a sense of place in Ordsall

The ideas reflected a strong connection with the Ordsall triangle and adjacent Islington. People celebrated their sense of place, often with fondness and seeking amusement in the process. Peter (55) and Paul (55) decided to take a tongue-in-cheek view of the Ideas4Ordsall project and created a character called 'Lord Puglington' who they said was initially 'quite snobby' about the area, but gradually came to like and value it after meeting people involved in the project and finding out about their work. Peter dressed as Lord Puglington, wearing a dog mask and black cape. He was filmed by Paul exploring different locations and chatting to people. The duo brought a spirit of fun and laughter to the project and created a lovely film that reflected the sense of connection and community that emerged from exploring the area.

Figure 5.7. Thanking participants at the close of the play about Ordsall.

Photo by Jessica Symons.

Mary (28) and Angela (44) were part of a theatre company run by disabled people and they created a film that celebrated the activities in their local community centre and in the local area. Mary wanted to give a perspective from her point of view and so connected the camera to her wheelchair. This film focused on the warmth and affection generated by the group and the people that worked with them.

Sharing knowledge in Ordsall

Passing on existing experience and knowledge in craft, cooking, music and bikes was also important to people. Many of these activities were presented as workshops for people to develop their skills, such as in cooking or bicycle maintenance. When the 'ideas people' did not have the experience themselves, they used the project money to buy in support from others. Dave (36) wanted to help people fix their bikes, so he organised a series of drop-in sessions for people to come along and learn how to pump up tires and check brakes. He hired a bike mechanic to help out with more difficult jobs.

Carrie (18) was a local woman born and raised in the area who remembered going to craft workshops as a child at the local arts organisation. Now an adult, she wanted to give back to her local community and lead her own craft workshops for kids, which she did in the local arts organisation.

Figure 5.8. Inspired by a WW1 memorial in Ordsall to tell the story of Edith Cavell.

Photo by Jessica Symons.

Steve (42) was a passionate cook who had moved into the area to settle down with his partner and their child. He was well known locally for running cooking workshops at the community centres. Steve wanted to set up a cooking school and used this project as an opportunity to buy equipment and work on his business model. He ended up working with a food project exploring using vegetable waste for running cooking sessions. They passed the cooked food onto a homeless charity for distributing in the city.

For Ordsall, it's a culture of 'care'

The ideas developed by people in Ordsall demonstrate a local emphasis on supporting each other that can be framed as an 'ethic of care' (Gilligan 1982). Here was a community of limited means demonstrating how they wanted to support each other and recognising that they are 'in it together' (Gilligan 2014). In all cases, the 'ideas people' responded to our offer of funding by focusing on socially motivated activities, even though we did not specify this as a requirement. They were also very fair with distributing the funding, sharing it evenly between them.

Following Geertz (1973), we can see how the context provides insight into the meaning and how people responded to ambiguities and challenges in their community. These activities demonstrate the underlying 'patterns' that make up local cultural practices. Despite limited incomes and in an area where criminal activity was an ever-present undercurrent, people demonstrated a strong sense of social responsibility—a culture that emphasised caring and supporting each other.

Gilligan (2014: 103) suggests that "the ethic of care guides us in acting carefully in the human world and highlights the costs of carelessness." She observes that while an 'ethic of care' might be associated with women, it should not be characterised as a 'feminine' voice but one that emphasises ways of engaging with people differently. While I encountered primarily women during fieldwork, with generations of mothers socialising together in the local café, sitting chatting and caring for older and younger relatives and a community worker noting, 'the mams and nans run this place'; there were men around as well. The ones I met were self-employed, retired or on benefits, but husbands, brothers and sons were talked about and clearly played a role in the lives of their friends and families.

Similarly, other anthropological research, such as that of Lewis, in the east of Manchester, reveals how people are keen to recall rich social dynamics, which are the outcome of generations of families forming communities that all worked for the same employer. Lewis draws out the ongoing importance of former factories to local residents as people remember fondly a time when they all worked together for the same employer (Lewis 2016). People value co-dependent support and relationships particularly when they are facing difficult circumstances.

Similarly, in North Manchester, Smith also identifies a strong concern with fairness among people in a low-income area. She describes the complex reciprocal interdependencies such as money lending between people in the community, regulated by a sense of fairness (Smith 2014). In Ordsall, the community members who developed ideas exhibited a strong desire for providing care to the community, by entertaining, sharing knowledge and providing resources.

In the former mill town of Bacup in Lancashire, Edwards has also found a community interwoven with a "keenness to observe justice and fairplay". As an informant put it, 'They're all a good lot in their own ways, they'll help you out if they have to' (Edwards 2000: 160). This longstanding culture of care in working-class communities stands in stark contrast to the individualism of contemporary times (Edwards, Evans and Smith 2012).

During the research period, Ordsall was not the only place in Salford to demonstrate a strong sense of solidarity and a focus on supporting community. In 2016, a major flood from the river Irwell led to a rapid mobilisation of local people who came together to help with toys, food, cleaning up, accommodation and more: people 'come together' when needed. The local newspaper, the Salford Star, was trenchantly supportive of socialism and has fiercely criticised the regeneration initiatives that left out local people.[8] Several community organisers and political figures in the area were closely associated with the growing Momentum movement and Corbyn's 2015 appointment to leader of the Labour party. This political emphasis explicitly reconnects with socialist principles of solidarity and co-dependency (Pitts and Dinerstein 2017).

Conclusion

This research gives valuable insight into how cultural practices in the UK come to be situated in a class-based hierarchy, where some types of cultural activities are valued over others. It also shows how people react when the hierarchy is revealed. Decision makers working to develop the 'cultural industries' recognise the lack of representation from working-class areas in the cultural agenda and want to change their approach, but they need a conceptual framing that allows for *both* culture as the arts, music, theatre *and* culture as how people live their daily lives. It is by understanding culture as how people make their lives meaningful, that the connection can be made and this connection is beginning to change how economic development can progress through the promotion of projects of cultural participation.

Similarly focused on the disconnection between policy models and their implementation, anthropologist, David Mosse, in his analysis of development workers in India (2004), finds, much to the chagrin of his development-worker colleagues, that they pay "surprisingly little attention" to how models manifest in practice (Mosse 2004: 640). He showed how communities he encountered in India reshaped around the development models to match the changing policies. Mosse argues that rather than support already-existing autonomous activities in these communities, development funding was subverting cultural practices and creating unequal hierarchies that were counterproductive in the overall aims of the projects.

My own research has shown how a rhetoric of failure, criticism and judgement in low-income areas in Salford has stifled local people's attempts to build on their own understandings of cultural worth. A lack of recognition for the importance of co-dependent relationships, born from necessity and maintained by a sense of solidarity and community, interrupts people's attempts to gain support for their own ideas and cultural priorities. When given resources, support and freedom, people enthusiastically embrace the opportunity to develop activities, building on local aspirations and priorities.

In this community in Salford, the paradox of communities remaining persistently on the Social Deprivation Indices despite multiple government interventions could be explained not just by the economic transformations associated with post-industrial decline, and unemployment, but by also recognising that while people remain attached to familial obligations, they have a different 'taste' for democratic participation (Edwards 2009), which prioritises local needs and social relationships. Culture in Ordsall was not going to the theatre, it was supporting friends and family. This research raises questions about what other assumptions underpin engagement with people in this area. The words used to describe these communities contain implicit judgements about the people involved—'hard to reach' and 'deprived' are loaded terms. The approach should not be, how to get people engaged with culture but instead should be how to support people to express themselves in a way that they find meaningful.

The emphasis in Ordsall on family and community can be seen as a 'culture of care', where people generate meaning through supporting each other to develop and grow as people. This kind of cultural activity is as important as those found in the 'cultural industries' and the two are connected by recognising culture as meaning-making. Whether an artist or carer, performing a song or having a cup of tea, the cultural value generated by these activities should elicit the same level of support and resource in government policy and civil society.

Acknowledgements

I would like to thank the people of Ordsall for their wisdom and insight, for challenging the project and its preconceptions and for making the research richer and stronger. I'd also like to thank Professor Beth Perry and Dr Vicky Simpson for their creative and adaptive approach in managing and supporting the research team. I hope that my subsequent work sharing of insight from the project honours the time they put into making it happen.

Notes

[1] Hannah was a local legend in the community. She was ostensibly leading a local charity carrying out engagement activities but her real value lay in her wisdom and practical support. Her discretion meant people could trust her with their stories and her 20-year staying power in the same job demonstrated significant commitment. Many people identified with her as a mother figure (and called her 'mam').

[2] This research project was part of a large UK initiative called 'Connected Communities' intended to encourage academics to carry out research with community partners. Over £30 million of government funding supported 280 projects exploring different ways of carrying out research with communities.

[3] http://dclgapps.communities.gov.uk/imd/idmap.html

[4] http://www.culturalintermediation.org.uk/

[5] The names used in this chapter are pseudonyms to obscure people's identities.

[6] http://www.manchester.gov.uk/news/article/5399/manchesters_cultural_ambition

[7] https://www.gov.uk/government/publications/culture-white-paper

[8] http://www.salfordstar.com/

References

Boal, A. and McBride, C. A. L. (2008) *Theatre of the Oppressed*, London: Pluto Press.

Davies, A. 2009. *The Gangs of Manchester: The Story of the Scuttlers, Britain's First Youth Cult.* Preston: Milo Books.

Delaney, S. (2014/1958) *A Taste of Honey.* London: Bloomsbury Publishing.

Desena, J. N. (2018) 'Swimming against the Tide': Working-Class Discourse on Gentrification in North Brooklyn. *The Palgrave Handbook of Urban Ethnography.* Springer.

Edwards, A. (2009) '"Tastes" for political participation: A lifestyle approach to democratic design'. *Representation*, 45: 39–52.

Edwards, J. (2000) *Born and Bred: Idioms of Kinship and New Reproductive Technologies in England.* Oxford: Oxford University Press.

Edwards, J., Evans, G. and Smith, K. (2012) 'Introduction: The middle class-ification of Britain'. *Focaal*, 2012: 3–16.

Evans, G. (2006) *Educational Failure and Working Class White Children in Britain.* Basingstoke: Palgrave Macmillan.

Evans, G. (2012) '"The aboriginal people of England": The culture of class politics in contemporary Britain'. *Focaal*, 2012: 17–29.

Facer, K. and Enright, B. (2016) *Creating Living Knowledge: The Connected Communities Programme, Community-University Relationships and the Participatory Turn in the Production of Knowledge*, Bristol: University of Bristol/AHRC Connected Communities.

Geertz, C. (1973) *The Interpretation of Cultures.* New York: Basic Books.

Geertz, C. (2003) (1973). Thick Description: Toward an Interpretive Theory of Culture. In: Lincoln, Y.S. and Denzin, N.K. (eds) *Turning Points in Qualitative Research: Tying Knots in a Handkerchief.* Walnut Creek, CA: Altamira Press.

Gilligan, C. (1982) *In a Different Voice*, Cambridge, MA: Harvard University Press.

Gilligan, C. (2014) 'Moral injury and the ethic of care: Reframing the conversation about differences'. *Journal of Social Philosophy*, 45: 89–106.

Gilmore, A. (2014) Raising Our Quality Of Life: The Importance of Investment in Arts and Culture. In: STUDIES, Centre for Labour and Social Studies.

Gilmore, A. (2017) 'The park and the commons: Vernacular spaces for everyday participation and cultural value'. *Cultural Trends*, 26: 34–46.

Greenwood, W. (2008/1933) *Love on the Dole: A Tale of Two Cities.* London: Random House.

Harrison, J. (2014) 'Rethinking city-regionalism as the production of new non-state spatial strategies: The case of Peel Holdings Atlantic Gateway Strategy'. *Urban Studies*, 51: 2315–2335.

Kidd, A. J. and Wyke, T. (2016) *Manchester: Making the Modern City*, Liverpool: Liverpool University Press.

Koch, I. (2016) 'Bread-and-butter politics: Democratic disenchantment and everyday politics on an English council estate'. *American Ethnologist*, 43: 282–294.

Leadbeater, C. (2009) 'Original modern: Manchester's journey to innovation and growth'. *Provocation*. London: National Endowment for Science, Technology and the Arts (NESTA).

Lees, L., Shin, H. B. and Morales, E. L. (2015) *Global Gentrifications: Uneven Development and Displacement*, London: Policy Press.

Lewis, C. (2016) '"Regenerating community"? Urban change and narratives of the past'. *The Sociological Review*, 64(4): 912–928.

Lewis, C. and Symons, J. (2017) *Realising the City: Urban Ethnography in Manchester*. Oxford: Oxford University Press.

Maw, P. (2013) *Transport and the Industrial City: Manchester and the Canal Age, 1750–1850*. Manchester: Manchester University Press.

Mosse, D. (2004) 'Is good policy unimplementable? Reflections on the ethnography of aid policy and practice'. *Development and Change*, 35: 639–671.

Parkinson-Bailey, J. J. (2000) *Manchester: An Architectural History*. Manchester: Manchester University Press.

Paton, K. (2016) *Gentrification: A Working-Class Perspective*, London: Routledge.

Peck, J. and Ward, K. (2002) *City of Revolution: Restructuring Manchester*. Manchester: Manchester University Press.

Pitts, F. H. and Dinerstein, A. C. (2017) 'Corbynism's conveyor belt of ideas: Postcapitalism and the politics of social reproduction'. *Capital & Class*, 41: 423–434.

Pratt, A. C. (2011) 'The cultural contradictions of the creative city'. *City, Culture and Society*, 2: 123–130.

Pratt, A. C. (2017) *New Horizons for Culture, Creativity and Cities*. Amsterdam: Elsevier.

Ravetz, A. (2003) *Council Housing and Culture: The History of a Social Experiment*, London: Routledge.

Smith, K. (2012) *Fairness, Class and Belonging in Contemporary England*. Basingstoke: Palgrave Macmillan.

Smith, K. (2014) '"You don't own money, you're just the one who's holding it": Borrowing, lending and the fair person in North Manchester'. *Anthropology of Britain Decennial Workshop*. University of Exeter.

Symons, J. (2017) '"We're not hard-to-reach, they are!" Integrating local priorities in urban research in Northern England: An experimental method'. *The Sociological Review*, doi: 0038026117717432.

Vaisey, E. (2016) Culture White Paper. London: Department for Culture, Media & Sport.

Wacquant, L. (2008) 'Relocating gentrification: The working class, science and the state in recent urban research'. *International Journal of Urban and Regional Research*, 32: 198–205.

Webb, R. (1990) *Manchester and the Age of the Factory: The Business Structure of Cottonopolis in the Industrial Revolution.* London: Croom Helm.

Young, M. and Wilmott, P. (2013/1957) *Family and Kinship in East London.* London: Routledge.

Chapter 6

Making Space in Urban Interstices

Making, wage labour and place-making in Newcastle upon Tyne

Abigail Schoneboom, Newcastle University

Abstract

This visual ethnographic project explores the making of a vibrant and highly sociable 'Maker Space' in the Newcastle upon Tyne's urban centre. Specifically, this study examines the relationship between the interstices that exist in routines patterned on wage labour (many of the makers fit their making activity around jobs in fields such as computer programming) and the creation of alternative spaces within urban 'cracks' in the city's shopping district. In an era where urban centres are increasingly highly commodified and homogeneous, and where organisational theory might benefit from exploring the parkour-like practices in urban placemaking that disrupt anesthetized settings, this study is particularly concerned with the way in which the makers populate the makerspace with a spontaneous, unfettered creativity and physicality that some of them feel is missing from their paid work.

***

Introduction

This visual ethnographic project explores the making of a vibrant 'Maker Space'—a collaborative, user-owned workspace for making things, from hi-tech LED displays to upcycled quilts—in Newcastle upon Tyne's urban centre. Carried out over two years of participant observation, it involved a series of recorded conversations with makers and a collaborative photographic exploration. Although the wider study looked at many aspects of making in relation to place and sustainability, this chapter specifically examines the relationship between interstices in routines and practices of wage labour (many of the makers fit their making activity around jobs in fields such as computer programming) and the creation of alternative spaces within urban 'cracks', the former commercial spaces left empty by economic recession, which become opportunities for exploring alternative use of space in the city centre.

In an era where urban centres are increasingly highly commodified and homogeneous (Augé 2008; Dale and Burrell 2002), and where, as Daskalaki *et al.* (2008) argue, organisational theory might benefit from exploring parkour-like practices that disrupt anesthetised settings, this study is particularly concerned with the way in which the makers populate Maker Space with a spontaneous, unfettered creativity and physicality that some of them feel is missing from their paid work.

Capturing this moment by exploring the meanings attached to objects created in the space and the organisational practices that emerge alongside making, the study traces how these messy yet regulated, social yet individually absorbed processes disrupt non-place (Augé 2008) and promote urban vitality. In keeping with Augé's analysis, non-place is understood here as overly commodified, unvaried, commercially oriented space that stifles vibrant creativity and human flourishing. Specifically, Maker Space is located in a rather drab stretch of Newcastle's shopping district, where precarious small businesses have fallen into decline, leaving empty storefronts as the backdrop to a row of grimy bus stops that line the narrow sidewalk.[1] City plans that have earmarked the street for redevelopment have created a temporary opportunity for arts organisations such as Maker Space to occupy the empty stores at low rent, changing the streetscape into one of the unusual and relatively non-commercial offerings.

Existing literature on makerspaces (Halverson and Sheridan 2014; Lindtner 2015; Richardson *et al.* 2013; Rosner and Fox 2016) has not examined the relationship between these spaces and paid employment, and has tended to focus on educational, normative and supply chain dimensions of making. While this literature explores aspects of organisation, creativity and production, how actors juxtapose making with their day job (where they need to earn a living outside of the makerspace) has not been specifically explored. Theoretically, this study makes experimental links between what goes on at Newcastle's Maker Space and the work of Arendt (1998) and Gorz (2005) on the satisfaction that derives from creating tangible, enduring and wholly executed things, particularly highlighting the makers' enjoyment of their ability to make physical things to behold, treasure and share with others. This contrasts with their largely immaterial (Hardt and Negri 2000) wage labour in occupations such as computer programming, where the product—such as a body of code—may yield professional satisfaction but lack the immediate physicality and integral wholeness of a hammered together picture frame or a hand-soldered circuit-board, designed and built from scratch or through a process of ingenious repurposing of found objects. This physicality resonates with recent work on lively materials (Carr and Gibson 2016), the notion that working intimately with materials, where sufficiently autonomous, nurtures a powerful sense of agency and a conviction that the physical environment is malleable. In this sense, the things that emerge from Maker Space, intertwined with the organisation's messy and playful form are conceived as potentially reenergising and transforming the cityscape.

As a cityscape, Newcastle upon Tyne (population 0.3 million) boasts a lively shopping and eating district that, especially at the weekend, bustles with life. Its main shopping district hosts glitzy restaurant chains, high-end department stores, and bijou outfitters but these "brilliant shops" (Engels 1952) and high rates of fashion spending (Savills, 2016) mask persistent unemployment and poverty (Newcastle City Council 2010). Sharp post-industrial decline and joblessness in the 1980s, have given way to a largely service-based economy with some economic recovery but increasingly precarious, low-skilled employment. Nevertheless, there are affluent pockets with stable professional employment in knowledge-based professions such as computer programming, accounting, academia and healthcare—members of Maker Space tend to come from this group. The city centre has shown resilience against recession but its bite is evident in empty shopfronts that blight the main shopping street, and a steep rise of temporary or bargain basement stores, particularly in the streets that branch off the main thoroughfare. Also, deep cuts to libraries and museums mean that recreational time in the city centre increasingly revolves exclusively around spending money in the shops and restaurants.

Drawing parallels between the above scholarship of work and literature on 'non-place' (Daskalaki *et al.* 2008; Farrar 2011; Paterson 1997), this study situates Maker Space as a contrast to the prevailing landscape of Newcastle's shopping district—as a locus where processes of memory, story and participation that transcend the commodity form are nurtured and celebrated. As such, this chapter reflects in an explorative fashion on concepts of materiality, alienation and place-making, also suggesting possibilities for a post-work urbanism.

Maker Space and Welcome Wednesday

Maker Space is an independent, user-owned resource in Newcastle upon Tyne's city centre that occupies a former storefront opposite the city library. Focused on diverse making activity from laser-cut constructions to theatrical costumes, it offers a workspace with tools and a readymade community. Its 52 members are predominantly white male, of working age, with many fitting in their making around full-time jobs in engineering or information technology. Some are of relatively working-class origin, having grown up around the city's heavy industrial base, with some of the interviews revealing class mobility gained from technical aptitude, leading to careers in engineering or computing, supported by the region's growing information technology sector.

Maker Space operates an open membership policy where anyone can join and pay the monthly membership fee of 10 pounds (this can be discreetly modified for those who are less able to pay) and, on Wednesday evenings, the space is open to non-members. This research project was inspired by the buzzing creativity and exchange that is experienced at Maker Space's Welcome Wednesdays, which create a vibrant hub of creative and social activity that—visible through the large shopfront windows—brightens up an otherwise lifeless and grimy streetscape.

Figure 6.1. Welcome Wednesday.

The social buzz of the space is palpable from inside and out. Photo by Julian May.

Newcastle's Maker Space has grown organically over the last few years out of a very small group of makers who came into contact at local show-and-tell events such as 'Dorkbot'. Two of the founding members had an existing office space that they opened up for maker meetings. As the group grew and opportunities arose, the makers moved to the current storefront location, sharing the rent by pooling their monthly membership dues.

Newcastle's Maker Space is part of a movement that comprises 1,400 active makerspaces globally, around 500 of which are located respectively in Europe and North America (Lou and Peek 2016). A makerspace, broadly speaking, is 'a collaborative work space inside a school, library or separate public/private facility for making, learning, exploring and sharing that uses high tech to no tech tools' (Makerspaces.com). Within this broad definition, there is some debate about whether the terms 'makerspace' and 'hackerspace' warrant distinction (Cavalcanti 2013), however, these labels are very often used interchangeably and, in this chapter, 'makerspace' is used to denote both. While Newcastle's Maker Space reflects the collectivist or non-profit ethos of many makerspaces, for-profit versions such as the 'Techshop' chain also exist. Best-selling books such as Chris Anderson's *Makers* (2013), coupled with popular 'Maker Faire' events that take place in large cities across the world, promote the idea of a broadly unified (if heterogeneous) worldwide maker movement oriented to reviving the art of tinkering—from 'make-and-mend' upcycling to amateur technology development—as a hands-on, sociable way of transforming the world for the better (Dougherty 2012). Many of those interviewed have been 'tinkerers' since childhood, with some discussing family role models or Newcastle's famous 'makers' such as inventor Joseph Swan (and the Literary and Philosophical Society where he and others exchanged ideas) as key influences in their Maker Space involvement.

Recent literature has explored many facets of the 'Maker Movement', from its role in education (Halverson and Sheridan 2014) to its potential to transform supply chain design (Waller and Fawcett 2014). Ethnographic study of hackspaces has produced textured accounts of making practice, showing infusion of hacker norms with feminist (Rosner and Fox 2016) and Chinese cultural (Lindtner 2015) characteristics. Focusing on cities, Richardson *et al.* (2013), suggest that distributed local making can transform urban landscapes, a perspective that is shared via arts-based initiatives such as DIWO, or Do-It-With-Others, (Furtherfield 2015).

While aspects of this literature connect making to emancipatory social practices, the fluid relationship between the making of objects, community building and placehood warrants closer unpacking. Little attention has been given to how makers juggle their makerspace activity and paid work. Existing studies touch on the relationship with work, but are more centrally concerned with exploring makers' shared political vision, whether in terms of reflecting Chinese culture (Lindtner 2015: 861–862) or promoting gender equality in the face of the "dark, unromantic, slightly humiliating side of modern motherhood" (Rosner and Fox 2016: 5). Richardson *et al.*'s (2013) article observes the impact of making (including making as a form of work) in Detroit but lacks fine-grained analysis of how this occurs, calling for further sociological study of the processes via which making nurtures urban resilience. This article therefore seeks to construct a more explicit link between, on the one hand, the act of making in the interstices of paid labour and, on the other hand, the emergence of a form of place-based organisation that is oriented to urban vitality. Reflecting the ethnographic tradition, the methodology and findings are presented in the following sections, drawing out emerging themes that inform the theoretical discussion in the final section of the paper.

Methodology

The predominantly inductive and interpretivist research design involved participant-observation on Welcome Wednesdays over a two-year period by Dr Schoneboom and a more intense period of conversations and photography (with Julian May) during December 2015–January 2016. The study explored the relationship between makers and their creations, the surrounding texture of sharing and organisation, the relationship between this activity and paid employment, and the impact of Maker Space on the streetscape. Dr Schoneboom has been a member of Maker Space since March 2014 (after being coaxed through the door by her 8-year-old son) and has received many hours of guidance on various construction projects from Maker Space members. The research is therefore also informed by a reflexive meditation on her participation in the space.

Maker Space has no single gatekeeper and permission to conduct the study was sought/granted by posting the details of the planned research on the Maker Space-admin mailing list (which is open to all members), fielding questions, and being permitted to proceed in the absence of objections. Several members immediately volunteered to participate in the research as part of this discussion process while other participants were part of a convenience sampling process based on those who were around during the photographic engagement. The interviews/conversations attracted members who have a founding or very active role in the space. All except one of those interviewed are male, which is broadly representative of the male-female gender ratio of the membership (this imbalance would make an interesting future study).

The photographic engagement took place on Welcome Wednesday at the Maker Space Christmas party. Recognising that photographic meanings are contingent and subjective (Pink 2014: 75), we aimed at a strategy of looking (Lyon 2013: 25) that was casual and responsive to the direction of makers, using photography as a "can-opener" (Collier and Collier 1986) that enabled makers to share their feelings during the social flow of the party, establishing a conversational rapport in the subsequent recorded conversations. Initially, Julian created collaborative portraits with individual makers, intentionally focused away from the face to emphasise our interest in the sensual hands-on aspects of making. These photos were aimed at understanding members' feelings about the things they had made through their manner of holding their creations and the features they wanted to show to the camera.

As part our emphasis on understanding the sensory dimension of place, we also combined photography and movement to "attend to elements of the ways that people experience and give meanings to their environments" (Pink 2014: 81). Julian was guided around the space by different makers, capturing aspects of the language of objects and signage (Sudjic 2009) that were meaningful to them. Drawing on the author's reflection on Maker Space's impact on the street and how it feels to approach Maker Space from the outside, Julian also photographed the movement and energy of members as transmitted through the windows.

Informed by the photographic engagement, 10 audio-recorded semi-structured conversations between the author and individual makers of 25–40 minutes were conducted at Maker Space or—when the space was too noisy—across the street at the City Library, which overlooks Maker Space. After transcription, these were shared with participants for their validation.

As in much ethnography (Duneier 2000; Van Maanen 1991), where the reflexive dimension is a central dimension of the work that must be interrogated in order to establish integrity of the study, the author/photographer's subjectivities were treated as an integral aspect of this research and, rather than trying to excise this, the write-up focused on articulating feelings and experiences in a way that makers would read as a reasonable interpretation of their world. Drawing on Pink (2009), whose work on slow cities, for example, illustrates the need to capture the physical and sensory entanglement of people and things in a place, the research design drew on an emplaced sensory methodology, acknowledging the "sensuous interrelationship of body-mind-environment" (Howes 2005: 7) that can inform a fluid and dynamic understanding of people and place. Interviews were conducted in the space wherever possible so that machine noise and social interruptions worked their way into the conversation and the transcripts.

As such, we aimed to generate textured data based on a fluid engagement with the space. The transcribed data, fieldnotes and images were coded using NVivo with emergent themes identified using techniques drawn from grounded theory (Strauss and Corbin 1990). The interpretation of the data, while somewhat inductive, is also deeply informed by the author's critical theoretical orientation (in particular, an interest in critical theoretical evaluations of the work ethic and the meaning of work that grow out of Marxist/Weberian discourses), which is in turn entangled with her efforts to learn how to solder and use a drill. The study attends to this layered interpretation of social reality and tries to retain the richness with which makers expressed their passion for making things, resisting the tendency to reduce or resolve its contradictory aspects (Van Maanen 1988: 116).

Findings

The findings are divided into two parts: the first is about makers' reflections on their making projects at Maker Space in relation to the activity that earns their living and the second is a commentary on the messy yet regulated, socially and physically vibrant Maker Space that emerges from this freewheeling creative activity.

Making and Making a Living

As noted earlier, many of the makers have careers in engineering or IT, with a smaller number working in education. For those makers who have a relatively structured 'day-job' as well as some others who work in a contract-based freelance capacity, key distinctions were made between paid work and their activity at Maker Space, emphasising the less instrumental, more freewheeling and tangible nature of making at Maker Space as opposed to their wage labour. Several interrelated themes thus emerge from exploration of the relationship between making activity and paid employment of Maker Space members: the tangibility or physicality of made things; the opportunity to make something from scratch or make the entire thing; the enduring and/or unique quality of made things; the sense of creative autonomy and non-instrumentality of the making process; and the flow of skills and materials between Maker Space and the workplace.

Tangibility and physicality of made things

Tim[2], a regular to the space, is passionate about his computer-oriented job, but finds his projects at Maker Space often offer a more satisfying level of tangibility. He does a lot of hands-on metalwork and woodwork at Maker Space, in contrast to his computer-oriented job and, during the fieldwork process, he was engrossed in a quadcopter project, launching his creation for its maiden flight at the Christmas party. Celebrating this tangibility, he remarks that at work it is sometimes frustrating not to see things making visual progress, whereas in making his quadcopter, "I can see a result. There's a physical thing and that's the difference. It's not a digital thing, it's a physical thing".

Ben, a software engineer, shares this desire to make something physical, noting that a computer program he writes is 'real, but not real in the sense you can pick it up and lift it, show people, tell people about how you've made it with your hands.' A prolific maker, Ben is usually to be seen working with fabric, wood or metal in the space, leaving no outward clue to his computer programmer identity. He recently started dabbling in sewing but was soon running Maker Space's sewing nights, learning how to do new practical things with dexterity and focus. During the fieldwork period, he made an impressively diverse selection of things, including a unique, collage-style quilt constructed from pieces of clothing that his kids had grown out of, along with several toys and bags.

Figure 6.2. Tim's quadcopter.

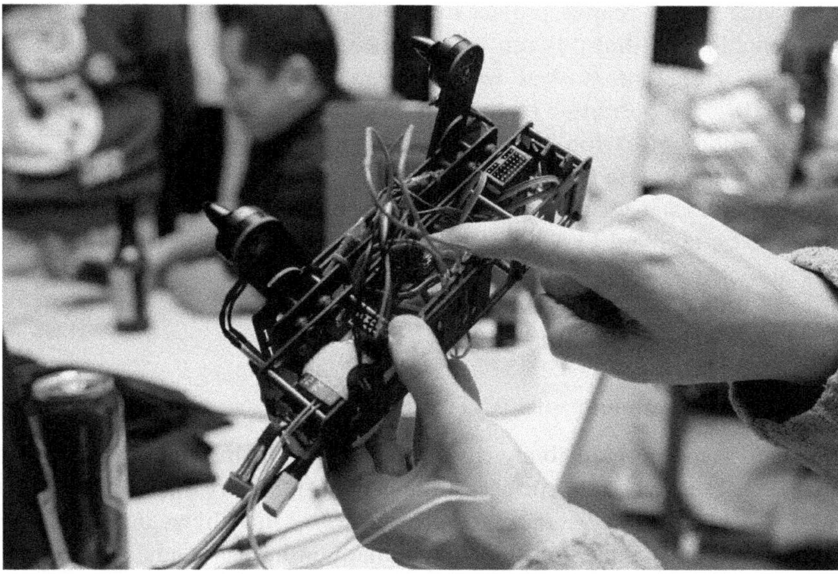

"It's not a digital thing, it's a physical thing". Photo by Julian May.

Malcolm, a software developer, presents a slight contrast to Ben and Tim, since he does not feel such a strong urge to make physical objects: "I'm very happy living inside my head a lot of the time, thinking about things". However, one of the reasons he is drawn to Maker Space is that he wants to complement his virtual expertise as a programmer with what he calls "real world stuff", the practical side of working with materials and understanding how to manipulate them effectively. This has been part of his motivation to build a 3D printer. He is working on developing a slicer, a computer programme that will make stronger 3D-printed objects—he is focused on the code but this is intertwined with his enjoyment of the physical side of the 3D printing process.

The opportunity to make something from scratch or make the entire thing

As well as physical tangibility, some makers highlighted an ontological need, in the sense of something connected to their sense of being and unfolding themselves in the world, to make something from scratch. Mark, a multitalented maker who is currently working on a 3-D printed robot hand, comments that although he likes his current job in the IT field, he does not get to build things from first principles any more, which can be frustrating: "Physically creating something from a component level, I don't get to do that at work anymore. I used to. I used to build PCs and things, but not in the current job I'm in, which annoys me a little bit".

Carrying out a creative project from beginning to end was also valued: Mark highlighted that this can be less achievable in the workplace, where different people are tasked with different aspects, sometimes causing delays. He is not permitted to do things at work that he knows how to do but are somebody else's job, whereas he feels that Maker Space allows him creative autonomy to get on with things and use his full range of skills. The sense of creative satisfaction in puzzling something out from beginning to end was exemplified by Rob, another maker and IT specialist, who noted that at Maker Space he sometimes purposely avoids using existing tutorials in order to set himself more of a challenge and learn more, developing a sense of mastery of the entire process.

Enduring and/or unique quality of made things

Linked to the idea of tangibility, the importance of making an enduring, well-built thing is a value that surfaced in several of the interviews. In particular, Ben, who is a very active maker, expressed regret that things are no longer built to last and contrasted this with something he has made, which "you don't want to just throw away because you know you've invested a lot of time and effort into making it". The sense of beholding an object that he has crafted is deeply satisfying: "You can pick it up, you can show people you've got something there that you've made, that you can keep forever". Ben enjoys the knowledge that his kids have unique, treasured toys that will last and will not be so readily disposed of. As he holds the bus proudly up towards the camera, his pleasure at showing off his creation is palpable.

In a similar vein, things that are made at Maker Space are also valued for their uniqueness—Evie, an educator who is relatively new to the space, notes that she relishes the idea of her friends and family having jewellery that she has crafted herself: "they wear it and it's totally unique because I don't really like to make the same thing twice". During one of our fieldwork sessions, she was using the laser cutter on felted wool to create coasters that she planned to give as Christmas gifts, filling the air with a slightly charred yet pleasant aroma that, we agreed, would add to their uniqueness.

Figure 6.3. A one-of-a-kind toy bus.

"You can pick it up, you can show people you've got something there that you've made, that you can keep forever". Photo by Julian May.

Figure 6.4. Laser-cut felt and jewellery.

"I don't really like to make something the same thing twice". Photo by Julian May.

Creative autonomy and non-instrumentality of the making process

Bill, a long-time maker who is currently making a miniature arcade game, comments that although he very much enjoys his paid employment as an engineer, the specifications he is working to in his paid capacity are for the needs of the business: "it's not my creative process, it's not my personal project, it's something I'm just being paid to design and make". His miniature arcade game, which forms part of a series of classic arcade games that he has constructed in different sizes is, by contrast, part of a lifelong habit of pursuing his own creative projects: "I've always been a maker, I've always been a maker of things".

Within this relatively self-directed process, several makers commented that they enjoy taking their time with making projects as opposed to the tighter deadlines at work. As Malcolm the software developer notes, there is a sharp contrast between his personal projects and paid gigs in terms of timescales for product delivery: "In terms of what I do on a day-to-day basis there's always a goal in a couple of weeks max and it's got to be delivered by then". He enjoys the desultory aspect of his making projects—the unbounded nature of his 3D printer project, which is not oriented to an immediate business or personal need—pleasantly allows room for experimentation and dabbling.

Figure 6.5. Rob's beautiful cube of white LEDs.

"They serve no purpose at all whatsoever". Photo by Julian May.

Flow of skills and materials between Maker Space and the workplace

With many Maker Space members fitting in their making activity around jobs in engineering or electronics there is a two-way flow of skills and resources between the two arenas. For most of those interviewed, the relationship between personal making projects and paid work is not embattled, but rather comes across as symbiotic and mutually beneficial. Rob comments that scrap material from his IT job that would otherwise be thrown out often ends up in the space: "I often joke that my boss sponsors the Maker Space with the amount of stuff that ends up in there from work". Similarly, skills such as programming, soldering or operating machinery often pass seamlessly between the Maker Space and places of paid employment.

In spite of this cross-pollination, several of those interviewed intentionally keep the spheres somewhat separate in order to enjoy their making more. Tim, focuses on hands-on projects such as his quadcopter, intentionally avoiding doing projects related to his day job in network engineering: "I do try and keep away from what I do at work and leave work for work". Similarly, Ben's efforts to stay away from programming at Maker Space, where he is customarily engaged in woodwork or sewing, remind him that this is a separate world from his day-job, creating a clearer boundary between paid employment and his personal making projects.

Making Maker Space

Resonating with these values of enduring tangibility and creative autonomy, organisational practices and a spatial reality emerge at Maker Space, creating a vibrant place that disrupts the blandness of the streetscape and militates towards a revitalised urban centre. This study suggests a synergy between, on the one hand, the unmet desires and needs that exist in the interstices of paid labour, and cracks in urban centres where these desires are indulged and alternative spaces flourish. Maker Space emerges physically and organisationally around the act of making, with a fluid, unfinished quality that extends from individual making projects to the making of a richly textured and storied space.

Maker Space comprises two rooms with an array of workbenches and tables of different heights that allow workers to work side by side while chatting. This mixture of concentrating on whatever one is making while connecting with what others in the room are doing creates a friendly, playful atmosphere where, nevertheless, serious work is getting done. Boxes of 'hackable' items overflow with possibility, creating a cornucopia of bits and bobs that makers can rummage in. Yet, from the labels on boxes to the silhouettes that remind makers where to replace any tools they use, there are clear signs of organisation.

Figure 6.6. Makerspace consumables.

Colour-coded boxes provide order to shared resources in the space while preserving a rich sense of variety and treasure-hunting to those who scavenge their contents. Photo by Julian May.

The space that emerges is thus messy yet regulated, something that is also reflected in Maker Space's flat organisational structure, which is oriented to ensuring that all members have a say, without getting bogged down in decision-making processes. As one of the founding members comments, this is designed so that "we don't have to get everybody to agree". Tasks such as tidying the kitchen get done through this flexible approach to rules, for example, mugs in the cupboard are accompanied by a sign that urges a workable compromise: "We are never going to agree if cups should be stored bottom up or bottom side down... The solution is to do both".

Normatively, this framework allows makers to get on with their creative projects, also enabling 'crazes' to develop as ideas spread contagiously in the small space. Physically, things in the space take on a storied and even enchanted quality. For example, emerging from the absorption of some of the makers in customising quadcopters, an 'obstacle course' of picture frames took shape, suspended from the ceiling. The daring voyages of the quadcopters also created a social focal point, with moments of "dread and excitement" becoming the stuff of memory, of enjoyable time spent at Maker Space.

Figure 6.7. Tim's quadcopter launch at the Christmas party.

A moment of "dread and excitement". Photo by Julian May.

Figure 6.8. Safety warning on the laser cutter.

Humour and homespun signage 'soften' the regulatory features of the space. Photo by Julian May.

There has been some tension around aspects of health and safety, for example where makers have stored dangerous chemicals in the fridge. Regulating this type of activity has been difficult, as Malcolm puts it, "people don't feel that they want all that organization". This need for rules without dogma is apparent in humorous signage such as the Laser Cutter warning that reads, "Big Scary Laser: Do not look into beam with remaining eye". These efforts maintain the sense that, in spite of rules, things in the space are dynamic and open to interpretation. One is left with the sense that the makers, as in their individual projects, approach organisation and space playfully, as a puzzle to solve.

Maker Space's 'storefront' underscores the connection between the individual work of makers and its richly social quality, which enlivens not only the inside space but also impacts the urban streetscape. Aside from the buzz of sharing and 'show and tell' that occurs within the space, the display of quirky objects, including plastic ducks and 3D printers, offers a curious visual feast that lures children away from their parents at the nearby bus stops.

Figure 6.9. One of several 3D printers.

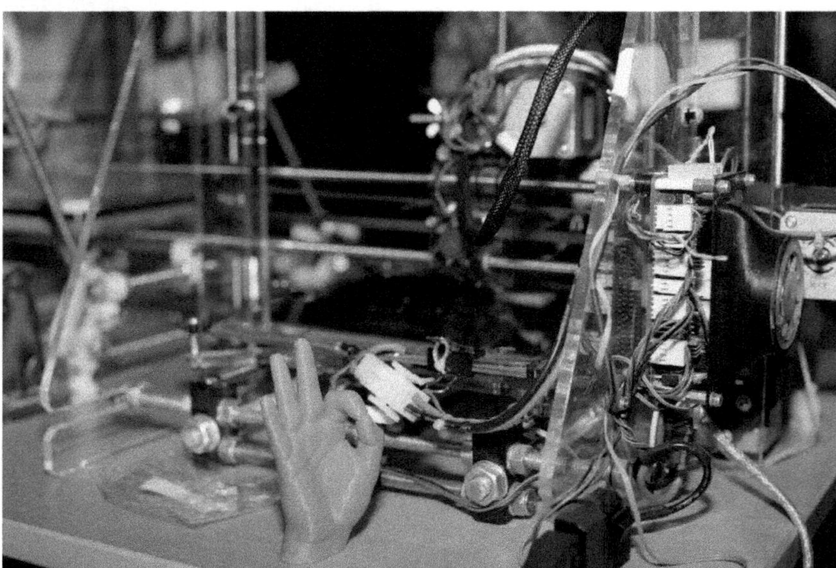

Excitement over particular technologies creates 'crazes' at Maker Space. Photo by Julian May.

At Christmas-time, many passers-by stopped to admire the makers' mechanical construction of penguins traversing Rob's laser-cut Tyne Bridge. As Ben comments, "we do get a lot of families, a lot of kids, looking in and really enjoying what they're seeing through the window".

Figure 6.10. 3D-printed penguins crossing a laser-cut Tyne Bridge.

Members devoted countless hours to devising this elaborately constructed moving Christmas window display. Photo by Julian May.

Discussion: Interstices in wage labour / cracks in urban space

Theoretical characterisations of the ontological need to make things (as an essential part of being or becoming human) and the social, place-based nature of this process provide a useful starting point for reflecting on the buzzing activity that goes on at Maker Space. The research invoked meditation on the link between the critical scholarship of work that theorises alienation and immaterial labour (Arendt 1998; Aronowitz *et al.* 1998; Gorz 2005; Hardt and Negri 2000; Marx 2001; Sayers 2013; Weeks 2011) and the scholarship of place and organisation (Burrell and Dale 2003; Daskalaki *et al.* 2008; Paterson 1997; Paton 2013).

For Hegel (1975: 31), humans are distinguished from animals by our ability to "double" ourselves in the things we create—this externalisation of the self means we can confront ourselves as a separate other, giving rise to a capacity for reflection. By representing ourselves in an object of our creation, we can think about ourselves in relation to the world. Deferred gratification, whereby we work upon the world by transforming the object rather than immediately consuming it, gives us a unique relationship to nature and to other humans. Through shaping and transforming the world, we separate ourselves from an object which is perceived as other, but also come to recognise ourselves in that which we have created, overcoming this 'alienation' of self from nature and thus becoming at home in the world (Sayers 2013: 17–18).

The creation of material objects that confront us as separate existences, as part of the unfolding of man's species-being, is central to Marx's youthful Hegelian writings on alienation. Emphasising man's ability to conceive of plans in his mind and will them into action, Marx (2001) argues that, where it retains its free and spontaneous character, our labour connects us to nature and to the species, enabling us to share in the riches of our fellow men and of the earth. By contrast, under capitalism, the worker is stunted by his labour, which becomes a fragmented and impoverished process, stripped of the dynamic of positive self-realisation and cut off from that movement towards becoming at home in our world. Notwithstanding ethnographies that, alongside the grime and tedium, celebrate the fulfilling dimensions of manufacturing work (Dennis 1969; Kornblum 1974; Mollona 2009), Marx's account captures the dehumanising nature of industrial labour.

It is important to note that, opposed to 'craft idiocy', by which he invokes the narrow and limited purview of feudal craft-based production (Marx 1978: 138), Marx does not romanticise the parochialism of the artisan within the feudal historical moment, conceiving dialectically of the development of industry to the point where most necessity can be met by machines, leaving us with a shortened work day that gives us liberty to pursue our own creative activity (Marx 1993: 706). Although Sayers (2013) uses Marx's abhorrence of craft-based production to remind us that Marx is not specifically enamoured of material labour, this study would suggest, in keeping with Hardt and Negri (2000) or Gorz (2005), that hands-on work with materials is a key part of the human endeavour, as explored further below.

It must also be noted that, as Sayers (2013) reminds us, making a useful, tangible thing such as a table is not central to Hegel's or Marx's conception of fulfilling work. All types of activity that are not based on immediate animal gratification fit within their self-realising purview. Work may involve fabrication of material objects, but it may also be an activity that transforms the world less tangibly through social activity (Marx 1978). Furthermore, work does not have to serve a practical need but rather encompasses all kinds of deliberate activity such as play, with art (when not done to put bread on the table) constituting the freest and highest form of work.

The importance of making physical things as vital to human self-realisation has been hotly debated, with critique of the modern labour process exemplified by Hardt and Negri's (2000) concept of immaterial labour, which argues that the contemporary labour process robs us of the transformative sense of working on the world that is key to self-realisation. In response to Hardt and Negri, Sayers argues that immaterial labour is a superfluous and misleading concept since, in Hegel and Marx's conception, all labour transforms matter in some way: "Symbolic labour is no exception: it involves making marks on paper, making sounds, creating electronic impulses in a computer system, or whatever ... it has material effects which produce and reproduce social and economic relations and alter consciousness" (Sayers 2013: 43).

Sayers argues forcefully that affective and symbolic labour—even housework—transform social and economic relations and are thus potentially a source of self-realisation in the Hegelian sense. This argument makes some logical sense and protects us from over-simplifying the potentiality for computer programming to offer the programmer a rich and fulfilling sense of having worked on the world. However, the distinction made by Tim and Ben, for example, between the feeling that derives from making a tangible thing such as a toy bus offers interesting insight into the loss of tangibility experienced by those whose work is based on the movement and manipulation of code.

Reflecting also on the notion of making durable things that emerged from the study, we must keep in mind Sayer's (2013) critique, which upholds that even intangible, ephemeral work processes can be fulfilling. However, other theorists have emphasised the importance of creating durable objects to human development. The making of artefacts is central to Arendtian thought, which exudes a fascination with the artificial world of durable objects that man builds on earth. Arendt laments that we are caught up in a production-consumption cycle, 'where all things swing in changeless, deathless repetition' (Arendt 1998: 96) and where 'a chair or a table is now consumed as rapidly as a dress and a dress is used up almost as quickly as food' (Arendt 1998: 124).

Distinct from Marx, she places particular value on the creation of objects that endure outside of this cycle of man's metabolism with nature. Durable objects, for Arendt, stabilise our existence against a backdrop of production and devouring that, in an era of abundance, absorbs humanity in mindless consumption. In this analysis, creation of enduring things is existentially vital, countering Heraclitean—in terms of the idea that one cannot stand in the same river twice—uprootedness (Arendt 1998: 137), reclaiming our social responsibilities and political capabilities. These objects prevent descent into an animalistic existence based on continuous and thoughtless devouring. Here, Ben's reflection on his creations as something he can hold up and keep forever and Evie's pleasure at seeing her family and friends adorned in her keepsake jewellery, exude this sense of the made object as stabilising the self.

Adding to this, Gorz problematises the practico-sensory deprivation inherent in, for example, working on a VDU, arguing that this represents an impoverishment of human experience. Referring to Hegel's conception of alienation (and contrary to Sayers position on this), he argues that the material impact of such work is too "distant and mediate" to provide the exteriorisation (*Entäusserung*) necessary for self-realisation in the Hegelian sense. Rather, in much contemporary knowledge-based labour, workers' "practico-sensory activity is reduced to the barest minimum, their bodies and sensibilities bracketed out of the operation" (Gorz 2005: 2).

In a related vein, Gorz problematises the ephemeral or "evanescent" quality of much contemporary labour, in which—as in much service work as well as knowledge work—the product is consumed as quickly as it is produced, never taking on any truly graspable form. Echoing Hegel's doubling of the self, this evanescent, intangible quality of work means for Gorz that there is no moment of contemplating the self as other that, in turn, makes one at home in the world: 'Seldom can these workers say: "Here's what I have done. This is the piece of work I've made. This was my doing" (Gorz 2005: 2). This loss of the sense of work as a physically tangible *oeuvre* links to the theme of building something enduring and unique that emerged from the study. Ben pictures his toy bus being handed down rather than thrown out, experiencing this product differently from the computer programs he writes at work; Evie relishes seeing her artistic creations out in the world, being worn and treasured by her friends enjoying the palpable sense that she is imprinted on the world.

This emphasis on practico-sensory deprivation is developed further by Carr and Gibson's (2016) recent analysis of the geographies of making, which argues that hegemonic capitalist interests have generated a mode of production that cuts us off from the vitality of materials. Carr and Gibson uphold that those who make things hold the key to orienting society toward more sustainable outcomes, calling for micro-level analysis of our relationship to materials that re-focuses attention in this area. As such, they urge, "ecological crisis demands more, rather than less, attention to materials and making processes" (Carr and Gibson 2016: 298). Indeed, a further study that looked more closely at the connection that develops between makers and the materials they work with would be a worthwhile future research direction.

Consideration of Maker Space as a realm of productive leisure also invokes reflection on Weeks' recent call for the sociology of work to refocus attention away from the binary of wage labour and care-giving. Weeks urges us to redirect our attention toward social processes that help us claim 'the time to reinvent our lives, to reimagine and redefine the spaces, practices, and relationships of non-work time' (Weeks 2011: 168). Within this reflection, the potential of Maker Space membership in decentring the professional work ethic as the centre of existence and forging time outside of wage labour for "what most pleases us" (Aronowitz *et al.* 1998) becomes a compelling theme for exploration. This is particularly pertinent in a context where, as Gorz, Aronowitz and others argue, we have reached a technological stage where full employment is no longer viable and paid work makes less sense as the organising principle through which human dignity is either earned or taken away.

The enviable absorption of makers in their creative projects, and their devotion to puzzling over and building intriguing and beautiful objects resonates with the critical theory that orients our attention toward human emancipation as spending as much time as we can on that which delights us (Aronowitz *et al.* 1998; Marx 1993). Furthermore, the seamless link between making objects and connecting to people and place, echoes conceptions of unalienated production as an intrinsically social and ecological practice (Marx 2001). Linking both to Arendt (1998) and Gorz (2005), and against the immateriality and evanescence of contemporary knowledge work, maker identity is stabilised by the tangible object, which may be held up, shown to others, and kept forever.

Emerging from interstices in the labour process, where the need for something more tangible, enduring and whole are indulged, is a process of place- and community-building that takes place in urban cracks that exist in the city's commercial centre, dominated by shops and offices. Place-making is here understood as emerging from the vibrant energy of making activity, coupled with the 'messy' organisational elements that enable the makers' individually absorbed yet richly social practice. Maker Space, as a space that emerges from this process, is rich with a sense of possibility, discovery and surprise. The cheeky signage and overflowing scrap boxes arise from the making process, in turn nurturing and inspiring the makers, as well as enlivening the streetscape through the maverick window displays.

When framed in terms of alienation, there is tremendous resonance between scholarship of work and that of place. Augé's (2008) claim that the relationship between individual and place has become increasingly contractual and objectified, mirrors Marx's characterisation of the estranged worker. The uniformity and predictability of commercially driven urban spaces mirrors the commodified relation between the worker and his or her product. In the theory of 'non-place', loss of an intimate, vibrant sense of place numbs the critical faculty by providing a landscape that, however dazzling, is not readable by its denizens, who are thus incapable of authentic connection with it (Dale and Burrell 2002; Daskalaki *et al.* 2008). Similarly, in Marx's analysis, the alienated worker becomes stunted and cut off by his labour, even when the product itself is beautiful.

Just as theorists of work have analysed the worker who is isolated from his fellow men and from nature, theorists of place such as Paterson (1997) and

Farrar (2011) envision the denizen who has no authentic connection to place, becoming atomised and incapable of civic engagement. Reflecting on this in relation to corporatized urban space, Daskalaki *et al.* (2008) lament the 'superficial formalism' of placeless places. For Farrar (2011: 727), this loss of connection amidst 'paralysing uniformity' foments political amnesia and resignation to 'what is', as subjects are not sufficiently connected to their environment to be able to read it, losing the ability to imagine what might be possible. This work on place echoes Gorz's work on practico-sensory deprivation inside the labour process as well as evoking Arendt's notion of the need for an anti-Heraclitean relationship to our world.

Using parkour as a provocation, Daskalaki *et al.* (2008) highlight the power of parkour-style interventions in disrupting this anesthetised state by physically and sensorially engaging the body in space, yielding creative and critical potential. Maker Space, as a site that is richly textured and highly legible to its members, who continually inscribe themselves in it, often though embodied practices of re-use and upcycling, can be framed as a type of parkour, fomenting a deep and lasting connection to space alongside the creation of lasting things.

Maker Space activity is distinguished from paid work by virtue of its time-rich, creatively autonomous and tangible characteristics, but is also sustained economically and materially by some of the members' day jobs in fields such as engineering and computing. It is an alternative organisational form that emerges from the interstices of everyday life and existing patterns of work and consumption, existing alongside these structures. Yet, as a space that is 'unruly, uncertain, unfinished, collaborative, alive' (Farrar 2011: 732), it is also disruptive in terms of challenging the imagination to consider what could be rather than being imprisoned in what is (Paterson 1997: 84), suggesting the type of richly textured urban spaces that are possible. Alongside this, it suggests what our productive activity, and our cities, might look like if we were less constrained by the exigencies of making a living and more able to spend more time doing what most pleases us.

Notes

[1] Following the conclusion of the research, Maker Space was evicted from the location featured in this chapter.

[2] The names used in this chapter are pseudonyms to obscure people's identities.

Acknowledgements

We would like to extend a very hearty thanks to the Makers at Newcastle's Maker Space who gave up their extremely valuable making time to help with this project. Julian's photographic work was funded by Northumbria University's Social Science Department.

References

Anderson, C. (2013) *Makers: The New Industrial Revolution.* New York: Random House Business.

Arendt, H. (1998) *The Human Condition.* Chicago: University of Chicago Press.

Aronowitz, S., Esposito, D., DiFazio, W. *et al.* (1998) The Post-Work Manifesto. In: Aronowitz, S. and Cutler, J. (eds) *Post-Work: The Wages of Cybernation.* New York: Routledge.

Augé, M. (2008) *Non-Places.* London: Verso.

Burrell, G. and Dale, K. (2003) Building Better Worlds? Architecture, Space And Organisation. In: Alvesson, M. and Willmott, H. (eds) *Studying Management Critically.* London: Sage.

Carr, C. and Gibson, C. (2016) 'Geographies of making: Rethinking materials and skills for volatile futures', *Progress in Human Geography,* 40(3): 297–315.

Cavalcanti, G. (2013) 'Is it a Hackerspace, Makerspace, TechShop, or FabLab?'. Available at: http://makezine.com/2013/05/22/the-difference-between-hackerspaces-makerspaces-techshops-and-fablabs/.

Collier, J. and Collier, M. (1986) *Visual Anthropology: Photography as a Research Method.* Albuquerque: University of New Mexico Press.

Dale, K. and Burrell, G. (2002) 'An-aesthetics and architecture', *TAMARA: Journal of Critical Postmodern Organization Science,* 2(1): 77–90.

Daskalaki, M., Stara, A. and Imas, M. (2008) 'The 'Parkour Organisation': inhabitation of corporate spaces', *Culture & Organization,* 14(1): 49–64.

Dennis, N. (1969) *Coal Is Our Life.* London: Routledge Kegan & Paul.

Dougherty, D. (2012) 'The Maker Movement', *Innovations: Technology, Governance, Globalization,* 7(3): 11–14.

Duneier, M. (2000) *Sidewalk.* New York: Farrar, Straus and Giroux.

Engels, F. (1952) *The Condition of the Working-Class in England in 1844.* London: Allen and Unwin.

Farrar, M. E. (2011) 'Amnesia, nostalgia, and the politics of place memory', *Political Research Quarterly,* 64(4): 723–735.

Furtherfield. (2015) 'DIWO – Do It With Others: Resource'. Available at: http://archive.furtherfield.org/projects/diwo-do-it-others-resource.

Gorz, A. (2005) *Reclaiming Work: Beyond the Wage-Based Society.* Cambridge: Polity Press.

Halverson, E. R. and Sheridan, K. M. (2014) 'The maker movement in education', *Harvard Educational Review,* 84(4): 495–504.

Hardt, M. and Negri, A. (2000) *Empire.* Cambridge, MA: Harvard University Press.

Hegel, G. W. F. (1975) *Aesthetics: Lectures on Fine Art.* Oxford: Clarendon Press.

Howes, D. (2005) 'Introduction', in Howes, D. (ed.) *Empire of the Senses: The Sensual Culture Reader.* Oxford: Berg.

Kornblum, B. (1974) *Blue Collar Community.* Chicago: University of Chicago Press.

Lindtner, S. (2015) 'Hacking with Chinese characteristics: The promises of the maker movement against China's manufacturing culture', *Science, Technology & Human Values,* 40(5): 854–879.

Lou, N. and K. Peek. (2016) 'By The Numbers: The Rise Of The Makerspace'. Available at: http://www.popsci.com/rise-makerspace-by-numbers.

Lyon, D. (2013) The Labour of Refurbishment: Space and Time, and the Building and the Body. In: Pink, S., Tutt, D.E. and Dainty, A. (eds) *Ethnographic Research in the Construction Industry.* London: Routledge.

Makerspaces.com. 'What is a makerspace?'. Available at: https://www.makerspaces.com/what-is-a-makerspace/.

Marx, K. (1978) *The Poverty of Philosophy.* Peking: Foreign Language Press.

Marx, K. (1993) *Grundrisse.* New York: Penguin Books.

Marx, K. (2001) *The Economic & Philosophic Manuscripts of 1844.* New York: International Publishers.

Mollona, M. (2009) *Made in Sheffield: An Ethnography of Industrial Work and Politics.* New York: Berghahn Books.

Newcastle City Council. (2010) 'Equality statistics, research and information'. Available at: https://www.newcastle.gov.uk/your-council-and-democracy/statistics-and-census-information/equality-statistics-research-and-information.

Paterson, D. D. (1997) 'Community building and the necessity for radical revision', *Landscape and Urban Planning,* 39(2–3): 83–98.

Paton, D. A. (2013) 'The quarry as sculpture: The place of making', *Environment and Planning A,* 45(5): 1070–1086.

Pink, S. (2009) *Doing Sensory Ethnography.* London: Sage.

Pink, S. (2014) *Doing Visual Ethnography.* London: Sage.

Richardson, M., Elliott, S. and Haylock, B. (2013) 'This home is a factory: Implications of the Maker movement on urban environments', *Craft + Design Enquiry,* 5: 141–154.

Rosner, D. K. and Fox, S. E. (2016) 'Legacies of craft and the centrality of failure in a mother-operated hackerspace', *New Media & Society,* 18(4): 558–580.

Savills. (2016) 'Newcastle & Birmingham top UK ranking for fashion spend'. Available at: http://www.savills.co.uk/_news/article/72418/207844-0/9/2016/newcastle-and-birmingham-top-uk-ranking-for-fashion-spend.

Sayers, S. (2013) *Marx and Alienation.* Basingstoke: Palgrave Macmillan.

Strauss, A. and Corbin, J. (1990) *Basics of Qualitative Research: Grounded Theory Procedures and Techniques.* London: Sage.

Sudjic, D. (2009) *The Language of Things.* London: Penguin.

Van Maanen, J. (1988) *Tales of the Field: On Writing Ethnography.* Chicago: The University of Chicago Press.

Van Maanen, J. (1991) The Smile Factory: Work at Disneyland. In: Frost, P. J., Moore, L. F., Louis, M. R. *et al.* (eds) *Reframing Organizational Culture*. Thousand Oaks, CA: Sage.

Waller, M. A. and Fawcett, S. E. (2014) 'Click here to print a maker movement supply chain: How invention and entrepreneurship will disrupt supply chain design', *Journal of Business Logistics*, 35(2): 99–102.

Weeks, K. (2011) *The Problem with Work: Feminism, Marxism, Antiwork Politics, and Postwork Imaginaries*. Durham, NC: Duke University Press.

Chapter 7

"You make do with what you've got"

Makeshift structures and the moral economy of affective labour in post-industrial Manchester

Luciana Lang, Manchester Metropolitan University

Abstract

Friedrich Engels once described Cheetham Hill, in North Manchester, as a "girdle" of working people's quarters beyond which lay the comfort and clean air enjoyed by the bourgeoisie. The great transformations over the next 160 years presented the worker with streamlining of factory work, stronger trade unions, and the emergence of a support network with the welfare system. However, the ruination that Engels perceived in the urban landscape of industrial Manchester resurfaces in the post-industrial era with the demise of work. Drawing on ethnographic material produced in a community centre in Cheetham Hill, this chapter treats people's involvement with constructing makeshift outbuildings, growing food, keeping animals, and creating spaces of mutual help as instances of "affective labour", here understood as the production of relations rather than goods (Muehlebach 2011: 61). I argue for the subversive potential of affective labour and the do-it-yourself culture in enabling productivity in a post-work scenario. The resulting effect is an alternative form of economy guided by a moral duty of giving back what one receives freely. In the process, the precariat forges a moral economy based on makeshift and 'make do', and the rise of affective labour grants social recognition and personal accomplishment in an otherwise infertile terrain. In a landscape where jobs are scarce, the possibility of being productive reawakens a class consciousness, not based on political activism but on a shared experience of a precariousness that binds this social fabric in its making.

***

Figure 7.1. The conversation room.

Makeshift living room put together by volunteers. Photo by Luciana Lang, 2016.

Introduction

In an article for the New Left Review in 2010, the cultural historian Michael Denning suggested that "Under capitalism, the only thing worse than being exploited is not being exploited". Denning is referring to the decline of manufacturing in the Global North in the late 1970s associated with post-industrial societies. This decline is commonly characterised by a new globalised work force, flexible labour regimes, and the emergence of what has been described as the precariat (Gorz 1999; Standing 2011; Weston 2012). Denning is also calling attention to the tragic condition of the formerly working classes who are more likely to be 'workless' in a society that now sees them as worthless. Evans (2012) unpacks and critiques the concept of 'worklessness', which makes unemployment in contemporary capitalism appear to be a moral condition of the 'feckless' and situates it instead in the context of the destructive political economy of post-industrialism.

In 2003, in a study on the dynamics of capitalism, André Gorz identified this vulnerable fraction of the population as the *précaires* (Gorz 2003 cited in Granter 2009: 125). He was referring to workers who relied on flexible and contingent employment in contrast to the certainties still enjoyed by fully employed elites. However, it was not until 2011 that Guy Standing characterised the precariat as a feature of advanced global capitalism, supposedly replacing the proletariat associated with industrial societies. Standing saw society in late capitalism as a division between the salariat, whose members enjoy the job stability that older generations took for granted, and the precariat, a "class-in-the-making" (2011: 8) for whom uncertainty is part of everyday life.

Over a century ago, Friedrich Engels analysed another turning point in British history when the proletariat emerged as a class by the introduction of machinery (1969 [1845]: 46). Engels describes how the invention of the spinning jenny by a weaver in 1764 had brought about radical changes for textile workers, who went from being rural farming-weavers, whose working lives were embedded in familial sociality, to becoming exploited, urban-dwelling wage-based weavers without autonomy or access to land (ibid.).

Whether the political-economic moment spawns the proletariat or the precariat, the classic analysis of Engels famously showed that attention must be given to the perspective from below, and while forms of labour are distinctively different in the industrial and post-industrial eras, parallels can be traced regarding forms of resistance by the poor in moments of financial distress. In an analysis of the food price crisis of the eighteenth century, historian E. P. Thompson observed how the streets became the stage for mobilisation. This political reaction, which Thompson described as "the moral economy of the English crowd" (1971), was driven by the grassroots perspective who powerfully resisted an economic model grounded in unfair relations, and believed economic reason ought to be moral. Although we still lack the benefit of hindsight to appropriately evaluate the effects of the crisis faced by the non-worker in late capitalism, Evans (2017) has analysed the outcome of the 2016 referendum in Britain to leave the European Union as a post-industrial protest vote that reveals the contemporary crisis of political, economic and social alienation. Evans's work is just one example of how the ethnographic method is uniquely positioned to unveil understandings of everyday struggles, coping strategies, and changes in the moral economy.

Drawing on material from interviews and on participant observation conducted in my capacity as an ethnographic researcher and as a volunteer over the course of two years at the Welcome Centre—an education and food distribution charity in Cheetham Hill, North Manchester—I explore, in this chapter, the forms of unpaid work that unemployed people engage with and I ask what motivates this act of labouring. Problems with unemployment and homelessness were common amongst participants in the research, and according to the Centre's reports, the service that grew the most over the last 18 months was "advice and advocacy", which points to the high levels of benefit claimants in the area (Lang 2018).

The 2011 census ranked Cheetham Hill ward amongst the 20 per cent most deprived areas in the UK. The levels of poverty found therein also reflect the effects that austerity measures had on welfare provision throughout the country following the post-2008 financial crisis. While Manchester boasts historical capital for having been a centre of the industrial revolution and for being a cultural powerhouse in popular music and television in the post-war period, the austerity measures of the Conservative central government are currently experienced by local councils as extreme budget cuts with tremendous impact on the region. After securing enough votes to take office as the Labour mayor of Greater Manchester in 2017, Andy Burnham told The Guardian newspaper that devolution and homelessness should be top of the political agenda (Helm 2017). Manchester's success at securing grants over the previous decades has fostered in the city a model of "entrepreneurial urbanism" (Quilley 2000; Ward 2003), which prompted the City Council to invest in areas like Cheetham Hill as part of its wider policies of social cohesion and economic regeneration, albeit often in a highly constrained and symbolic fashion, such as funding the annual Cheetham Festival (Stone and Milan 2012). The trope of 'revolution' re-emerged in 2015 in the context of devolution plans for the city region announced by the UK Chancellor George Osborne and the Leader of Manchester Council Sir Richard Leese. That said, the effects of their vision of a 'Northern Power House' are yet to be felt by the poor, particularly in peripheral areas like Cheetham Hill.

The Welcome Centre is a direct outcome of the political-economic scenario summarised above: it fills the vacuum left by changes in the welfare state and by the introduction of austerity measures. This chapter explores what may emerge from this vacuum. In other words, what form does resilience take in neighbourhoods where urban planning and government support are absent and socio-economic relations must, of necessity, adapt to the withdrawal of responsibilities on the part of the state? I argue that people's involvement with growing and handling food, looking after chickens and fish, transforming indoor and outdoor spaces, and constructing makeshift structures not only nurtures shared values in this racially and ethnically diverse collective space, but also gives people a possibility of being productive and recognised for what they do. I treat people's activities as instances of "affective labour", described by Muehlebach as unwaged labour that produces "good feeling" and relations, rather than goods (2012: 61).

The chapter has three parts: first, I give a contextual background to my field site and locate participants in terms of their socio-economic trajectories; second, I converse with the literature related to labour and its permutations in late capitalism; and finally, I present ethnographic excerpts to argue for the subversive and productive potential of people's involvement with autonomous urban design and alternative forms of moral economy.

Contextual background

Cheetham Hill is one of the most ethnically diverse neighbourhoods of the UK; it was once a major textile hub in industrial Manchester, as noted by Engels in his analysis of the proletariat in England (1969 [1845]). According to records at the Manchester Jewish Museum, there was a continuous flow of migrants moving into the area since at least 1780, when the first Jews arrived followed by traders from Germany and Holland. From 1830s onwards, Sephardi merchants from the Middle East and the Mediterranean came to Cheetham Hill attracted by the textile trade and cotton mill industries (Lang 2017). The twentieth century witnessed the arrival of Russian and Austro-Hungarians fleeing poverty and violence, World War II refugees, and Egyptians, Hungarians and Iranians after the 1950s. According to the 2011 census, 44 per cent of the 22,562 residents of Cheetham Ward were born outside of the UK (Lang 2018).

More recently, with the decline in manufacturing, local trade turned to retail, evidenced in the way factory-turned-wholesalers now display a wide range of merchandise, from clothes, to wigs and hats. Food-related retail accounts for 33 per cent of local trade and it is significant that 21 per cent of the local economy is constituted by solicitors' services specialising in immigration law (Hall *et al.* 2015: 3). These sectors are followed by beauty and clothing (11 per cent) and technology (5 per cent). According to the 2011 UK Census, the highest migrant contingent is of Pakistani origin, followed by Polish and Other European, and African origin (Office for National Statistics

2011). While unemployment in the area is rife, an entrepreneurial Pakistani contingent accounts for a large proportion of proprietors (41 per cent) and were often mentioned in interviews as the most commonly found landlord (Lombard and Lang 2016).

The first time I walked up to Cheetham Hill from the city centre, I was approached by a string of young men ushering me surreptitiously into doorways set back from the road. Because I was relatively new to this area, I was puzzled by this unfamiliar interactional street dynamic and despite my curiosity, I declined their offer. A local taxi driver later clarified the scenario to me: "They sell counterfeit! It's illegal but the police have more important things to do."

It was not until a few days later when I was again walking down the same road on a weekend, after seeing dozens of people going inside the units clearly enjoying a family day out to explore the wide range of fake goods, from televisions to '10-quid' pairs of Adidas trainers, that I felt comfortable to satiate my curiosity. Having been described as the "counterfeit capital of Great Britain" (Scheerhout 2016), the hidden units on this particular road are regularly raided by the police. Described as a "dark economy" in the mainstream press (ibid.), this versatile market also constitutes a thriving informal economy in the face of precarity.

Located just off Cheetham Hill Road, the Welcome Centre caters for more than 63 nationalities, a figure often mentioned by both volunteers and staff. Among this highly diverse contingent, there is a significant number of both non-white and white British nationals, as well as migrants, refugees, and asylum seekers at different stages in terms of residence status. The centre offers free lunches three times a week to an average of 100 people per day; English and computer classes; furniture and bike repair workshops, and massage and beauty treatment, to name a few of its activities. Visitors enjoy a great deal of autonomy, so the activities on offer may vary according to what people are willing to contribute with. Thus a pop-up hairdresser in a small room of the building may give place to an exhibition of photographs and drawings by visitors to the centre.

My involvement with the Welcome Centre, which started with voluntary work in their community garden in 2015, developed into subsequent university–community collaborations. In 2016, I carried out a study with 30 participants about housing precarity and strategies among low-waged workers and the unemployed. The analysis shows that people's precarious housing conditions mirrors their work situation and vice-versa, locking them in a vicious cycle of precarity that only a 'decent job' could break. In the words of Kamil, a middle-aged interviewee: "I'm now on a zero-hour contract. There's no stability, I can't plan what I will do tomorrow".

While there were only two officially homeless people out of the 30 we interviewed, other six people were under the category 'free of charge', which stands for people who are living in other people's houses, sleeping on floors and sofas, either having to rely on their host's good will or giving something back in return, such as doing cleaning in exchange for free accommodation. Life trajectories show that while cultural and social backgrounds are varied, the overall experience of uncertainty is a constant, either because of difficulty in finding paid work or because of short-term contracts for those lucky enough to find jobs. Lack of job security and unemployment not only affects people's sense of self-respect and wellbeing, but also has a direct impact on the type of housing they are able to access: if they do not have an address, they cannot get benefits; housing benefit may be denied if they do not work enough hours; the type/size/quality of accommodation depends on how much residents are earning and, most importantly, the fact that there is no job security also means that there is no guarantee that they will be able to keep up rental payments. In addition, landlords pick and choose who they will take, so if they sense that the person is likely to go onto benefits, they tend to reject the person as a potential tenant (Lombard and Lang 2016). The trajectory of most interviewees was marked by constant moving from place to place. Tomas, a participant from Slovakia, summarised his work trajectory after the fall of socialism in former Czechoslovakia:

> Until 1989, all properties, museums, agricultural yields used to belong to the state. It was better with the socialist regime; the situation got worse and worse after 1989. When I was 19 I worked as a driver, then I did military service for 2 years, and after that I trained to be an electrician and worked until 1993 when I became unemployed. There was big unemployment then. I went to Bratislava to find work, and I worked as a truck driver for 1 year. After that, I worked as an electrician until 2007 receiving a very low wage. In 2008, I went to Denmark to work in a distribution service. After the crisis in 2008, I returned to Slovakia to work in security systems for 1 year, and in October 2010, I came to the UK looking for a job.

Cyryl, a participant, born in 1974 in Poland, spent most of his adult life changing jobs and places of residence. He worked as a journalist for a radio station in Poland, organised trips for tourists, and managed an NGO related to heritage and history of industrial machines and railways. Cyryl left Poland in 2006 because there was no funding to keep his organisation and no jobs. He went to the Czech Republic to work in a factory making mobile phones, then to Amsterdam where he worked in warehouses and in a juice factory. People he knew there talked about life in the UK, and how easy it was to find a job, so he came to the UK. After a few odd jobs, he found work at a large supermarket in Hull, and for one year and six months, he commuted between the two cities, starting at 6:00 a.m. in the morning. He was pleased with the work, because it paid a good salary and was relatively stable, but he eventually lost that job and was only able to find agency work. Filip, another participant from Poland, came to the UK in 2012 to escape problems with drugs and the law. When he arrived in Manchester, he pitched a tent next to the river near Victoria Station. He soon learned that people were not too keen on sharing public spaces with the homeless: "I figured out that it was better to put the tent in a place away from the city, so I pitched my tent in the cemetery".

Filip had a few jobs in the UK, but his longest term of employment was two and a half months getting £10 a day for clearing skips. He expressed bitterness when recalling that experience and a strong sense that people did not respect his labour: "How can you pay someone £10 for a whole day of physical work in England?" Rifat, an interviewee from Syria, left Damascus in September 2014 after his house was bombed. He took a bus to Lebanon, then a plane to Turkey, a boat to Greece, and a plane to Dublin, in Ireland. He decided to come to Cheetham Hill after being offered asylum because he knew about the textile history of Manchester and thought it would be a good place to find work. He used to have a business trading textile machines back in Damascus, which boasted 1,200 customers. However, because his asylum status was granted in Ireland, there had been delays in the processing of his claim. At the time of our interview, his wife and three children were still in Damascus living underground, and he was homeless, sleeping rough, or occasionally, at the Mosque, a favour he would only ask from a personal friend when he was desperate for a good night sleep. Rifat now needed to find work so he could get his family to join him.

The pervasiveness of work and its social utility

It has been noted that workless capitalism represents an ontological challenge (Muehlebach 2011; Castel 1996) insofar as people's understanding of their being in the world is so often through what they do. Labour is not only a result of the human drive to satisfy one's needs (Marcuse 1973), but it also mediates the exchange between humans and nature (Marx 1976 [1867]) constituting the very essence of the economic and productive unit, the *oikos*, and of subsequent relations of production. The sociologist Robert Castel (1996) gives an overview of the different roles workers had over the centuries noting that while the labouring classes were previously perceived as the dangerous classes, the indictment of vagrancy is evidence of an ideology of social utility before the industrial revolution. This view became pervasive in the twentieth century when the equation between work and worth turned wage employment into the basis of social recognition and paved the way to greater social protection and more robust labour laws (Castel 1996). In this shift from economic utility to social recognition, the factory worker went from being reduced to the condition of a machine to playing a political role in the class struggle and becoming a member of a class for itself (Thompson 1991 [1963]). The shop floor, albeit the setting for unequal power relations and alienation through an artificial division of labour, did provide the working class with a sense of belonging through long-term work relations. Later, Henry Ford, founder of the Ford Motor Company in the United States, forged a moral high ground for the worker, who was promised the benefits of becoming a consumer through his merit as a producer.

In the 1930s, John Keynes (1963) predicted that eventually people would work less and have more leisure time, but the positive evaluation of this future-directed phenomenon now presents itself with a twist. The process of land enclosures and privatisation of common ground that started in the eighteenth century (Polanyi 1944), spawning a landless class stripped of its means of production, has persisted such that the logic of dispossession and exclusion now makes this landless class also a workless class. The broader consequences of alienation from labour process among white-collar workers also constitute an emergent trend described as the proliferation of well-paid "bullshit jobs" (Graeber 2014). By contrast, David Harvey (2016) highlights the ever-growing sector of insecure, low-paid jobs that bring no fulfilment to workers, such as call centres and fast-food restaurants. The range of concepts explored in work-related studies in late capitalism is wide and points to the general realisation that the work force will have to reinvent itself: "compassionate labour" (Muehlebach 2011: 61); volunteering (Malkki 2015; Rozakou 2016); the "end of work" (Granter 2009; Gorz 1999); post-work (Weeks 2011); the precariat (Gorz 2003; Standing 2011; Weston 2012) and "immaterial labour" (Hardt 1999: 90; Lazzarato 1996), which is characterised by a focus on the consumption and manipulation of information technology, were some of the framings found in the reviewed literature.

In Cheetham Hill, the social and cultural value derived from labour is pervasive despite high levels of sustained unemployment. This is true across different social groups, and sheds light on the motivation for people to engage with wageless labour. If in the past non-remunerated occupations were classed as non-work (Castel 1996), in the post-industrial scenario these forms of unwaged labour are rehashed as civil duties, and gain value under the new conceptualisation of "affective labour" (Muehlebach and Shoshan 2012). The concept of was first used by Michael Hardt to define a "productive circuit of affect and value" (1999: 89) surrounding caring and kin work, occupying an increasingly dominant position in the global economy. As it evolved, the concept came to describe 'labour that produces or manipulates affects' (Hardt and Negri 2004: 108). Of interest here is the more recent reframing by Andrea Muehlebach, who elaborates on the concept to refer to unwaged labour that produces good feeling and relations rather than goods (2011: 61). Muehlebach warns, however, that while creating new forms of sociality, these forms of work can also potentially exploit free labour (2011).

With that caveat in mind, there is a need to contextualise affective labour, given that it does not stand in an isolated era of globalisation. Instead, it is in constant dialogue with the "ghostly presence" (Muehlebach 2011: 62) of Fordist structures, even if only to haunt people's aspirations and feed their sense of nostalgia, associated with the way places change "symbolically and culturally" (Savage 2010: 23) in relation to a former sense of belonging. Reminiscences by British residents, such as that described by an older participant, included both a longing for the camaraderie amongst shop floor workers and for the freedom of their youth when they could just "walk in and out of jobs without a worry", a comment often repeated by Pete, a participant born and raised in the north of England. The nostalgia sensed in the accounts by Tomas, Cyryl and Filip is also fuelled by feelings of uselessness and unfairness felt while waiting in benefit offices where claimants are constantly blamed for being workless (Foster 2014; Smith 2012).

In this scenario of post-industrial precarity, affective labour emerges not only as a mitigating strategy to cope with shortcomings brought about by uncertainty, but by fostering trust and reciprocity it offers an alternative logic to the competitiveness inherent to the free global market, an aspect that is not lost amongst participants who reiterate that they work for free because they want to help, as the ethnographic excerpts below indicate. Framed as civil duty, unwaged labour such as volunteering turns the 'useless' (Castel 1996) into social citizens, transforming their home-spun *oikos* into a moral economic and productive unit.

In the field

It was a bright sunny day at the Welcome Centre and there were quite a few of the regular visitors in the garden. Two Polish ladies who could not speak English pointed to the raspberries excitedly and prompted me to try one of the berries. A group of visitors was talking around a table:

> Pat: Where are you from?
>
> Jamila: I'm from Somalia

Pat: I don't like Somalis. Nothing against you though. Moss Side is full of Somalis now; before there was a community there. Like, my father came from the West Indies and when I was growing up Moss Side was a community, with drugs like and gang fights.

The conversation then digresses to how different cultures have changed Manchester and the way blacks of West-Indian origin are treated. One of the kitchen workers joins in and gives her take on how ethnic-oriented constraints changed food practices at the centre:

Louise: We were given lots of chicken but I couldn't use it because we were told that all the meat has to be Halal.

Carole: That is not fair. The food isn't just for Muslims, you know.

Laiba: I'm a Muslim and I think this isn't right. You would have to use a different pan to cook it, but I don't see why they should have only Halal food here.

Carole: There's no thinking about Caribbeans in this place. They just think about the Muslims.

The exchange makes me think of Standing's suggestion (2011) that because the precariat is constituted by a wide range of groups in terms of age, culture, and social background, mobilisation and solidarity amongst its members can be curtailed. However, despite the heterogeneity amongst visitors to the centre, there is a sense of commonality between people exactly because of the uncertainty they share, suggesting that the supposed class-in-the-making is bound by precarity.

Luke, a white middle-aged British man who calls himself a "posh tramp", arrives on his bike. His bicycle frame is a bricolage of animal plastic figures, bike accessories, and a sound system wired to his Bluetooth playing a compilation of rock and blues. His dog is tied to a leash and runs along while he peddles. With a background in engineering, Luke used to service different types of machinery, running his own business for years. For a number of reasons, some related to his mental and physical health, he gave it all up and said he is happy not having the spare cash to squander. I probed him asking if he misses work: "You're not worth your own time when you have a job. I don't think you need to work; you need to know how to survive".

As it turns out, he does keep himself busy by helping people out, repairing burst washing machine pipes or fridges that stopped working. I overhear Luke arranging a visit to an elderly lady to service her computer and realise that the exchange of goods and services is what binds the social fabric here. This logic chimes with the "what goes around comes around" in the ethnography by Carol Stack (1974) in a North American black neighbourhood in the 1970s where networks of support created kin-like bonds as a survival mechanism in the face of poverty. Two years ago, the centre was given five chickens and Amy, a regular visitor to the centre, volunteered to look after them. Amy suffers from anxiety and had her children taken away to foster homes years ago. She thinks the chickens are good for her mental health, and says, "they keep me busy". The chicken and ducks have given her a new lease of life:

> They are like my kids. And I gained all this knowledge! I've learned all sorts, from ways to get different breeds, to feeding and housing. I didn't know there's no need for heating with them. There are more than 20 Facebook groups that I joined just to swap tips about chickens. I spend hours reading them. I made a third generation of chickens!

She praises the 'hands on experience' she acquired. Along with her husband and another two volunteers, Pete, a former trawlerman from Newcastle, and Antoni, a builder from Poland, they built a chicken coop:

Figure 7.2. Chicken coop.

Built by Tony, Amy, Jan and Pete. Photo by Luciana Lang, 2016.

Amy now has two ducks at home and a baby chick in the incubator and has learned to look after ill chickens. She found out that you can give them Epsom salt. She also knows now how to tell the males from the females and says that "you can determine the sex through the feathers". She explains her hypothesis to me: "I reckon that a chicken can turn herself into a male. They are transgender when they are born, hermaphrodites like". I asked her what she gets out of her work with the chickens: "*Not eggs!*", and she bursts out laughing at the frustrating fact that other people get to the eggs before she does in this communal space.

Pete, the person in charge of the community gardens both at the Welcome Centre and at the Irish Centre up the road where locals were given a plot of land to work on, tells me what he gets out of unpaid labour: "It makes me feel good. It keeps me busy". He points to three guys dismantling a shed who are paid volunteers from Shaw Trust, a national charity that helps people get back to work through paid internships:

> It's different for those lads that are helping now with the greenhouse. They're only doing it because they get paid. For me what I do here is like a job because I'm working full days three times a week. It's just that I don't get nowt for it. I just get my veg and I help other people through learning them. If I get spuds and sprouts, that's what I'll eat for dinner.

A woman overhears him and adds: "You make do with what you've got, ain't it, love?"

The DIY mentality

If precarity is a lived experience in terms of work and housing, people's attempt to 'make do with what you've got' also follows a logic informed by the DIY mentality as a means of being productive beyond the constraints of the state and the market (Lang 2017; Pickles *et al.* 2014: 450; Purdue *et al.* 1997). In common with the urban occupation of plazas and other public spaces across post-financial-crisis Spain (Corsín Jiménez and Estallela 2011), the dynamics that fuel the collaborations at the Welcome Centre are based on practices of exchange, including food, plants and seeds, building materials, animals, and on the do-it-yourself culture with interventions being both provisional and open-ended (Pickles *et al.* 2014: 459) where "amateurs can become agents of change" (Richardson *et al.* 2013: 141). Other parallels can be made: if the camps in Spain produced a library, a kitchen, a nursery, a centre for food and drinks, a legal desk, a cleaning squad, and a medical-emergencies space (Corsín Jiménez and Estallela 2011), the Welcome Centre voluntary hub created a hair salon, a beauty parlour, a clothes exchange point, a bike repair container, a furniture repair space, and a circuit of translators on request. The way related materials and equipment are sourced and worked follows a do-it-yourself mentality, while scavenging for materials is recognised and praised as the most viable and sustainable approach.

However, different from the #SpanishRevolution encampment, the do-it-yourself at the Welcome Centre is not driven by an overt political agenda. Instead, it emerges organically, informed by a desire to be productive, and in many cases, to give something back to the space that welcomed participants in times of need. With little possibilities of changing the prospect of precarious work and housing, affective labour and makeshift structures also emerge as an adaptive option. In this new scenario, being "useless" (Castel 1996), as vagrants were described in the past, is no longer the necessary outcome of being workless, and social citizenship is no longer exclusive to workers.

Out of 30 interviewees, 11 volunteer at the Welcome Centre on a regular basis, helping with a number of activities, and almost all occasionally join in a number of activities, sometimes making a contribution outside the centre. A participant from Angola who came to the UK as a refugee started volunteering at the Welcome Centre first as an English class assistant, then in the kitchen, introducing salads to the lunch-time menu, and finally, she became the food parcel coordinator. She also goes out in her spare time to distribute food to the homeless. She says this is a way of giving back some of what she received at the centre and in this country: "I like to help in the kitchen because they have helped me".

A couple from Lithuania who built the fishpond in the garden are now self-employed doing painting and decorating, as well as delivering food for the Centre. Another visitor, Michael, used to come to the centre only in the afternoons, when the space is used by the West-Indian community:

> I normally come to the centre to play dominoes, but one day I saw that the garden needed more help. You see, back home in the Caribbean, I always helped my family in the garden. And here, people can actually eat this food. There are many people here who need this.

Michael also helped build the greenhouse where he now grows tomatoes, courgettes and bell peppers:

Figure 7.3. Self-built greenhouse.

Greenhouse built by Michael and other volunteers. Photo by Luciana Lang, 2016.

Such instances of affective labour make people realise their capacity to be productive in a scenario where they are constantly being denied this opportunity. Contrary to Gorz's view that these social actors would be anti-productive and anti-state (Gorz 2003 cited in Granter 2009: 125), what the interventions at the Welcome Centre suggest is a subversion of the formal manner of interacting with the market and the state, rather than merely negating them. The market is present, insofar as most of the food consumed and materials used were donated by outlets, but people do not pay for the goods. Likewise, the land is leased from the council, but people have a high level of autonomy that is granted through a benevolent form of authority from the part of the centre's management. These are examples of labour producing sociality rather than goods, as suggested by Muehlebach.

No place like home

Following a pilot study on the housing conditions of migrants at the Welcome Centre, Lombard and Lang (2016) produced a report, which helped to secure funds to buy a used ship container. This led to the next stage of the collaboration between the Welcome Centre and the University of Manchester, now focusing on designing alternative housing led by a lecturer in Architecture and Global Urbanism. An event was held at the Centre to discuss the follow-up with users of the centre. The lecturer explained the challenge he set for students: to force them to reflect and understand the real social fabric of the people they would be designing for and with. In order to do that, they needed to find out what resources were available locally, understand the local infrastructures and networks, and map empty dwellings and available sites locally.

With that in mind, students presented three pilot projects at the end of the academic term: a) an emergency pod for people who find themselves homeless, which would be situated on the grounds of the Welcome Centre; b) an emergency house using a mobile container that would move between empty sites in Cheetham Hill accompanied by a map of available empty sites; and c) a model pod fitted with a series of post-boxes that also functioned as an emergency pod to deal with the critical issue of the catch-22 situation when people cannot claim benefits because they lack a postal address.

In early 2017, volunteers at the centre started the construction of the first idea, the emergency pod, since this was the design for which they had all the materials, namely, pallets and tyres donated by local businesses, such as the local pub and the Irish Centre. After the course finished, Jan, a regular visitor to the Welcome Centre who used to teach telecommunications in the Czech Republic, took charge of the construction of a shower room and a sleeping pod. Dawid, an illustrator and graphic designer who came to the UK three years ago because of the economic situation in Poland, became a volunteer and Jan's main assistant after losing his job as a printing-machine operator. They had complete autonomy throughout the construction period and were helped occasionally by other volunteers. They explained the construction process:

> Jan: We used around 8 pallets as construction blocks for the sleeping pod, and tyres to lift the pod off the ground. The size of the pallets is given, so the design followed those dimensions. I followed my head for the design; the plan I had in my mind. There's limited money. If you want anything you improvise, you need a piece, but you have to do it with two

> pieces, which is then weaker. Mark [the manager at the Welcome Centre] was a spiritual father; he advised on better approaches.
>
> Dawid: It was a no-budget job; we used everything that we could find. We had to find stuff to use, like screws on the floor that we could straighten up.

Jan enjoyed the process, seeing it develop "slowly, slowly". Students from the university visited once and gave suggestions for the roof. I asked them about how they sourced the materials and what motivated them to work on the constructions:

> Jan: What motivated me? I have free time and my heart is in this house. I like doing something good for England and for this house.
>
> Dawid: There's a lot of people around who need help. I think the idea around this sleeping pod is pretty cool. There are a lot of homeless people around without any hope or help. Also, I love power tools, like drill, jigsaw. I was involved in similar jobs in the past. [As for the wood], you have to ask Mark, he was the magician who finds things.

An event was held at the centre to show the product of this collaboration between the university and the community. The lecturer leading the project introduced the concept of "social architecture" in Latin America, a concept that sits within a broader movement in support of "the right to the city" (Harvey 2012). With an estimated forecast of 3 billion people living in precarious housing in the next few years, he explained the need to 'recuperate the use-value' of housing and to promote the 'ethos of self-built'. Visitors to the event included two local councillors; housing association representatives; local leaderships; representatives of the Jewish Museum and the New Testament Church; as well as the regular visitors to the Welcome Centre. Taking place just a week before the surprise elections called by Theresa May in 2017, seen by some as a gamble to increase her slim majority in the House of Commons, the Labour councillors made sure they were present, eager to show support for grassroots initiatives in the community.

Figure 7.4. Occupod.

Model for a sleeping pod developed by Isobel Robertson, Celia Cooper, Xinming Ma, and Ross Nea for the Prefigurative Architectures course (2016) convened by Dr Leandro Minuchin at the Manchester School of Architecture. With permission of Dr Leandro Minuchin, 2016.

Figure 7.5. Actual pods.

External view of actual sleeping pod and shower room, the latter disguised as a bike-cleaning facility, constructed by volunteers. Photo by Luciana Lang, 2016.

Having "radical infra-structures" as a topic of interest on his course, the lecturer was excited with the autonomous materialisation of an idea by volunteers, a feeling that was perhaps not shared by the higher management at the Welcome Centre, more concerned with the legal implications of a makeshift product that did not comply with any health and safety rules. It is noteworthy that strategic arrangements were made to disguise the overall appearance of the pods so that they could be presented as a carpentry unit (the sleeping pod) and a place to wash bikes (the shower room), lest there be a health and safety monitoring from the council:

Figure 7.6. Inside the sleeping pod.

The sleeping pod, disguised as a joiner's workshop. Photo by Luciana Lang, 2016.

This made me reflect on the forms of knowledge circulating at the Welcome Centre and the issue of emancipation. The Argentinian lecturer was bringing to North Manchester the "self-built ethos" inspired by the informal architecture of slums in Latin America, which was informing the construction of makeshift structures by people of Polish, Lithuanian, and Czech origin. If informal architecture offers an opportunity for agency and productivity (Bayat 2004; Moser 2009), a dialogue with the Global South on this matter is fruitful since it promotes what has been described as "reverse flows" of theory (Yiftachel 2006: 216) and *techne*, here referring to knowledge and craftsmanship, from other parts of the world. In other words, a discussion that originated in the Global South, where precarity is often a feature of post-colonial development, can now illuminate a phenomenon in the Global North, inverting the usual north-south flow of theories and technologies. Here, the local and the global feed on each other, revealing a tension that simultaneously rejects and reinforces globalisation (Purdue *et al.* 1997), while the material interventions point to the dialectical outcome of austerity measures. I argue that this, along with the sense of autonomy over what is created, represents a subversive response to austerity.

Against this backdrop, informal constructions and the DIY culture emerge as the potential for agency and productivity, without however undermining the political-economic constraints underlying it. The issue of legality and its subversion, regarding the construction of informal structures, takes centre-stage insofar as it refers to different legal models that operate within distinct logics, that of the post-industrial Global North and the post-colonial Global South.

The sleeping pod is now being used regularly, but people take the mattress away every morning. The container that was bought after our initial research is currently being used to store the belongings of some homeless visitors, and to hide the mattress used in the pod. A compost toilet was bought a few months ago and is being used by male visitors, leaving the inside toilet for female visitors only. The last time I visited the centre, two visitors used the shower room in the space of two hours. They were given clean towels and a set of shampoo and shower gel, which had been previously donated by a hotel chain. In a recent community engagement event at the centre, we gathered in the main room to listen to Jan doing a PowerPoint presentation of his learning experience with the makeshift structures. Sammy, a British-born middle-aged woman from Pakistani parents who regularly visits the centre was watching the presentation not quite understanding what it was about—"too technical", she said. I explained that Jan had learnt a great deal through making things, and asked her if she had learned anything at the centre: "I socialise and learn about people", she said.

Conclusion

To conclude, the ethnography gives evidence to the suggestion made by Muehlebach that affective forms of labour can produce forms of unalienated labour. By focusing on relations, the unpredictable outcome of the dialectical encounter between the non-worker and the globalised free market could prove wrong Michael Denning's (2010) claim that opens this paper: we may adapt to wage-less work and to producing relations rather than goods. While the beginning of workers' protection and rights marked the end of exploitation, the possibility of being productive in late capitalism grants some social recognition and a sense of personal accomplishment in an otherwise infertile terrain. I have also argued that autonomous forms of affective labour, such as the process of designing and constructing a shower room and a 'sleeping pod', are evidence of the subversive potential of home-spun strategies in precarious scenarios. The resulting effect is an alternative form of economy guided by a moral duty of giving for free what one receives freely.

The DIY culture, whether used for politics (Corsín Jiménez and Estalella 2011), music festivals and local trading systems (Purdue *et al.* 1997), or community playgrounds (Lang 2017), is driven by a desire to reciprocate, to be self-sufficient, to exercise autonomy, and to create an alternative collective that does not rely on the state and its agencies. During the construction of the shower room and the sleeping pod, informality surfaced as a means of bypassing constraints around housing initiatives. Through the use of recycled materials, often exchanged rather than purchased; and affective labour, dissociated from wages as exchange value, people subverted mechanisms they normally have no control over, engaging with creative labour, and enabling productivity in a post-industrial landscape. The cultural flows that characterise global capitalism with resulting experiments of alternative urban design emerge as the silver lining in this ethnography of precarious livelihoods, enabling alternative versions of the good life and of a moral economy. If the precariat is a class-in-the-making, as Standing suggests, perhaps under fertile conditions, it can become a class for itself.

Acknowledgements

I am grateful to the Welcome Centre and its visitors and volunteers who gave valuable contributions to this chapter. A special thank you goes to Mark Greenwood, a 'magician' and 'spiritual father' in the words of some participants in this research. I am also indebted to Dr Leandro Minuchin, whose architecture classes at the centre provided food for thought, to Dr Melanie Lombard, who gave me the opportunity for extended fieldwork at the centre, and to Dr Gillian Evans, who gave valuable suggestions for the chapter's final draft. All names have been changed to protect people's identity. All photographs were taken by the author.

References

Bayat, A. (2004) Globalization and the Politics of the Informals in the Global South. In: Roy, A., Alsayyad, N. (eds), *Urban Informality: Transnational Perspectives from the Middle East, Latin America and South Asia.* Lanham, VA: Lexington Books.

Castel, R. (1996) 'Work and usefulness to the world'. *International Labour Review* 135: 615–622.

Corsín Jiménez, A., and Estalella, A. (2011) '#SpanishRevolution'. *Anthropology Today,* 27: 19–23.

Denning, M. (2010) *Wageless Life.* New York: New Left Review.

Engels, F. (1969) *Condition of the Working Class in England.* Moscow: Panther Edition.

Evans, G. (2012) '"Worklessness": A family portrait'. *Anthropology in Action,* 19: 3–16.

Foster, J. (2014) 'Engagement and alienation amongst Manchester's unemployed'. Anthropology Matters. Available at: anthropologymatters.com/index.php/anth_matters/article/view/478/597.

Gorz, A. (1999) *Reclaiming Work: Beyond the Wage-Based Society.* Cambridge: Polity Press.

Graeber, D. (2014) *Bullshit Jobs.* New York: Simon & Schuster.

Granter, E. (2009) *Critical Social Theory and the End of Work: Rethinking Classical Sociology.* Aldershot: Ashgate.

Hall, S., King, J. and Finlay, R. (2015) City Street Data Profile on Ethnicity, Economy and Migration: Cheetham Hill, Manchester, Super-diverse Streets: Economies and spaces of urban migration in UK cities. London School of Economics and Political Science, London.

Hardt, M. (1999) 'Affective labor'. *Boundary* 2(26): 89–100.

Hardt, M. and Negri, A. (2004) *Multitude: War and Democracy in the Age of Empire.* New York: Penguin Books.

Harvey, D. (2012) *Rebel Cities: From the Right to the City to the Urban Revolution.* London: Verso.

Harvey, D. (2016) Why We Need a Moneyless Society. Available at: youtube.com/watch?v=3L36F8qvNqs.

Helm, T. (2017) Interview Andy Burnham: 'This is Jeremy Corbyn's moment.' The Guardian.

Keynes, J. M. (1963) Essays in Persuasion. In: *Economic Possibilities for Our Grandchildren.* New York: W.W. Norton.

Lang, L. (2017) Making and Enabling the Commons: Shared Urban Spaces and Civic Engagement in North Manchester. In: Lewis, C. and Symons, J. (eds), *Realising the City: Urban Ethnography in Manchester.* Manchester: Manchester University Press.

Lang, L. (2018) '"Sometimes you don't know how to move": Cultural savviness and learning the ropes of bureaucracy'. *Journal of Organizational Ethnography*. Online edition: https://doi.org/10.1108/JOE-01-2018-0005.

Lazzarato, M. (1996) Immaterial Labor. Generation Online. Available at: http://www.generation-online.org/c/fcimmateriallabour3.htm.

Lombard, M. and Lang, L. (2016) *Housing Experiences and Aspirations Among Low-Paid Migrant Workers in Manchester*. Manchester: Wai Yin.

Malkki, L. (2015) *The Need to Help: The Domestic Arts of International Humanitarianism*. Durham, NC: Duke University Press.

Marcuse, H. (1973) 'On the philosophical foundation of the concept of labour in economics'. *Telos*, 9–37.

Marx, K. (1976) *Capital: A Critique of Political Economy*. London: Penguin.

Moser, C. (2009) *Ordinary Families, Extraordinary Lives: Assets and Poverty Reduction in Guayaquil, 1978–2004*. Washington, DC: The Brookings Institution.

Muehlebach, A. (2011) 'On affective labor in Post-Fordist Italy'. *Cultural Anthropology* 26: 59–82.

Muehlebach, A. and Shoshan, N. (2012) 'Post-Fordist affect'. *Anthropological Quarterly*, 85: 317–344.

Office for National Statistics (2011) UK 2011 Census.

Pickles, J., Casas Cortes, M. and Cobarrubias, S. (2014) The Commons. In: Nonini, D. (ed.), *A Companion to Urban Anthropology*. Wiley, New York.

Polanyi, K. (1944) *The Great Transformation: The Political and Economic Origins of Our Time*. New York: Farrar & Rinehart.

Purdue, D., Dürrschmidt, J., Jowers, P. and O'Doherty, R. (1997) 'DIY culture and extended milieux: LETS, veggie boxes and festivals'. *Sociological Review*, 45: 645–667.

Quilley, S. (2000) 'Manchester first: From municipal socialism to the entrepreneurial city'. *International Journal of Urban and Regional Research*, 24: 601–615.

Richardson, M., Elliott, S. and Haylock, B. (2013) 'This home is a factory: Implications of the maker movement on urban environments,. *Craft + Design Enquiry*, 5: 141–154.

Rozakou, R. (2016) 'Crafting the volunteer: Voluntary associations and the reformation of sociality'. *Journal of Modern Greek Studies*, 34: 79–102.

Savage, M. (2010) *Identities and Social Change in Britain since 1940: The Politics of Method*. Oxford: Oxford University Press.

Scheerhout, J. (2016) Cheetham Hill named the counterfeit capital of the UK. Manchester Evening News.

Smith, K. (2012) *Fairness, Class and Belonging in Contemporary England*. Basingstoke: Palgrave Macmillan.

Stack, C. B. (1974) *All Our Kin: Strategies for Survival in a Black Community*. New York: Harper & Row.

Standing, G. (2011) *The Precariat: The New Dangerous Class*. London: Bloomsbury Academic.

Stone, C. and Milan, A. (2012) 'Empowering communities in the 'big society': Voluntarism and event management issues at the Cheetham Hill Cross – Cultural Festival'. *International Journal of Management Cases*, 14: 317–326.

Thompson, E. P. (1971) 'The moral economy of the English crowd in the eighteenth century'. *Past & Present*, 50: 76–136.

Thompson, E. P. (1991) *The Making of the English Working Class*. Toronto: Penguin Books.

Ward, K. (2003) 'Entrepreneurial urbanism, state restructuring and civilizing New East Manchester'. *Area*, 35, 116–127.

Weeks, K. (2011) *The Problem with Work: Feminism, Marxism, Antiwork Politics, and Postwork Imaginaries*. Durham, NC: Duke University Press.

Weston, K. (2012) 'Political ecologies of the precarious'. *Anthropological Quarterly*, 85: 429–455. https://doi.org/10.1353/anq.2012.0017

Yiftachel, O. (2006) 'Re-engaging planning theory? Towards "South-Eastern" perspectives'. *Planning Theory*, 5: 211–222.

Chapter 8

Green is not always perfectly green

Temporality, decay and open spaces in riverside Turin (Italy)

Lucilla Barchetta, University of Turin

Abstract

Inspired by the study of urban political ecology, this chapter explores the relationship between temporality and material decay in Michelotti Park, an open space in post-industrial Turin, Italy. By retracing the non-linear re-configuration of the park from a zoological garden to a waste space, the study explains how prevailing constructs of time and normative representations of decay reinforce discursive divisions between urban and natural processes and reproduce the moral geographies of human-nonhuman relations, which contribute in many ways to degradation.

***

Political ecology in urban studies: the life cycle of metropolitan natures

The transformation of nature in urban environments and the production of ecological imaginaries provide an interesting lens through which to observe the profound effects of socio-political restructuring in post-industrial cities over recent decades. Since the 1980s, the rise of *landscape urbanism* (Mostafavi and Najile 2004) has disclosed a new scenario for metropolitan change that follows the transition of many cities in the West, from the industrial to the post-industrial age, and the opportunities generated by processes of industrial abandonment and urban redevelopment (Waldheim 2006).

As a response to the ecological risks of planetary urbanisation and the change in worldwide metropolitan infrastructure investment, urban natures such as parks and areas of spontaneous vegetation, wastelands and other interstitial spaces along watercourses form illuminating 'playgrounds' for the biophysical and socio-spatial transformation of the contemporary city. They are also fundamental components in urban design and regional planning imperatives, boosterism initiatives (Smith 2014, 2017; Clark 2003), and other ways forward to achieving the socio-ecological sustainability of the urban environment by providing "Nature-Based Solutions" (EU 2015) and "designing city systems as biological metabolisms" (De Block 2016: 368).

In the last three decades, the bodies of research of geography and urban environmental history have enriched to a great extent investigations that merge studies of ecological processes with those of the city (Rose, 2004; Braun, 2005). The literature of urban political ecology (Heynen 2013, 2015, 2017), with its specific focus on metropolitan natures as socio-ecological constructions, examines how natures become transformed into different types of landscape of the modern city and constitutive elements of its metamorphosis (Gandy 2002; Heynen *et al.* 2006; Kaika, 2005; Robbins; 2007).[1] Urban political ecology, as part of a broader political and conceptual approach provides the ground to move away from a nature–culture binary by developing political, historicist and anti-essentialist understandings of natural processes.

Research has shed light on how urban natures, from urban parks to wastelands, are incorporated into human settlements as circumscribed spaces that in turn embody the "socio-cultural construction of nature as either destructive or redemptive", but always as separate and oppositional to the city (Millington 2013: 287). By focusing on the study of visual representations of wilderness in Detroit, Michigan, Nate Millington suggests that images of nature reclamation, produced by photographers and journalists, "are co-constructers" of Detroit's "business of decay" (ibid.). The formation of such post-industrial imaginary reduces the complexity of ecologies, while also leading to the "dismantlement of natural environments" from the city (ibid.), which in turn "neutralize the processes that are presently constructing Detroit's landscape, most notably virulent racism and industrial restructuring" (ibid.).

Focusing on various forms of socio-ecological processes, the approach from urban political ecology research shows that urban natures are always the result of the interdependencies of the everyday and its material realities, including biophysical processes (atmospheric variation; the role of water; the variety of plants, animals and soil formation), technological networks, governance structures, the associated cultural perceptions and practices, and the ideologies and representations through which socio-natures are incorporated into public and political discourse.

Most interestingly, this body of research has highlighted how a "brown/green antinomy" (Gandy 2013: 2) naturalises an organic evolution of urbanisation that cyclically reproduces an opposition between "green fields" and "brown fields", desirable natural landscapes of ecological, economic and aesthetic value versus undesirable spaces of abandonment, neglect and socio-ecological degradation. Gandy (2016) is thus able to explain the manners through which utilitarian approaches concerning unproductive places and their supposed "emptiness" narrowly frame urban open spaces, by exacerbating oppositional relations between planned (parks and gardens) and unplanned natures (wastelands and other fragments of spontaneous vegetation) waiting for development. Building on this critique, the chapter thus explains how prevailing modalities of temporality, in contemporary public and planning debates, often reduce the life of open spaces into a sequential and one-directional organisation of cycles: from brown to green and vice versa.

The oppositional relation between desirable and undesirable open spaces is itself a socio-cultural construction that ascribes open spaces with aesthetic, moral and discursive evaluations, which in turn model and monitor the lived experiences and political management of urban environments.

Gandy (2012) and Patrick (2014) also demonstrate how the relationship is regulated between the life cycle of open spaces and the formation of urban subjectivities. While showing the ethico-political and ecological alliances between queers and plants, the authors also argue that heritage discourses in the case of London's Abney Park Cemetery and novel forms of gay and ecological gentrification in the case of New York's High Line become matters of human and non-human displacement, which provide a challenge to plants and human diversity.

Inspired by this approach, I focus in this chapter on the life cycle of open spaces and the formation of urban subjectivities in post-industrial Turin, Italy. I argue that the environmental change of open spaces, and especially their material decay, leads to an emergent and unpredictable cycle of urban development and socio-environmental change, which makes and re-makes the city through a series of colliding and overlapping spatialities and temporalities. In this chapter, the geographies of abandonment of a post-industrial amenity space—the Michelotti Park—are analysed at the intersection of ecological, political and socio-spatial dynamics. In addition, ethnographic field notes and other materials, such as newspaper articles, books and images have been systematised to develop the narrative of the chapter, which also includes reflexive notes. I focus on the processes through which material decay in urban spaces operates to mediate human-environment relations in the riverbank space of the Italian, prototypical one-factory-town. I explore the relation between material decay and temporality to unravel the ways in which a riverside park is shaped and framed by non-linear processes of development and socio-ecological change.

The Riverbanks of Turin

Turin is a city in the northwest of Italy, capital of the Piedmont region, nestled between the Alpine Wall and the hills surrounding the plain of the Po River.

The city's hydrographical network is based on the basins of four rivers—the Po River and its tributaries: Stura di Lanzo, Dora Riparia and Sangone. In Turin, the FIAT car factory intensely informed the spatial, economic and social dimensions of the urban space (Pizzolato 2008; Bagnasco and Olmo 2011). At the riverbank, the automotive plant colonised peripheral spaces by establishing the infrastructures, such as industrial landfills and scrapyards that served to regulate and sustain local industrial production. These spaces along the riverbank emerged as a response to the rapid industrialisation of the city in the late nineteenth century, even before the automobile industry was established in 1899. Some tracts of riverbank spaces, and notably the ones adjoining the Po River, became integral parts of the visions of future modernisation and protagonists of the *mise en scène* of the city. Riverbank spaces, however, were not only places to celebrate refined architectural features; during the nineteenth and twentieth centuries, the riverbanks were also the work sites of generations of millers, laundry women, fishermen and ferrymen, a recreational and festive place for its inhabitants, as well as a place of sport due to the birth of rowing clubs.

Figure 8.1. The riverine features of Turin.

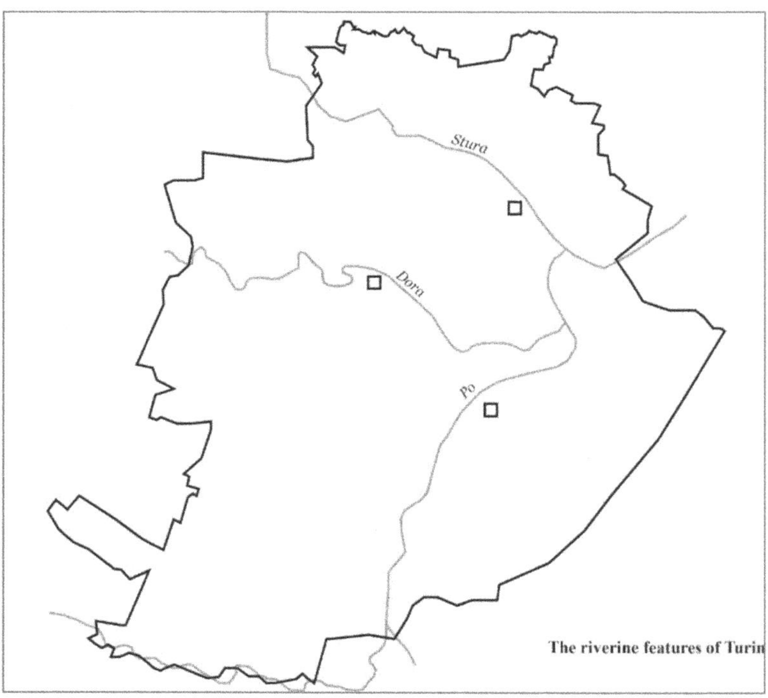

Elaboration of the author, 2017.

The modernisation of the city during the Fordist age, founded on a model of synoptic rationality of urban planning and economic organisation, decisively reshaped watercourses and their adjoining spaces. The river was not only used as a source of energy, but also as a place to dump waste products and watercourses thus became part of an organic machinery, which served the urbanisation and the spatial distribution of the automotive plant. Sand extraction sites were also built along the riverbanks to serve the construction of residential building during the housing boom of the 1950s and 1960s. This led to the emergence of large subsidised housing estates as devices for the development of the Fordist city and its workers coming from the Italian *Mezzogiorno*—the southern part of the peninsula (Adorni *et al.* 2017; Di Biagi 2008; Garda *et al.* 2015).

The industrial development of Turin also re-organised the leisure spaces of everyday life. The proliferation of spontaneous allotment gardens and other recreational activities, such as fishing and bathing, became the socio-cultural expression of the Fordist city built on the spaces of leisure and subsistence. However, it is the cultural memory of the people washing their cars beside the Po River that seems to vividly condense the myriad of meanings about urban-riverine relationships during the rapid industrialisation of the city.

From the 1970s, the gradual crisis of Fordism, due to the intertwined factors of oil crisis effects on the local automotive market and the increased global competition in the car sector, led to dramatic changes in the socio-economic basis of city life in Turin. Both elements, in fact, resulted in industrial delocalisation policies and subsequent major job losses in town. This rapid state of urban decline eventually became visible in the proliferation of urban industrial wastelands and ruins, some of them in the riverside areas of both the city-centre and periphery. The effects of deindustrialisation reached their highest point in the 1980s; however, the dismantlement of industrial brownfields, which started 40 years ago, still continues and the rehabilitation of the riverbanks, in particular, have not yet been concluded. The post-industrial transformation of Turin has slowly developed in relation to regional government strategies to turn it into a regional and national node of culture and technology. Various initiatives of urban change-making have attempted to redefine the international image of the city leading, in 2006, to the hosting of the Winter Olympic Games, which represented an attempt on the part of city politicians and national government to emulate other post-industrial cities in Europe that have tried to turn around a city's fortunes through the hosting of urban mega-events (Horne and Manzenreiter 2006).

From the 1990s, municipal renewal initiatives were put in place, which aimed to "re-colour the greyness", and "demolish the ugliness" of long-term inner-city decay through the upgrade of streets and public plazas of great historical and architectural interest. Simultaneously, in 1994, the establishment of the program—Turin City of Waters—proposed a long-term plan for the creation of a blue-green system with a 74-km riverine park of bicycle and pedestrian pathways, along the Po River and its tributaries. While the project reinforced the need to conserve and revitalise the local natural heritage by restoring and enhancing the pre-existing network of open green spaces, it concurrently proposed ambitious interventions of environmental restoration and massive clean-ups of brownfield sites and abandoned spaces. After decades of spontaneous use, neglect, abuse and removal of the riverine system, the formation of a new discourse of nature moved open public spaces, and especially riverbank spaces, to centre stage. Riverbank spaces have played a decisive role, not only in driving the reconfiguration of the urban fabric after the crisis of Fordism, but also in changing perceptions of the relations between the city and its green landscapes, shedding light on the processes through which attempts were made to internationalise the city and, at the same time, forging the city's image in relation to local residents (Vanolo 2017). Nonetheless, despite a period of optimism, the project of riverine change and uplift has corresponded with difficulty in materialising a systematic and homogeneous program of waterfront rehabilitation. What has emerged in Turin instead is a programme of scattered and intermittent interventions, which have operated in a disconnected manner with the other areas of riverbank, exacerbating the physical, ecological and social fragmentation of riverside spaces.

Turin City of Waters benefited from the huge amount of money that poured into the city to implement different urban projects, but in the last two decades, municipal interventions have declined and political momentum has progressively waned. Today, Turin City of Waters remains a political slogan, whose articulation into political debates and planning practices seems to be merely evocative. The result is the presence of tracts of riverbank spaces where intermittent developments, as well as forms of controlled abandonment, have determined a peculiar condition of temporal suspension, which is illuminated by the manifestation of peculiar configurations of 'waste' and 'blight' space.

Michelotti Park

Michelotti Park is located on the southern banks of the Po River, in proximity to the historic centre of the city. Famous for its urban zoo, from 1957 to 1987, the life of this place has been characterised by the provision of habitat for a wide range of animals and shown the complex and paradoxical reconfiguration of natural spaces in light of shifting notions about public welfare and leisure (Atkins 2013). My research with the archival materials clearly highlights the idea of the municipal zoo as a flagship project for the area, and more broadly, for the whole city (Maschietti *et al.* 1990).

Dorothee Brantz describes the emergence of botanical and zoological gardens in most European and American cities as, "a marker of the rising bourgeois society of the late nineteenth and early twenty century," the expression of particular "cultivations of nature" as they constituted places "to educate to the flora and fauna of foreign lands". Additionally, they materialised the ways in which, "the urban space is divided into distinct arenas that separate work and leisure, the public and the private, and daily practices of production and consumption" (2007: 208–209).

The zoo, as a new urban institution, functioned as the emblem of the rising middle class in a Turin inseparable from the Fordist expansion of the city. The provision of amenity spaces imposed a different aesthetic, introducing sensorial features and rhythms into an urban space where the prosperous workers now had time and money to take their leisure. The park rises over the ruins of a canal that was built in 1817 as an energy resource for the nearby areas. In the early decades of the twentieth century, the canal was covered with debris and the area became an open space, where poplar, willow and plane trees were planted and leisure activities progressively took place. This transformation thus opened a window for the large urban renewal programs that accompanied the political and economic changes that were affecting the city.

Figure 8.2. Picnic at Michelotti Park.

Photo by Rossella Bono, 1931.

The creation of the Murazzi waterfront area, in whose name the place for the public promenade was inaugurated, decisively contributed to change the nearby area of the Michelotti Park, where many proto-industrial activities (especially small factories and mills) were located. The area remained, however, an “interstitial space” (Brighenti 2016), whose uses and meanings overlapped with the attempts to conceptualise it as a ‘traditional’ public open space. Another example is the geographical metaphors used in archival documents describing the area with a certain degree of uncertainty; sometimes it is described as a park, other times as an ‘open space lined with trees’, or a set of woods. The reputation of the area was equally ambivalent: the woods were considered grim and insalubrious, populated by the phantoms of the dead found in the canal. Elsewhere, the park is described as an evocative place for lone walks.

Figure 8.3. A topographic exploration of Michelotti Park.

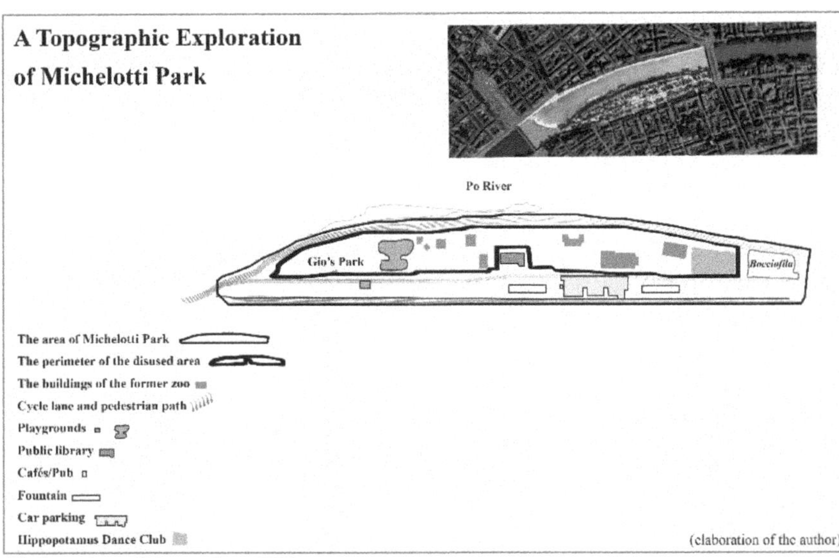

Elaboration of the author, 2018.

Michelotti remained a space lacking a specific function, though some portions were used for the leisure activities of local residents. From this perspective, the presence of the river was essential. The riverbanks were in fact a popular site, where various uses co-existed. The emergence of the zoological garden, which came after long negotiations between the municipality and the Molinar Company (one of the most important collectors of wild animals in Turin and, more broadly, in Italy), overlapped with the invisible traces of a pre-existing informal playground. The designation of the zoo radically changed the perception of the area, from a little used and unkempt field to a distinctive place of popular public attraction.

The multiple fates of Michelotti Park

"I was posting the fence, where the playground is, with the Assemblea Michelotti advertisements. An old man approached me and asked me what I was doing. We discussed about the current situation of the park. He was very sorry about the closure of the zoo and the park in general. He told, in a deeply nostalgic tone, that he has been working for the zoo over 30 years as a monkey keeper. He used to feed the animals and keep the cages cleaned. The monkeys were happy and the visitors too. He then stretched his hand and showed me a deep wound caused by working at the zoological garden." (Maria, early 40s, activist)

Today, park-goers, including residents and casual visitors, recall the zoo, and more broadly the park, as popular destinations during weekends. Although it catered for the Sunday visits of the 'FIAT families and children', the zoo and park were also leisure spaces for tourists and occasional visitors. In many cases they remember the zoo when talking about their childhood, whether it was experienced directly or indirectly through fond family memories. Roberto (45 years old) is one of the owners of a *piola*, a traditional and popular place to eat and drink in Turin that is located beside the park. Roberto's parents opened it in 1965, and many persons consider it a historic place of the city. Here, you can meet the old and new inhabitants of the Borgo Po neighbourhood. It is in this place that I encountered many of the park-goers I interviewed for my research.

Although Roberto stopped visiting the park when he was a teenager, he continues to watch the flow of park life from the backyard of his piola, where one can catch a glimpse of the park and the river. He sat back here as he talked about his own memories of the park, which he used to visit regularly to play football with his friends on the adjoining lawns. A vivid detail for him was climbing the fence to retrieve the ball, even without the zookeeper's permission, because it would repeatedly fall down into the zoo during these afterschool games. This 'crossing the lines without permission' created the sense of both trespassing and belonging. In this sense, the zookeepers played an important role in mediating and creating the inside-outside interstitial space of the park. In the recounting of these memories, the role of zookeepers emerged, "as a fundamental component of introducing the institution of the zoo and the animal other into the urban space" (Reinert in Losquaderno 2016: 31).

> When there was the zoo, we had troubles with the animals, elephants especially. I mean, not because of their sounds but because of the unpleasant smell of excrements.
>
> (Federico, the manager of the Bocciofila, early 70s)

> I loved to wake up in the morning and see giraffes out of my window. I mean I loved that feeling of being in a urban savannah.
>
> (Claudia, 80 years old)

The construction of the zoo generated the physical and ecological fragmentation of the park, by building fences and walls that are still visible today and that narrowed its physical proximity to the river. The area, in fact, can best be described by the juxtapositions of the strips of land parallel to the Po River, which contain very diverse environments in terms of the design of space and landscape aesthetics. Despite the fragmentary topography of the space, residents and park-goers recollect the past configuration of the park as continuously redefined by fixity and movement from very different sensorial environments—outside to inside (and vice-versa). Reminiscence about the park, for example, often emerges through the various forms of a human-animal nexus, whether this emotional and sensorial encounter was the result of an exciting or frightening experience. I met Piera (80 years old) while she was sitting on a bench watching the passers-by, on her daily visit to the park. She looked at me with suspicion when I first approached her, but after introducing myself, she relaxed and opened up. When I asked her to recount her memory of the park when the zoo was still open, we decided to have a walk together along the lane. Piera's most vivid memories were in relation to the animals and how people used to feed them from the outside. These spontaneous conversations with senior users were invaluable in reconstructing the memory of the landscape of the park, the geographies of smell, sound and tactile experience, such as the smells of animals, their bites, and the nuisances caused by their sounds.

The topographical explorations during go-alongs, in fact, threw light on the temporal development of this urban leisure-scape and unfolded the potentials of walking as a valid instrument to investigate urban spaces and develop knowledge (Kusenbach 2003). Chiara is 35 years old. We first met along the wall of the former zoo, when she was taking her dog out for an evening walk in the central promenade. After I stopped her and introduced myself as a researcher, I asked if she was available to talk about the park and her experience of it. Ethnographic encounters are never straightforward in public spaces, but Chiara was enthusiastic about my project and she invited me to join on her walk. Her descriptions combined individual memories and media representation as she retraced the multifold histories of the place.

Figure 8.4. The stone wall surrounding the old zoo.

Photo by Lucilla Barchetta, 2017.

On my way to Regina Bridge I pass the Giò's Park. An association had managed the space, it was a lively play yard, but I was a bit too grown up for it; today, I only have noticed the rusty playground equipment. Someone, I can't remember who, have told me that in the 1990s a cultural centre was established in the house of the tiger… Ah, of course who can forget the scientific exhibition, it was a great success for the city. Here, there is ample parking place. People living in trailers often stop.

Figure 8.5. The old zoo buildings.

Photo by Lucilla Barchetta, 2017.

The eventual closure of the municipal zoo in 1987 set the pace for a variety of planning initiatives and temporary uses that overlapped with the zoo's archaeology; some of these plans came to fruition and others did not—most notably a failed attempt to build a theatre. In the 1990s, the first step towards the renovation of the park took place. Giò's Park led to one portion of the ex-zoological garden being converted into a playground and a bicycle path was built along the Po River afterwards. These renovation initiatives added new value to the amenity space, while also verifying local attempts to create a new image of the city through a waterfront enhancement plan. The rehabilitation initiative was, in fact, part of Turin City of Waters' programmed interventions. Unfortunately, however, these initiatives crystallised the spatial segmentation of the area and accentuated the physical fragmentation both inside and outside the former zoo. Progressively, a confused landscape formed. Today, if it were not for the rusty boards and signs on display directing the public to 'the house of the tiger' or 'the house of the giraffe', it would be difficult to guess that the place used to be a zoo.

Fragments of heaven and patches of decay

Public and private actors of various kinds, from loosely organised associations to formal organisations and companies, have at different times managed the zoo. The former zoo hosted a myriad of music and art shows and a number of exhibitions. From 2000 to 2005, the area became the site of the scientific exhibition 'Experimenta' promoted by the Piedmont Region. In 2012, the project Street Art Museum, both a collective and self-financed project of urban regeneration, challenged the 'past-ness' of the place by organising street art interventions to cover the buildings where the animals were kept. Layers of materials vividly maintained and challenged the memory of the place. In 2014, a 'Jurassic Park' on the riverbank was built when the former zoo hosted the children's exhibition 'Dinosaurs'. In the same period, the dance club 'Hippopotamus' closed. Over time, the spatial inscription of diverse practices of property emerged through multiple geographies of material decay.

However, it was poor city maintenance and declining municipal initiatives that set the basis for the gradual state of neglect characterising the area, while also progressively exacerbating the non-integration, both physical and social, of Michelotti Park into the urban design of Turin. For more than a decade, the zoo area lived in a sort of limbo, a silent permanence regulated by "different regimes of visibility and invisibility", including media representations, and public perceptions of disgust, fear and nostalgia (Brighenti 2008). Today, disorder defines the institutional and everyday framing of the place, where the presence of different types of waste constitute the "material affordances" (Ingold 2000) through which people make sense of the current condition of the park. It is around the matter of waste and the related conceptualisations of waste space that the collective senses and perceptions are continuously formed and situated. Waste and wildness are characteristic features of the ways the abandoned zoo overflows from its boundaries into the "material excess" and "re-contextualization of things", especially weeds, rubbish and objects (Edensor 2005).

Antonio (early fifties) walks with his dog along the central promenade and down by the riverbank every day. At various times, he stops to look around and smoke a cigarette, careful to keep the former zoo out of his vista.

However, the uncontrolled growth of branches, the consistent amount of leaves and the residual objects that he observes in the park and through the fences of the former zoo affect his sensual and emotional encounter with the park. "For me, it's like the abandoned park overflows and run onto the city. Waste disperses. It's such a shame. I would like to burn this park—it's disgusting". These things escape the dirt control system and invade his body, causing feelings of physical revulsion. Waste is thus a peculiar feature of the deployment of discourses of blight and obsolescence as a decisive material logic involving different bodies as well as the corporeal dimensions of space.

Nevertheless, the discursive affiliation of blight with wildness, in the form of spontaneous vegetation and wild animals, is not always a neutral backdrop of neglect and absence of control. Blight is not a fixed attribute of bodies and places, and can generate various affective responses. At times, it appears to be negotiable or, conversely, to create clashes between river ecologies and human interests.

The case of *myocastor coypus*, for example, semiaquatic rodents coming from South America and introduced to Italy by fur ranchers, reveals the complex attitude of humans towards wild animals; depending upon the public and scientific representation of their reputation as dirt, waste or nuisance. It also relates to the significant role of human feeders in urban environments and their implicit attempts to domesticate portions of unplanned nature. Near Michelotti Park, the *coypus* have become the object of a popular attraction for lonely seniors, despite the public warning against this species as sources of bacterial infections for other animals, persons and water.

Giovanni is a 70-year-old retiree. He is one of the *meridionali*, as Southern migrants were called, that arrived in Turin to work at the FIAT's factories. Whereas staying at home can be boring, he says, he prefers strolling by the river, sitting along the grassy banks and feeding the animals. Recently, he also built a small fence to let children play safely with *coypus*. These instances show how "the *improvement* of animals through domestication", in fact, helps to put various natures under control in the city, as well as regularizing deviant human others and spaces" (Atkins 2013: 15, emphasis of the author).

Formal and informal attempts to establish "normative ecologies" (Brownlow 2006: 234)—areas discursively affiliated with control, order and maintenance—beyond their ecological impacts, always have social and political implications both in the everyday life of urban routines and in the various strands of civic activism around Michelotti Park. The park has constituted a sensitised zone for activist contestation, in which community groups have demanded the preservation of the land from financial speculation and animal exploitation for mass tourism. Indeed, in 2015 the area became the target of a plan for a bio-park privately run by a private corporation (Zoom S.p.a). And, over the last two years a number of activist groups, which include different types of environmental and animal-right organisations, as well as historic landscape preservation groups, have been following the legislative approval of the redevelopment plan. The activists' proposals for action and their practices of resistance shared two common claims: the attempted privatisation of public space and the forgetting of the massive protests, both at the local and national level, that actively contributed to the closure of the zoo. In addition, by bringing to light certain errors and omissions in the legal procedures, activist groups accused city authorities of colluding with private interests.

Figure 8.6. A walk inside the old zoo.

Photo by Lucilla Barchetta, 2017.

The ruins are repeatedly animated in community groups' walks and meetings, during which they argue, as Colombino and Vanolo (2017: 2) tellingly suggest, that the proposed project for a private bio-park created a "spatial amnesia", where "forgetting becomes a practice that illuminates the dynamics involved in current and past urban development process." The activist case of Michelotti Park staged the transition from an industrial to a post-industrial zoo that reflected a re-appropriation of a Fordist approach to the design and planning of nature and amenity spaces in cities. It confirmed a vision of metropolitan nature that retained the boundary between nature and the city through the creation of a landscape of consumption functionally and visually separated from residential areas and workplaces. The emergence of the association "Assemblea Michelotti" can be seen as the product of this period of civic mobilisation. In light of formal organisations constituting the majority of participants in the No Zoo Committee, the necessity arose to build up a grassroots form of activism, where deeply engaged activist and common citizens could participate.

During meetings, I had the opportunity to analyse how local activists interpreted the environmental revitalisation work, and how different ideologies underpinned the socio-cultural creation of new urban natures and with that, the redefinition of the park's ecology. Concerns not only relate to the aesthetic characteristics of nature. A heightened problem regarded the ways the decay of the ruined zoo was affecting the adjoining areas, along with the discourses and regulatory practices devised to regulate social life.

Figure 8.7. The path alongside the Po River.

Photo by Lucilla Barchetta, 2017.

The linear path along the bank of the river is a prime example. It is an open space of informal greenery characterised by spontaneous riparian woods, where the seasonal changes of the river embankments form gentle slopes and beaches, which between spring and summer become an extraordinary place for picnics, romantic encounters, chance meeting with mallards, herons and geese, and also a playground for children and dog. Yet, since August 2017, this area has been the target of a municipal by-law (in Italy this is called municipal *ordinance*)[2] whose primary aim was to curb access to the path. This by-law was a response to the reported level of public insecurity about the disorder that seemed to characterise the area due to the presence of homeless people living in the ex-zoo area; illegal activities, as well as the risk of injuries from falling trees and branches. In these instances, the derelict site becomes particularly problematic as the formerly cultivated space, through its unconfined growth, spills out of its boundaries.

These socio-ecological factors are intertwined and become the spatial markers of the disorder of the place (Patrick 2014; Tonnelat 2008). The ordinance has, therefore, restrained access to the ex-zoological garden and to the linear path after 8:00 p.m. and has established a cut off in the provision of water and public lighting to discourage people from occupying the building of the ruined zoo. This use of night spaces shows the manner in which the meanings of darkness in the urban environment could be "multiple, overlapping and contradictory, incorporating the myriad of social processes that constitute it" (Williams 2008). Furthermore, this development reproduces securitised and conservative views of public order that start to threaten the playful potentialities of this public space. As Laura (early thirties) says, "It's too dark and anything could happen, nobody could hear or see you from other parts of the park. I used to come here for the night-time walks with my dog, I used to meet other adventurous dog walkers like me". For many dog-walkers, the municipal regulation has, in fact, put an end to evening walks and to a place socially perceived as essential for ludic experiences.

In addition, fences and barriers, made up by plants and hedgerows, stonewalls, wire fences or low wood barriers, are the *knots* around which the relationships that make up the edging interfaces of the park's past and present are organised. It is around these fences and barriers that the resistance practices of community groups have been organised, and the everyday discourses on the park have been framed by multifold acts of looking, scrutinising and monitoring.

Figure 8.8. The central promenade of Michelotti Park.

Photo by Lucilla Barchetta, 2017.

In the central promenade, a fenced playground sits next to Giò's Park, while the old fence that separates them gathers the grievances of local users about the blight condition of the ex-zoo area. In these instances, 'ex-zoo' is the geographical synecdoche that substitutes one portion of the park for the whole area. Interestingly, this playground is the place where the majority of park-goers stop, sit or stand to play and converse. The playground not only "territorializes children's play" (Brighenti and Kärrholm, forthcoming book), by regulating "the rhythms of playing together", it also synchronises the rhythms of a mundane leisure space and the ruined playground. The wall that marks the perimeter of the former zoo is decorated with graffiti and is a place for teenagers to rock climb. It also serves as the site where strollers often stop to look out the ruined park and recount histories that are located somewhere between nostalgia for a fondly remembered past and an anxious future.

A green wall made of centennial gingko trees, ivy and other spontaneous plants keeps the area confined from the Po River. However, the presence of two holes in the fence of the former zoo discloses the secret life of the abandoned space, where the silent life of a small group of migrants, street artists and homeless people co-exists with the rambles of adventurous and nostalgic visitors. The traces of the ex-zoo, as well as its successive temporary uses (cages, moats and other buildings), exist side-by-side with the ruins of the playground equipment. The most established plants growing on the abandoned space, Phytolacca Americana and Artemisia Annua cover the archaeology of the place and sometimes spill out of the boundaries at the edges of the abandoned park.

During my ethnographic visits at the ruined park, I often met some of the persons living in the zoo buildings, and also occasional visitors. I rarely delved into deep conversations with random visitors, as a primal feeling of fear appeared to keep us at a distance. However, other kinds of encounters were possible. For instance, Michelotti Park is also a place for amateur botanists' excursions. These urban botanist explorers are anti-speciest activists that, through the discovery of the 'botanical inhabitants', experiment with the potentials of a spontaneous and libertarian place of freedom, and they create the basis for an imaginative re-interpretation of the urban space.

Over time, the uncertainty and the physical fragmentation of the space seem to have intensified. In addition, police patrols repeatedly remark the institutional framing of the area as out of order, thereby reinforcing common-sense depictions that render this space useless and disreputable. The formal park area has become the stage of a controlled urban life, where the social and symbolic barriers that divide the portions of Michelotti Park are simultaneously reinforced and blurred by the movement of persons, objects, animals and vegetation.

Uncertain futures

The life of Michelotti Park entered a new stage in its lifecycle on the 15th of December 2017 with the public announcement of the rescinding of the bio-park plan. The Five Star Party, the presiding party since 2016, announced a new season of participatory planning for the revitalisation of the park. Consequently, activist groups have since redefined their agenda, while starting a new interaction with municipal government and civil society around the remaking of the park. Uncertainty in the patterns of public participation and differences in priorities among common citizens and activists emerge in public debates and bring to the foreground the ideological dimensions underpinning urban natures and the divides in the political project of Turin environmentalism.

These emerging cultures of nature and leisure space-on-display provide an additional ground from which to view the metamorphosis of the industrial city through the forms of specific cultural and ecological valorisations of nature. Some citizens and activists are constructing a radical rethinking of the meaning of nature in the city, by rejecting the idea of a massive intervention of clean-up, which they claim would dismantle an 'island of biodiversity' and also its threads of memory; others groups show a preservationist ethic, which combines an interest to conserve wildlife with a priority for social and spatial order. Yet, local activist groups are not residents to the area. From the angle of activist stories, the existence of everyday residents and users seem to remain silent.

The work of urban political ecology has long been suggesting the role that the micro-politics of environmental discourse formations can have in the reconfiguration of the material conditions of urban space through the construction of landscapes and subjects in certain ways, while foreclosing others. In post-industrial Turin, the representations of blight produce an imaginary of environmental change as a matter of socio-ecological control in which human bodies, as well as botanical species and other material traces of the past, are viewed and represented as *victims of waste*, thereby over-reducing the responsibility towards abandoned spaces to sites merely waiting for removal or revitalisation, through supposed 'good-design' and nature conservation practices. Within this context, activist practices of "resistance" become often normalised and transformed into anaesthetised practices of "resilience" (Slater 2014), in the extent to which the reconfiguration of a park into a waste space frames environmental change as the negative effect of urban austerity, the actions of governing subjects and deviant individuals.

This, in turn, reproduces an understanding of public nature as an inert site of a mere consensus in which objects and persons circulate according to a shared horizon of comfort and happiness. In terms of the design of an urban green space, it over-reduces the complexity of nature into micro-patches of functional areas through which the division between nature and society is reproduced, even in certain attempts to overcome it.

However, the ethnographic exploration of Michelotti Park has highlighted a public space of "agitated togetherness", contingency and ambivalence that articulates different levels of struggle and expressions of desire. Within this context, discursive and corporeal affiliations with waste are negotiable, unpredictable and contradicting. Adventure, domesticity, discovery and excitement—not only fear, anxiety and nostalgia—can be practices of resistance that make way for a re-configuration of a supposed messy landscape into a space of complexity and multiplicity. It also provides a challenge to the re-organisation of persons as victims of waste, while highlighting the potentials of ordinary affects and sensory experience to create transformative articulations of public-ness and nature–people alliances.

Moving through the present and past circuits of routine practices and memories, the case study of the park shows that environmental changes do not correspond to a sequential organisation of periodicities. In the vicissitudes of many post-industrial cities of the West, one can notice the difficulty to bring a new future into being, which becomes visible through spaces that "litter" the ordered city. As a response, organic imaginaries of regeneration provide attempts to piece time and space back together into a framework of spatial-temporal continuity.

In this regard, the works of urban political ecology and environmental history, rather than trying to explain what a prevailing construct of temporality can *be*, have been studying what a dominant articulation of temporality can *do*. In this way, research has shown that time cannot be mapped on space but is part of the formation of the landscape. Multiple space-times form many different cultural expressions of industrialism and post-industrialism, by showing the present as a temporal collage, where ideas, natural flows, material traces and sophisticated systems of technologies circulate and come together in a continuous process of recombination.

At Michelotti Park, material traces have shown the potential to extend normative conceptions of temporality. The meanings and uses of traces are unstable, dispersed and always become something else. Nonetheless, the stories around Michelotti Park also suggest the manners through which meanings around traces can also sediment and stabilise through the everyday work of sensory memories, as well as through the politics and privilege of histories through which bits of present and past become absent or constrained. In this way, it can be suggested that micro-stories and geographies of waste spill out a particular sequence of abandonment as a single event along a chronological line of time.

Michelotti Park has shown a process of perpetual and unpredictable social and spatial change that provides a challenge to the brown/green antinomy, as a prevailing construct of urban development and traditional pattern of metropolitan change. A green space is not only hybrid concerning the types of green space contained by its form, but also concerning the patterns of socio-environmental change it can embody.

Ethnographic work has enriched significantly urban political ecology engagements with urban life, while contrasting and confounding the linearity of time. By engaging in an in-depth ethnographic work of the phenomenological, affective, atmospheric dimensions of socio-environmental change, this work endorses current calls for embodied and everyday approaches to the study of urban socionatures, and promotes it as a way to build narratives that trace out the threads of ordinary worlds and follows their convolutions, small and subtle moves.

Notes

[1] For example, Heynen, Swingedouw and Kaika (2006) illuminate the complexities of built-form–nature environment entanglements, while laying out a theoretical agenda that unifies sub-disciplines around a wide range of urban environmental concerns such as air, water and waste management; food privilege; open spaces; redevelopment processes and environmental justice. An additional body of research, rooted in the sub-field of environmental justice, explores the uneven distribution of environmental amenities as forms of injustice, or as constitutive grounds to negotiate new forms of justice (Holifield *et al.* 2017; Walker 2012).

[2] The proliferation of municipal ordinances as a feature of the regulation of public spaces in Italy have increased significantly in recent years. The article by Moroni and Chiodelli (2014) clearly shows the characteristics of such instrument, its diffusion and often arbitrary application by some municipalities to regulate behaviour in public spaces on the basis, as the authors writes, of "substantive" conceptions of the "good".

References

Adorni, D., D'Amuri, M. and Tabor, D. (2017) *La casa pubblica. Storia dell'Istituto Autonomo case popolari di Torino*. Roma: Viella.

Atkins, P. (ed.) (2013) *Animal Cities: Beastly Urban Histories*. Farnham: Ashgate.

Bagnasco, A. and Olmo, C. (2008) *Torino 011. Biografia di una città*. Milano: Mondadori Electa.

Brantz, D. (2007) The Natural Space of Modernity. A Transatlantic Perspective on (Urban) Environmental History. In: Lehmkuhl, U. and Wellenreuther, H. (eds), *Historians and Nature. Comparative Approaches to Environmental History*. Oxford and New York: Berg.

Braun, B. (2005) 'Environmental issues: writing a more-than-human urban geography'. *Progress in Human Geography*, 29(5): 635–650.

Brighenti, A. M. (2008) 'Visual, visible, ethnographic'. *Etnografia e Ricerca Qualitativa*, (1).

Brighenti, A. (2016) *Urban Interstices: The Aesthetics and Politics of the In-Between*. Abingdon: Ashgate.

Brighenti, A. M. and Karrholm, M., (forthcoming) *Animated Land. Studies in Territoriology*. Lincoln: University of Nebraska Press.

Brownlow, A. (2006) 'An archaeology of fear and environmental change in Philadelphia'. *Geoforum*, 37: 227–245.

Clark, T. N. (ed.) (2003) *The City as an Entertainment Machine*. New York: Lexington Books.

Colombino, A. and Vanolo, A. (2017) 'Turin and Lingotto: resilience, forgetting and the reinvention of place'. *European Planning Studies*, 25(1): 10–28.

De Block, G. (2016) 'Ecological infrastructure in a critical-historical perspective: From engineering "social" territory to encoding "natural" topography'. *Environment and Planning A*, 48(2): 367–390.

Di Biagi, P. (2008) *La Città Pubblica. Edilizia sociale e riqualificazione urbana a Torino*. Torino: Allemandi.

Edensor, T. (2005) 'The ghosts of industrial ruins: Ordering and disordering memory in excessive space'. *Environment and Planning D: Society and Space*, 23: 829–849.

European Union (2015) Towards an EU research and innovation policy agenda for nature-based solutions and re-naturing cities. Final Report of the Horizon 2020 Expert Group, Brussels.

Gandy, M. (2002) *Concrete and Clay. Reworking Nature in New York City.* Cambridge, MA and London: MIT Press.

Gandy, M. (2012) 'Queer ecology: Nature, sexuality, and heterotopic alliances'. *Environment and Planning D: Society and Space*, 30(4): 727–747.

Gandy, M. (2013) 'Marginalia: Aesthetics, ecology, and urban wastelands'. *Annals of the Association of American Geographers*, (September): 37–41.

Garda, E. *et al.* (eds) (2015) *Valigia di cartone e case di cemento. Edilizia, industrializzazione e cantiere a Torino nel secondo Novecento.* Torino: Celid.

Heynen, N. (2013) 'Urban political ecology I: The urban century'. *Progress in Human Geography*, 38(4): 598–604.

Heynen, N. (2015) 'Urban political ecology II: The abolitionist century'. *Progress in Human Geography*, 40(6): 839–845.

Heynen, N. (2017) 'Urban political ecology III: The feminist and queer century'. *Progress in Human Geography*, 42(3): 446–452.

Heynen, N., Kaika, M. and Swyngedouw, E. (eds) (2006) *In the Nature of Cities. Urban Political Ecology and the Politics of Urban Metabolism.* London: Routledge.

Holifield, R., Chakraborty, J. and Walker, G. (eds) (2017) *The Routledge Handbook of Environmental Justice.* New York: Routledge.

Ingold, T. (2000) *The Perception of the Environment. Essays on Livelihood, Dwelling and Skills.* London and New York: Routledge.

Kusenbach, M. (2003) 'Street phenomenology: The go-along as ethnographic research tool'. *Ethnography*, 4(3): 455–485.

Lehmkuhl, U. and Wellenreuther, H. (eds) (2007) *Historians and Nature. Comparative Approaches to Environmental History.* Oxford and New York: Berg.

Maschietti, G., Muti, M. and Passerin D'Entrèves, P. (eds) (1990) *Giardini zoologici: vicende storico-politiche degli zoo torinesi (1851–1989).* Torino: Allemandi.

Millington, N. (2013) 'Post-industrial imaginaries: Nature, representation and ruin in Detroit, Michigan'. *International Journal of Urban and Regional Research*, 37(1): 279–296.

Moroni, S. and Chiodelli, F. (2014) 'Municipal regulations and the use of public space: local ordinances in Italy'. *Cities, Territories and Architecture*, 1(11). doi: https://doi.org/10.1186/2195-2701-1-11

Patrick, D. J. (2014) 'The matter of displacement: A queer urban ecology of New York City's High Line'. *Social and Cultural Geography*, 15(8): 920–941.

Pizzolato, N. (2008) *Challenging Global Capitalism. Labor Migration, Radical Struggle, and Urban Change in Detroit and Turin.* Basingstoke: Palgrave MacMillan.

Smith, A. (2014) 'Borrowing public space to stage major events: The Greenwich Park controversy'. *Urban Studies*, 51(2): 247–263.

Smith, A. (2017) 'Animation or denigration? Using urban public spaces as event venues'. *Event Management*, 21(5): 609–619.

Vanolo, A. (2015) 'The Fordist city and the creative city: Evolution and resilience in Turin, Italy'. *City, Culture and Society*, 6(3): 69–74.

Walker, G. (2012) *Environmental Justice: Concepts, Evidence and Politics*, New York: Routledge.

Williams, R. (2008) 'Night spaces: Darkness, deterritorialisation of social control'. *Space and Culture*, 11(4): 514–532.

Index

D

E

F

G

H

I

J

K

L

M

N

O

P

X

Z

Ingram Content Group UK Ltd.
Milton Keynes UK
UKHW020021190423
420401UK00015B/233/J

9 781622 737680